The German Library: Volume 54

Volkmar Sander, General Editor

GERMAN ESSAYS ON RELIGION

Edited by Edward T. Oakes

CONTINUUM · NEW YORK

1994
The Continuum Publishing Company
370 Lexington Avenue, New York, NY 10017

The German Library
is published in cooperation with Deutsches Haus,
New York University.
This volume has been supported by Inter Nationes, and a grant
from the funds of Stifterverband für die Deutsche Wissenschaft.

Printed in the United States of America

Library of Congress Cataloging-in-Publication Data

German essays on religion / edited by Edward T. Oakes.
p.   cm. — (The German library ; v. 54)
Includes bibliographical references.
ISBN 0-8264-0734-X (alk. paper)   . — ISBN 0-8264-0735-8
(pbk. : alk. paper)
1. Religion.   2. Religions.   I. Oakes, Edward T.   II. Series.
BL50.G394   1994
200—dc20   94-13413
                                                                  CIP

Acknowledgments will be found on page 257,
which constitutes an extension of the copyright page.

To Frank Peters,
who taught me how
to get out three books in one year
without reducing my monthly intake
of movies.

Contents

JOHANN GOTTLIEB FICHTE

FRIEDRICH DANIEL ERNST SCHLEIERMACHER

GEORG WILHELM FRIEDRICH HEGEL

ARTHUR SCHOPENHAUER

LUDWIG ANDREAS FEUERBACH

KARL MARX

FRIEDRICH NIETZSCHE

Introduction

No other nation (or better: national culture) has produced a more influential corpus of writing on religion than Germany.[1] Even to list the names of some of the luminaries who appear in this book establishes this point: Freud, Marx, Nietzsche, Barth, Kant, Hegel, Feuerbach. No other nation or national culture could begin to match the influence of such thinkers in the issue of religion, and no major religion in the world remains untouched by the categories and judgments introduced by the German-speaking thinkers included in this volume of the German Library.

One of these writers, who probably achieved fame more for his personality and witness than his writings (though here too his achievement was considerable), is Albert Schweitzer, the biblical scholar and medical missionary in Africa. In one of his most famous books, a survey of (mostly German!) scholarship on the life of the historical Jesus, he described *en passant* the basis for this extraordinary influence. Now, coming from any other writer and describing any other national culture, he would have been written off as a crank or a chauvinist. But in this

---

1. Two of the authors in this book are Swiss (Barth and Balthasar), and two are Austrian (Freud and Wittgenstein), so it is more accurate to speak here of a national culture based on a common language than on one nation in particular, though one should bear in mind that both Barth and Balthasar pursued their doctoral studies for the most part in Germany itself, and Freud won the coveted Goethe Prize from the German government for achievements in the German language. And of course, Germany did not come into being as a fully formed nation-state until the latter half of the nineteenth century, so we must in any case speak of the general patrimony of the German-speaking nations, and this I have collectively identified as the German "national culture."

case he speaks accurately; and although he is discussing theology in particular and not the philosophy of religion as well, his description can in fact stand for an accurate assessment of the reason for Germany's dominating, all-pervasive influence in religious thought:

> When, at some future day, our period of civilization shall lie, closed and completed, before the eyes of the later generations, German theology will stand out as a great, a unique phenomenon in the mental and spiritual life of our time. For nowhere save in the German temperament can there be found in the same perfection the living complex of conditions and factors — of philosophical thought, critical acumen, historical insight, and religious feeling — without which no deep theology is possible.[2]

This of course need not imply, and indeed should not, that this influence has been either univocal or uniformly beneficial. Such an expectation would in any case be impossible, for the voices that speak in this book are astonishingly discordant. But also always — and equally astonishingly — inventive and insightful. One can find no better way of seeing why religion plays so tense a role in the human community today than by consulting the authors represented in this book, for they are the ones who have by and large defined the meaning and nature of that role.

Given the diverse positions and approaches that the authors have taken toward religion, I have tried to govern my choice of their respective works — to the extent it was possible — by confining the selections to a common theme. In philosophical terminology, this might be described as the problem of the One and the Many; or in theological terms, between faith and reason; or in abstract terms, between the universal and the particular. The central issue is this: just as no one speaks "language" but *a* language, so too no one belongs to, or is born into, "religion" but into *a* religion. As the world began to converge into one interlocking system of civilizations in the Age of Discovery, this

---

2. Albert Schweitzer, *The Quest for the Historical Jesus: A Critical Study of Its Progress from Reimarus to Wrede,* trans. W. Montgomery (London: Adam and Charles Black, 1911), 1.

issue — the "scandal of particularity," one might say — became paramount.

Of course it was phrased in different ways according to the approach and background of the author. With reference to Christianity, the issue tended to be discussed in terms of the universality of Christ's saving mission versus the all-too-obvious limited outreach of his mission and of the church. In the philosophy of religion, the issue was often formulated as a problem between faith and reason: faith is given only to some, while reason is part of the definition of the human animal, and is therefore universal. Do, then, the truths of faith serve only to *confirm* the already available truths of reason (especially for those whose rational faculties, by reason of endowment or historical fate, were underdeveloped), or do believers have *privileged access* to truths that no amount of rational argumentation could attain — or gainsay? And if the latter, what does this say about the nature of God?

Even atheism comes out of this debate, for to the extent this extended debate was resolved in terms of the One, or in favor of reason and universality, it set up reason to judge the many particularities of belief, thereby eventually calling them all into question. And then, of course, it devolved upon the believing thinker to point to atheism as the logical conclusion of favoring reason over faith. And thus the issue was joined, and out of it came the clash of ideas that this book has tried to capture.

It is always a happy duty, and one that I do hereby cheerfully discharge, to offer one's thanks for the help received during the writing of a book. My first debt of gratitude goes to Professor Yolkmar Sander of the German Department at New York University, who first offered me the chance to be the editor of this volume. Although I had a number of other projects on my plate at the time, something told me that this project would be both important and fun, and such it has proved (at least for me) to be.

I did most of my research for this book while on a "Study Visit Abroad" Grant from the Deutscher Akademischer Austauschdienst, an arm of the German government, whose Board of Directors I would like to thank for this most pleasant of opportunities. I spent the bulk of my Study Visit at the Philosophisch-Theologische Hochschule St. Georgen in Frankfurt. I am especially indebted to the Rector of the Hochschule, Prof. Dr. Werner Löser, S.J., and

xiv · *Introduction*

the Director of the library there, Dr. Georg Miczka, whose hospitality and expertise were artfully combined to provide the perfect setting for my research. And finally, I must thank Dr. Jill Claster, Director of the Center for Near Eastern Studies, and Dr. F. E. Peters, Chairman of the Department of Near Eastern Languages and Literatures, both of New York University, for offering me their own "office-hospitality" while I was living off the fat of the foundations.

E. T. O.

Immanuel Kant

With Immanuel Kant (1724–1804), philosophical reflection on religion in German emerges with a consistency of outlook and a maturity belied by its sudden appearance. With Kant, not only does the philosophy of religion as a generic concept make its first appearance in German philosophy, but it also "comes of age and takes its place among the basic parts of philosophy."[1] Much like Plato in the case of philosophy in general, or Shakespeare in the English theater, Kant of course had his predecessors, his "pre-Socratics," as it were; but only with him does philosophy of religion emerge as its own self-subsistent field of reflection, its own legitimate branch of philosophy, with distinct methodologies and themes.

And as in the case of Plato, it is the first emergence of the field that determines the course of all of its later development. The selections that follow are taken from two of Kant's last works, *The Strife of the Faculties* and *Religion within the Limits of Reason Alone,* and in them the reader will notice themes being adumbrated that will crop up again and again in the rest of the essays: particularly the strained and very tense relation between faith and reason, and the role of morality and revelation in humankind's religious life.

Kant very definitely favored the claims of reason and morality in these disputes over against what he took to be the rival claims of revelation and faith, but to understand the positions he adopts in the following selections one must first have some inkling of the prior metaphysical framework from which his views on religion

---

1. James Collins, *The Emergence of the Philosophy of Religion* (New Haven: Yale University Press, 1967), viii.

are generated. Kant's philosophy cannot be understood except in terms of the Newtonian worldview he inherited and that he struggled to humanize. Isaac Newton's *Principia Mathematica* (1687), with its mathematical specification of the law of gravity and its subsumption of all motion under this one law, caused an immense crisis for the European mind almost upon its publication. This is because it seemed to mechanize the entire physical universe, leaving only one apparent exception: the knowing subject that could recognize such a mathematically rule-governed mechanism. But this lone exception had then to look out on a world without value, one it could no longer call home. As Georg Simmel, a noted Kantian interpreter, says: "Because of the mechanistic principle of the natural sciences, reality seemed to be placed in complete contrast to all that previously had seemed to give meaning to this reality: it had no more room for ideas, values, purposes, for religious meaning and moral freedom."[2]

Kant's solution was fundamentally one of juxtaposition, indeed of outright dualism: subject over against object, mind over against matter, the freedom of the moral subject over against the law-governed behavior of physical bodies, and to some extent, the individual over against society (and therefore over against institutional religion).

Because the Newtonian universe was so relentlessly mechanical, the question immediately arose: Did the human mind also obey these same mechanical rules? If the answer were proven to be yes, then obviously free will was an illusion, as was the belief in the immortality of the soul. Kant set out not only to fight these implications but more crucially to do so *in terms of the reigning Newtonian paradigm,*[3] and his solution was ingenious: in Newton's world, space and time are "absolutes," that is, abstract grids or coordinates within which bodies careen and can be located. But in Kant's interpretation, space and time are "constituted" by the human mind; that is, the sensations of the physical world bombard the mind, but the mind *structures* these sensory data according to

---

2. Georg Simmel, *Kant und Goethe: Zur Geschichte der modernen Weltanschauung* (Leipzig: Kurt Wolff Verlag, n.d.), 9.

3. "It is not going too far to suggest that [Kant's] most basic problem was: *How are autonomy and free will possible in a deterministic Newtonian universe?*" (Walter Kaufmann, *Discovering the Mind,* vol. 1: *Goethe, Kant, Hegel* [New York: McGraw-Hill, 1980], 86; emphasis in original).

its own categories of understanding, the primary ones being the forms of space and time. In other words, the mechanical world-view of Newton is true but is itself constituted by the human subject's categories of understanding, which impose on the sense data the absolutes of space and time.

This "Copernican turn" of perspective, as Kant called it, at once alters the terms of the problem, for no longer is the subject enmeshed in the cause–effect nexus of the physical world but is rather the constituting foundation of it. But there was a price to be paid for such a finessing of the problem. First, any literally *meta*physical speculations regarding God, freedom, or the immortality of the soul were ruled out, because pure reason could reliably function only when it had sensory data to work with: the categories of understanding were meant to impose form and intelligibility upon sense data, without which they had no legitimate speculative function. But second, we could reach a *practical* certainty of such matters as the existence of God and the immortality of the soul through the practical action of leading moral lives, that is, by the defiant assertion of freedom in spite of the deterministic world revealed by Newton.

This is why for Kant what counts in religion is purity of heart and not speculative theology. For Kant, to adopt the religious attitude is to look on duties *as if* they are divine commands. But this is just a picturesque way of saying that duties have an unconditioned character. But since Kant thought he had already shown in the *Critique of Pure Reason* that knowledge of the suprasensible world is impossible, the whole meaning of belief in God and a future life is to be found in faithfulness to the moral norms it motivates. Kant thus dispenses with the historical elements of Christianity as having no importance in themselves: whatever is true in religion must come from moral reason, which is accessible to all men, and therefore the true religion is *natural religion*.

These views were first expressed in *Religion within the Limits of Reason Alone,* selections from which follow. They soon provoked the anger of theologians and, more importantly, of the Prussian authorities, and Kant was asked by his king, Frederick Wilhelm II, to refrain from further pronouncements on religion. But in Göttingen (outside Prussia), the liberal theologian C. F. Staüdlin asked him for a written reply for a journal he was editing, promising

Kant "unlimited freedom of the press" (letter, June 14, 1794), and from that came *The Strife of the Faculties.*

From The Strife of the Faculties

Part One
Concerning the Service of God in Religion in General

Religion is (subjectively regarded) the recognition of all duties as divine commands. That religion in which I must know in advance that something is a divine command in order to recognize it as my duty, is the *revealed* religion (or the one standing in need of a revelation); in contrast, that religion in which I must first know that something is my duty before I can accept it as a divine injunction is the *natural* religion. He who interprets the natural religion alone as morally necessary, i.e., as duty, can be called the rationalist (in matters of belief); if he denies the reality of all supernatural divine revelation he is called a *naturalist;* if he recognizes revelation, but asserts that to know and accept it as real is not a necessary requisite to religion, he could be named a *pure rationalist;* but if he holds that belief in it is necessary to universal religion, he could be named the pure *supernaturalist* in matters of faith.

The rationalist, by virtue of his very title, must of his own accord restrict himself within the limits of human insight. Hence he will never, as a naturalist, dogmatize, and will never contest either the inner possibility of revelation in general or the necessity of a revelation as a divine means for the introduction of true religion; for these matters no man can determine through reason. Hence the question at issue can concern only the reciprocal claims of the pure rationalist and the supernaturalist in matters of faith, namely, what the one or the other holds as necessary and sufficient, or as merely incidental, to the unique true religion.

When religion is classified not with reference to its first origin and its inner possibility (here it is divided into natural and revealed religion) but with respect to its characteristics which make it *capable of being shared widely with others,* it can be of two kinds: either the *natural* religion, of which (once it has arisen) everyone can be convinced through his own reason, or a *learned* religion, of which one can convince others only through the agency of learning (in and through which they must be guided). This distinction is very important: for no inference regarding a religion's qualification or disqualification to be the universal religion of mankind can be drawn merely from its origin, whereas such an inference is possible from its capacity or incapacity for general dissemination, and it is this capacity which constitutes the essential character of that religion which ought to be binding upon every man.

Such a religion, accordingly, can be *natural,* and at the same time *revealed,* when it is so constituted that men *could and ought to have discovered it* of themselves merely through the use of their reason, although they *would* not have come upon it so early, or over so wide an area, as is required. Hence a revelation thereof at a given time and in a given place might well be wise and very advantageous to the human race, in that, when once the religion thus introduced is here, and has been made known publicly, everyone can henceforth by himself and with his own reason convince himself of its truth. In this event the religion is *objectively* a natural religion, though *subjectively* one that has been revealed; hence it is really entitled to the former name. For, indeed, the occurrence of such a supernatural revelation might subsequently be entirely forgotten without the slightest loss to that religion either of comprehensibility, or of certainty, or of power over human hearts. It is different with that religion which, on account of its inner nature, can be regarded only as revealed. Were it not preserved in a completely secure tradition or in holy books, as records, it would disappear from the world, and there must needs transpire a supernatural revelation, either publicly repeated from time to time or else enduring continuously within each individual, for without it the spread and propagation of such a faith would be impossible.

Yet in part at least every religion, even if revealed, must contain certain principles of the natural religion. For only through reason can thought add revelation to the concept of a *religion,* since this very concept, as though deduced from an obligation to the will of a *moral* legislator, is a pure concept of reason. Therefore we shall be able to look upon even a revealed religion on the one hand as a *natural,* on the other as a *learned* religion, and thus to test it and decide what and how much has come to it from one or the other source.

If we intend to talk about a revealed religion (at least one so regarded) we cannot do so without selecting some specimen or other from history, for we must devise instances as examples in order to be intelligible, and unless we take these from history their possibility might be disputed. We cannot do better than to adopt, as the medium for the elucidation of our idea of revealed religion in general, some book or other which contains such examples, especially one which is closely interwoven with doctrines that are ethical and consequently related to reason. We can then examine it, as one of a variety of books which deal with religion and virtue on the credit of a revelation, thus exemplifying the procedure, useful in itself, of searching out whatever in it may be for us a pure and therefore a universal religion of reason. Yet we do not wish thereby to encroach upon the business of those to whom is entrusted the exegesis of this book, regarded as the summary of positive doctrines of revelation, or to contest their interpretation based upon scholarship. Rather is it advantageous to scholarship, since scholars and philosophers aim at one and the same goal, to wit, the morally good, to bring scholarship, through its own rational principles, to the very point which it already expects to reach by another road. Here the New Testament, considered as the source of the Christian doctrine, can be the book chosen. In accordance with our intention we shall now offer our demonstration in two sections, first, the Christian religion as a natural religion, and, second, as a learned religion, with reference to its content and to the principles which are found in it.

Section One
The Christian Religion as a Natural Religion

Natural religion, as morality (in its relation to the freedom of the agent) united with the concept of that which can make actual its final end (with the concept of *God* as moral Creator of the world), and referred to a continuance of man which is suited to this end in its completeness (to immortality), is a pure practical idea of reason which, despite its inexhaustible fruitfulness, presupposes so very little capacity for theoretical reason that one can convince every man of it sufficiently for practical purposes and can at least require of all men as a duty that which is its effect. This religion possesses the prime essential of the true church, namely, the qualification for universality, so far as one understands by that a validity for everyone, i.e., universal unanimity. To spread it, in this sense, as a world religion, and to maintain it, there is needed, no doubt, a body of servants of the invisible church, but not officials, in other words, teachers but not dignitaries, because in the rational religion of every individual there does not yet exist a church as a universal *union,* nor is this really contemplated in the above idea.

Yet such unanimity could not be maintained of itself and hence could not, unless it became a visible church, be propagated in its universality; rather is this possible only when a collective unanimity, in other words a union of believers in a (visible) church under the principles of a pure religion of reason, is added; though this church does not automatically arise out of that unanimity nor, indeed, were it already established, would it be brought by its free adherents (as was shown above) to a permanent status as a *community* of the faithful (because in such a religion none of those who has seen the light believes himself to require, for his religious sentiments, fellowship with others). Therefore it follows that unless there are added to the natural laws, apprehensible through unassisted reason, certain statutory ordinances attended by legislative prestige (authority), that will still be lacking which constitutes a special duty of men, and a means to their highest end, namely, their enduring union into a universal visible church; and the authority mentioned above, in order to be a founder of such a church, presupposes a realm of fact and not merely the pure concepts of reason.

Let us suppose there was a teacher of whom an historical record (or, at least, a widespread belief which is not basically disputable) reports that he was the first to expound publicly a pure and searching religion, comprehensible to the whole world (and thus natural). His teachings, as preserved to us, we can in this case test for ourselves. Suppose that all he did was done even in the face of a dominant ecclesiastical faith which was onerous and not conducive to moral ends (a faith whose perfunctory worship can serve as a type of all the other faiths, at bottom merely statutory, which were current in the world at the time). Suppose, further, we find that he had made this universal religion of reason the highest and indispensable condition of every religious faith whatsoever, and then had added to it certain statutes which provided forms and observances designed to serve as means of bringing into existence a church founded upon those principles. Now, in spite of the adventitiousness of his ordinances directed to this end, and the elements of arbitrariness in them, and though we can deny the name of true universal church to these, we cannot deny to him himself the prestige due the one who called men to union in this church; and this without further adding to this faith burdensome new ordinances or wishing to transform acts which he had initiated into peculiar holy practices, required in themselves as being constituent elements of religion.

After this description one will not fail to recognize the person who can be reverenced, not indeed as the *founder* of the *religion* which, free from every dogma, is engraved in all men's hearts (for it does not have its origin in an arbitrary will), but as the founder of the first true *church*. For attestation of his dignity as of divine mission we shall adduce several of his teachings as indubitable evidence of religion in general, let historical records be what they may (since in the idea itself is present adequate ground for its acceptance); these teachings, to be sure, can be no other than those of pure reason, for such alone carry their own proof, and hence upon them must chiefly depend the attestation of the others.

First, he claims that not the observance of outer civil or statutory churchly duties but the pure moral disposition of the heart alone can make man well-pleasing to God (Matthew V, 20–48); that sins in thought are regarded, in the eyes of God, as tantamount to action (V, 28) and that, in general, holiness is the goal toward which man should strive (V, 48); that, for example, to hate in one's heart is equivalent to killing (V, 22); that injury done one's neighbor can be repaired only through satisfaction rendered to the neighbor himself, not through acts of divine worship (V, 24), and that, on the point of truthfulness, the civil device for extorting it, by oath, does violence to respect for truth itself (V, 34–37); that the natural but evil propensity of the human heart is to be completely reversed, that the sweet sense of revenge must be transformed into tolerance (V, 39, 40) and the hatred of one's enemies into charity (V, 44). Thus, he says, does he intend to do full justice to the Jewish law (V, 17); whence it is obvious that not scriptural scholarship but the pure religion of reason must be the law's interpreter, for taken according to the letter, it allowed the very opposite of all this. Furthermore, he does not leave unnoticed, in his designations of the strait gate and the narrow way, the misconstruction of the law which men allow themselves in order to evade their true moral duty and, holding themselves immune through having fulfilled their churchly duty (VII, 13). He further requires of these pure dispositions that they manifest themselves also in *works* (VII, 16) and, on the other hand, denies the insidious hope of those who imagine that, through invocation and praise of the Supreme Lawgiver in the person of His envoy, they will make up for their lack of good works and ingratiate themselves into favor (VII, 21). Regarding these works he declares that they ought to be performed publicly, as an example for imitation (V, 16), and in a cheerful mood, not as actions extorted from slaves (VI, 16); and that thus, from a small beginning in the sharing and spreading of such dispositions, religion, like a grain of seed in good soil, or a ferment of goodness, would gradually, through its inner power, grow into a kingdom of God (XIII, 31–33). Finally, he combines all duties (1) in one *universal* rule (which includes within itself both the inner and the outer moral relations of men), namely: Perform your duty for no motive other than unconditioned esteem for duty itself, i.e., love God (the Legislator of all duties) above all else; and (2) in a *particular* rule, that, namely, which concerns man's external relation to other men as universal duty: Love every one as yourself, i.e., further his welfare from good-will that is immediate and not derived from motives of self-advantage. These commands are not mere laws of virtue but precepts of *holiness* which we ought to pursue, and the very pursuit of them is called *virtue*.

Accordingly he destroys the hope of all who intend to wait upon this moral goodness quite passively, with their hands in their laps, as though it were a heavenly gift which descends from on high. He who leaves unused the natural predisposition to goodness which lies in human nature (like a talent entrusted to him) in lazy confidence that a higher moral influence will no doubt supply the moral character and completeness which he lacks, is confronted with the threat that even the good which, by virtue of his natural predisposition, he may have done, will not be allowed to stand him in stead because of this neglect (XXV, 29)....

Section Two
The Christian Religion as a Learned Religion

To the extent to which a religion propounds, as necessary, dogmas which cannot be known to be so through reason, but which are nonetheless to be imparted uncorrupted (as regards essential content) to all men in all future ages, it must be viewed (if we do not wish to assume a continuous miracle of revelation) as a sacred charge entrusted to the guardianship of *the learned*. For even though *at first,* accompanied by miracles and deeds, this religion, even in that which finds no confirmation in reason, could obtain entry everywhere, yet the very report of these miracles, together with the doctrines which stand in need of confirmation through this report, requires *with the passage of time* the written, authoritative, and unchanging instruction of posterity.

The acceptance of the fundamental principles of a religion is faith *par excellence.* We shall therefore have to examine the Christian faith on the one hand as a pure *rational faith,* on the other, as a *revealed faith.* The first may be regarded as a faith freely assented to by everyone, the second, as a faith which is commanded (*fides imperata*). Everyone can convince himself, through his own reason, of the evil which lies in human hearts and from which no one is free; of the impossibility of ever holding himself to be justified before God through his own life-conduct, and, at the same time, of the necessity for such a justification valid in His eyes; of the futility of substituting churchly observances and pious compulsory services for the righteousness which is lacking, and, over and against this, of the inescapable obligation to become a new man: and to become convinced of all this is part of religion.

But from the point where the Christian teaching is built not upon bare concepts of reason but upon facts, it is no longer called merely the Christian *religion,* but the Christian *faith,* which has been made the basis of a church. The service of a church consecrated to such a faith is therefore twofold: what, on the one hand, must be rendered the church according to the historical faith, and, on the other, what is due it in accordance with the practical and moral faith of reason. In the Christian church neither of these can be separated from the other as adequate in itself; the second is indispensable to the first because the Christian faith is a religious faith, and the first is indispensable to the second because it is a learned faith.

The Christian faith, as a *learned* faith, relies upon history and, so far as erudition (objectively) constitutes its foundation, it is not in itself a *free faith* (*fides elicita*) or one which is deduced from insight into adequate theoretical proofs. Were it a pure rational faith it would have to be thought of as a free faith even though the moral laws upon which it, as a belief in a divine Legislator, is based, command unconditionally — and it was thus presented in Section One. Indeed, if only this believing were not made a duty, it could be a free theoretical faith even when taken as an historical faith, provided all men were learned. But if it is to be valid for all men, including the unlearned, it is not only a faith which is commanded but also one which obeys the command blindly (*fides servilis*), i.e., without investigation as to whether it really is a divine command.

In the revealed doctrines of Christianity, however, one cannot by any means start with *unconditional belief* in revealed propositions (in themselves hidden from reason) and then let the knowledge of erudition follow after, merely as a defense, as it were, against an enemy attacking it from the rear; for if this were done the Christian faith would be not merely a *fides imperata,* but actually *servilis.* It must therefore always be taught as at least a *fides historice elicita;* that is, *learning* should certainly constitute in it, regarded as a revealed credal doctrine, not the rearguard but the vanguard, and then the small body of textual scholars (the clerics), who, incidentally, could not at all dispense with secular learning, would drag along behind itself the long train of the unlearned (the laity) who, of themselves, are ignorant of the Scripture (and to whose number belong even the rulers of world-states). But if this, in turn, is to be prevented from happening, recognition and respect must be accorded, in Christian dogmatics, to universal human reason as the supremely commanding principle in a natural religion, and the revealed doctrine, upon which a church is founded and which stands in need of the learned as interpreters and conservers, must be cherished and cultivated as merely a means, but a most precious means, of making this doctrine comprehensible, even to the ignorant, as well as widely diffused and permanent.

This is the *true service* of the church under the dominion of the good principle; whereas that in which revealed faith is to precede religion is *pseudo-service*. In it the moral order is wholly reversed and what is merely means is commanded unconditionally (as an end). Belief in propositions of which the unlearned can assure themselves neither through reason nor through Scripture (inasmuch as the latter would first have to be authenticated) would here be made an absolute duty (*fides imperata*) and, along with other related observances, it would be elevated, as a compulsory service, to the rank of a saving faith even though this faith lacked moral determining grounds of action. A church founded upon this latter principle does not really have *servants*, like those of the other organization, but commanding high *officials*. Even when (as in a Protestant church) these officials do not appear in hierarchical splendor as spiritual officers clothed with external power — even when, indeed, they protest verbally against all this — they yet actually wish to feel themselves regarded as the only chosen interpreters of a Holy Scripture, having robbed pure rational religion of its merited office (that of being at all times Scripture's highest interpreter) and having commanded that Scriptural learning be used solely in the interest of the churchly faith. They transform, in this way, the *service* of the church (*ministerium*) into a *domination* of its members (*imperium*) although, in order to conceal this usurpation, they make use of the modest title of the former. But this domination, which would have been easy for reason, costs the church dearly, namely, in the expenditure of great learning. For, "blind with respect to nature, it brings down upon its head the whole of antiquity and buries itself beneath it."

The course of affairs, once brought to this pass, is as follows. First, that procedure, wisely adopted by the first propagators of the teaching of Christ in order to achieve its introduction among the people, is taken as a part of religion itself, valid for all times and peoples, with the result that one is obliged to believe *that every Christian must be a Jew whose Messiah has come*. Yet this does not harmonize with the fact that a Christian is really bound by no law of Judaism (as statutory), though the entire Holy Book of this people is nonetheless supposed to be accepted faithfully as a divine revelation given to all men. Yet the authenticity of this Book involves great difficulty (an authenticity which is certainly not proved merely by the fact that passages in it, and indeed the entire sacred history appearing in the books of the Christians, are used for the sake of this proof). Prior to the beginning of

Christianity, and even prior to its considerable progress, Judaism had not gained a foothold among the *learned public,* that is, was not yet known to its learned contemporaries among other peoples; its historical recording was therefore not yet subjected to control and so its sacred Book had not, on account of its antiquity, been brought into historical credibility. Meanwhile, apart from this, it is not enough to know it in translations and to pass it on to posterity in this form; rather, the certainty of churchly faith based thereon requires that in all future times and among all peoples there be scholars who are familiar with the Hebrew language (so far as knowledge is possible of a language in which we have only a single book). And it must be regarded as not merely a concern of historical scholarship in general but one upon which hangs the salvation of mankind, that there should be men sufficiently familiar with Hebrew to assure the true religion for the world.

The Christian religion has had a similar fate, in that, even though its sacred events occurred openly under the very eyes of a learned people, its historical recording was delayed for more than a generation before this religion gained a foothold among this people's learned public; hence the authentication of the record must dispense with the corroboration of contemporaries. Yet Christianity possesses the great advantage over Judaism of being represented as coming *from the mouth of the first Teacher* not as a statutory but as a moral religion, and as thus entering into the closest relation with reason so that, through reason, it was able of itself, without historical learning, to be spread at all times and among all peoples with the greatest trustworthiness. But the first founders of the *Christian communities* did find it necessary to entwine the history of Judaism with it; this was managed wisely in view of the situation at the time, and perhaps with reference to that situation alone; thus this history too has come down to us in the sacred legacy of Christianity. But the founders of the *church* incorporated these episodical means of recommendation among the essential articles of faith and multiplied them either with tradition, or with interpretations, which acquired legal force from the Councils or were authenticated by means of scholarship. As for this scholarship, or its extreme opposite, the inner light to which every layman can pretend, it is impossible to know how many changes the faith will still have to undergo through these agencies; but this cannot be avoided so long as we seek religion without and not within us.

Translated by Theodore M. Greene and Hoyt H. Hudson

From Religion within the Limits of Reason Alone

A.
The Distinctive Characteristic of the Theology Faculty

The biblical theologian proves the existence of God on the grounds that He spoke in the Bible, which also discusses His nature (and even goes so far into it that reason cannot keep up with the text, as when, for example, it speaks of the incomprehensible mystery of His threefold personality). But the biblical theologian as such cannot and need not prove that God Himself spoke through the Bible, since that is a matter of history and belongs to the philosophy faculty. [Treating it] as a matter of faith, he will therefore base it — even for the scholar — on a certain (indemonstrable and inexplicable) *feeling* that the Bible is divine. But the question of the divine origin of the Bible (in the literal sense) must not be raised at all in public discourses directed to the people; since this is a scholarly matter, they would fail completely to understand it and, as a result, would only get entangled in impertinent speculations and doubts. In such matters it is much safer to rely on the people's confidence in their teachers. The biblical theologian can also have no authority to ascribe a nonliteral — for example, a moral — meaning to statements in the text. And since there is no human interpreter of the Scriptures authorized by God, he must rather count on a supernatural opening of his understanding by a spirit that guides to all truth than allow reason to intervene and (without any higher authority) maintain its own interpretation. Finally, as far as our will and its fulfillment of God's commands is concerned, the biblical theologian must not rely on nature — that is, on man's own moral power (virtue) — but on grace (a supernatural but, at the same time, moral influence), which man can obtain only by an ardent faith that transforms his heart — a faith that itself, in turn, he can expect only through grace. If the biblical theologian meddles with his reason in any of these tenets, then, even granting that reason strives most sincerely and earnestly for that same objective, he leaps (like Romulus's brother) over the wall of ecclesiastical faith, the only thing that assures his salvation, and strays into the free and open fields of private judgment and philosophy. And there, having run away from the Church's government, he is exposed to all the dangers of anarchy. But note well that I am here speaking only of the *pure* (*purus, putus*) biblical theologian, who is not yet contaminated by the ill-reputed spirit of freedom that belongs to reason and philosophy. For as soon as we allow two different callings to combine and run together, we can form no clear notion of the characteristic that distinguishes each by itself. . . .

Appendix
The Conflict between the Theology and Philosophy Faculties, as an Example to Clarify the Conflict of the Faculties

1
Subject Matter of the Conflict

. . . The biblical theologian says: "Search the Scriptures, where you think you find eternal life." But since our moral improvement is the sole condition of eternal life, the only way we can find eternal life in any Scripture whatsoever is by putting it there. For the concepts and principles required for eternal life cannot really be learned from anyone else: the teacher's exposition is only the occasion for him to develop them out of his own reason. But the Scriptures contain more than what is in itself required for eternal life; part of their content is a matter of historical belief, and while this can indeed be useful to religious faith as its mere sensible vehicle (for certain people and certain eras), it is not an essential part of religious faith. Now the faculty of biblical theologians insists on this historical content as divine revelation as strongly as if belief in it belonged to religion. The philosophy faculty, however, opposes the theology faculty regarding this confusion, and what divine revelation contains that is true of religion proper. . . .

For this reason scriptural erudition in Christianity is subject to many difficulties in the craft of exegesis, and the higher faculty (of biblical theologians) is bound to come into conflict with the lower faculty over it and its principle. For the higher faculty, being concerned primarily for theoretical biblical knowledge, suspects the lower faculty of philosophizing away all the teachings that must be considered real revelation and so taken literally, and of ascribing to them whatever sense suits it. On the other hand the lower faculty, looking more to the practical — that is, more to religion than to dogma — accuses the higher of so concentrating on the means, dogma, that it completely loses sight of the final end, inner religion, which must be moral and based on reason. And so, when conflict arises about the sense of a scriptural text, philosophy — that is, the lower faculty, which has truth as its end — claims the prerogative of deciding its meaning. The following section contains the philosophical principles of scriptural exegesis. By this I do not mean that the interpretation must be philosophical (aimed at contributing to philosophy), but only that the *principles* of interpretation must be philosophical. For any principle — even those exegetical principles having to do with historical or grammatical criticism — must always be dictated by reason; and this is especially true here, since what the text yields for religion can be only an object of reason.

2
Philosophical Principles of Scriptural Exegesis for Settling the Conflict

If a scriptural text contains certain *theoretical* teachings which are proclaimed sacred but which *transcend* all rational concepts (even moral ones), it *may be* interpreted in the interests of practical reason; but if it contains statements that contradict practical reason, it *must be* interpreted in the interests of practical reason. Here are some pertinent examples.

The doctrine of the Trinity, taken literally, has *no practical relevance at all,* even if we think we understand it; and it is even more clearly irrelevant if we realize that it transcends all our concepts. Whether we are to worship three or ten persons in the Divinity makes no difference: the pupil will implicitly accept one as readily as the other because he has no concept at all of a number of persons in one God (hypostases), and still more so because this distinction can make no difference in his rules of conduct. On the

other hand, if we read a moral meaning into this article of faith
(as I have tried to do in *Religion within the Limits* etc.), it would
no longer contain an inconsequential belief but an intelligible one
that refers to our moral vocation. The same holds true of the doctrine that one person of the Godhead became man. For if we think
of this God-man, not as the Idea of humanity in its full moral
perfection, present in God from eternity and beloved by Him (cf.
Religion), but as the Divinity "dwelling incarnate" in a real man
and working as a second nature in him, then we can draw nothing
practical from this mystery: since we cannot require ourselves to
rival a God, we cannot take him as an example. And I shall not
insist on the further difficulty — why, if such a union is possible in
one case, God has not let all men participate in it, so that everyone
would necessarily be pleasing to Him. Similar considerations can
be raised about the stories of the Resurrection and Ascension of
this God-man.

Translated by Mary J. Gregor

Gotthold Ephraim Lessing

Gotthold Lessing (1729–81) was born five years after Kant but died a good twenty-three years before him. So most of his writings on religion antedated those of Kant (who took up the controversial implications of his philosophy as it bore on religion only toward the end of his life), and in fact he might well be considered the Socrates to Kant's Plato, especially as he was instrumental in publishing the posthumous writings of Hermann Samuel Reimarus (1694–1768). (Although Lessing gave those writings the title *Wolfenbüttel Fragments,* Reimarus had called them *Apology for the Reasonable Worshipers of God,* perhaps the most important "pre-Socratic" work in German religious thought.) Nonetheless, Lessing appears second in this Reader not only because the authors are arranged by their birthdates but also for a more fundamental reason: as Lessing himself admitted, he was not original in his thinking or scholarship.[1] As one of his English-speaking interpreters warns:

> In assessing the originality of his contribution to thought, it is important not to overestimate him. His criticisms of orthodoxy are not new; in all this he belongs to the second or third generation, and his originality in ideas is not great.... What is wholly original in Lessing is not the argument but the fire and force of its expression, the provocative, sharply formu-

---

1. "I am not a scholar, I have never intended to become a scholar; I could not be a scholar even if it were possible in a dream. All that I have managed to achieve is the ability to make use of a learned book in case of necessity" (*Lessing's Werke,* ed. Lachmann-Muncker, 16:535).

lated sentences, the constant irony, the parry and thrust of debate.[2]

Unlike Kant, Lessing was never a philosopher by training but a playwright by avocation and a librarian by profession. And indeed some of his most important ideas on religion are located in his plays, especially his brilliantly realized *Nathan the Wise;* that work, a plea for toleration among the religions, features highly allegorized heroes such as Nathan the Jew, Saladin the Moslem, and a Knight Templar representing Christianity. At the climax of the play, Saladin asks Nathan which of the three religions is true, and Nathan replies with a fable about an ancient Oriental potentate who possessed a priceless ring that had the power to render its wearer beloved by God. It was passed down from generation to generation to the eldest son, until it came into the hands of a legatee who had three sons all equally beloved of him. Not wishing to show favoritism, he had two replicas made and gave each of his sons one of the "rings." After his death, of course, the sons took to quarreling, and each one claimed he had the real ring, but the true ring could not be identified. (Did the father have it destroyed and give three simulacra out to his sons?) A judge called in to assay the rings said that by love and brotherly concern each son could show that he had the true ring.

This allegory neatly captures Lessing's genius: on the one hand, it fully reflects the already hoary Enlightenment notion that all the "positive" religions are equally true to those who believe them, equally false to the philosophers, and equally useful to the magistrate; but on the other hand, it is expressed in a deft narration and directness of style that popularized the idea far beyond the confines of scholarly controversy.

The German Library has a whole volume devoted to Lessing (volume 12), where this play appears in its entirety, along with several of his essays on religion, which should be read in conjunction with the following selections. To avoid duplication, I have selected essays that have not appeared yet in this series (with some minor overlaps).

The first selection is from his essay "New Hypothesis concerning the Evangelists," which shows the heavy influence of Reimarus on

---

2. Henry Chadwick, introduction to *Lessing's Theological Writings* (Stanford, Calif.: Stanford University Press, 1956), 45.

his thought. In the fragments that Lessing had published, Reimarus had insisted that the idea of a specific revelation granted to a select chosen people and necessary for salvation goes against reason, for it consigns children, pagans before the birth of Christ, members of other religions, and so on, to eternal condemnation for the arbitrary accident of not hearing this revelation. With that as his postulate, Reimarus then turned his critical eye to the Bible itself and professed to see in there only the occasional writings of men who never intended them to be the medium of revealed dogmas or absolute revelation. Lessing picks up from there and seeks to prove that the evangelists were fallible as historians, establishing a theme that has proven to be dominant in German scholarship ever since.

The other selections show how much Lessing was influenced by Leibniz in his theology of God. Because historical truth was based on fallible testimony, the truths of history were an inappropriate vehicle for divine truths, which could be obtained only through the faculty of reason, a theme that will also crop up time and again in the German Idealists — in fact, it is the central presupposition of all Idealist thought from Plato to the present.

From "New Hypothesis concerning the Evangelists Regarded as Merely Human Historians"

1. Contents

First the hypothesis will be set forth in plain, straightforward prose. Then the critical proof of it will be given, and all that follows on from it.

After this will be shown the advantage which this hypothesis could have in making intelligible various difficulties and in providing a more exact explanation of disputed passages, and the conclusion will subject it to a closer scrutiny....

It goes without saying that I acknowledge as my assessors and judges only those divines whose mind is as rich in cold critical learning as it is free from prejudices. I shall pay only little regard to the judgment of other members of this profession, however respectable they may seem to me on other grounds.

1. The first followers of Christ were pure Jews, and after Christ's example did not cease to live as Jews. The other Jews gave them the name Nazarenes....

2. Certainly the Jews may have given them this name out of scorn. But it was in profound accord with the mind of Christ's disciples that they did not reject a nickname which they had in common with their Master, but gladly accepted as an honorable title a name intended to discredit them.

3. Therefore also there was nothing they could do to suppress this name again in a short time. Rather must we believe that even when the name "Christians" had been accepted in Antioch and for a long time been universal, the Palestinian Jewish Christians would have preferred to keep their old name, Nazarenes, and would have been the more concerned to preserve it since it was convenient for distinguishing them from the uncircumcised Christians against whom they always had some slight hostility, many traces of which can be found in the New Testament.

4. Would it be safe to assume that those earliest Nazarenes, very early, very soon after the death of Christ, had a written collection of narratives concerning Christ's life and teaching, which arose out of orally transmitted stories of the apostles and all those people who had lived in association with Christ? Why not?

5. And how, speaking roughly, would this collection have appeared? Like a collection of narratives, the beginning of which is so small that the first originator can be forgotten without ingratitude; which by chance is enlarged by more than one and is copied by more than one with all the freedom that is usual with such works which are attributed to nobody — just as any other such collection, I say, would always appear. Basically it is always the same. But with each copy it is in some places enlarged, in some places abbreviated, in some places altered, according as the copyist or the possessor of the copy might believe that he had included more or better narratives from the mouths of credible people who had lived with Christ.

6. And when at last the process of increasing or altering the collection had to stop, because at length the contemporaries whose authentic narratives anyone believed he could include inevitably died out; how would this collection then be entitled? Either, I imagine, after the first authorities for the narratives therein contained, or after those for whose use the collection would chiefly

have been made; or after this or that man who first gave the collection an improved form or put it into a more intelligible language.

7. If it had been called after the first authorities, how would it have been entitled? The first authorities were all people who lived with Christ, and had known him to a greater or less degree. Among them were indeed a number of women, whose little anecdotes about Christ ought the less to be despised the greater the degree of their familiarity with him. But it was chiefly his apostles from whose mouth without doubt the most numerous and reliable narratives originated. Thus it would have been entitled, this collection (the word Gospel taken in the sense of a historical narrative of Christ's life and teaching) — *The Gospel of the Apostles.*

8. And if they were named after those for whose use they were particularly made: how would they have been entitled then? How else than *The Gospel of the Nazarenes?* Or among those who did not wish to use the word Nazarenes *The Gospel of the Hebrews.* For this name quite properly belonged to the Nazarenes as Palestinian Jews.

9. Finally, if it had been named after this or that man who first gave it an improved form or translated it into a more intelligible language; how would it have been entitled then? How else than the Gospel of this man and that man who had thus gained this credit?...

19. Admittedly the later Nazarenes were *called* heretics. But fundamentally they were no more heretics than the ancient Nazarenes to whom the name of heretics had not yet been given, as we may conclude from the silence of Irenaeus. For both the one and the other believed that the Mosaic ceremonial law must be maintained together with Christianity....

23. Is it conceivable that in this thirty years there was no written record of Christ and his teaching? that the first person who decided to write one, after so long a time sat down to write it merely out of his or others' memories? that he had nothing before him by which he could justify himself in case he had to vindicate his statements in this or that detail? That is simply not credible even if he was inspired. For only he himself was aware of the inspiration, and probably even at that time people shrugged their shoulders over those who pretended to know historical facts by inspiration.

24. Thus there was a narrative of Christ written earlier than Matthew's. And during the thirty years it remained in that language in which alone its compilers could have written it. Or to put the matter less definitely and yet more accurately: it remained in the Hebrew language or in the Syriac-Chaldaean dialect of Hebrew as long as Christianity was for the most part still confined to Palestine and to the Jews in Palestine.

25. Only when Christianity was extended among the Gentiles, and so many who understood neither Hebrew nor a more modern dialect of it were curious to have better information about the person of Christ (which, however, may not have been during the first years of the Gentile mission, since all the first Gentile converts were content with the oral accounts which the apostles gave to each one), was it found necessary and useful to satisfy a pious curiosity by turning to that Nazarene source, and to make extracts or translations from it in a language which was the language of virtually the entire civilized world.

26. The first of these extracts, the first of these translations, was made, I think, by Matthew. And that, as I have said in §12, is the conjecture which may boldly be included among the historical truths, if we have any of these things at all. For all that we know both of the person of Matthew and of his Gospel, or that we can reasonably assume, not only agrees completely with this conjecture; but also a great deal which is a recurrent problem that has been insoluble to many scholars can only be explained by this conjecture.

27. For in the first place Matthew is to be held without contradiction to be the first and earliest of our evangelists. But this, as already observed, cannot possibly mean that he was absolutely the first of all who put anything into writing about Christ which was in the hands of the new converts. It can only mean that he was the first who wrote in Greek.

28. Secondly, it is very probable that Matthew was the only apostle who understood Greek, without needing to receive knowledge of this language directly through the Holy Ghost.

29. Thirdly, in favor of this view is the occasion on which Matthew must have composed his Gospel. For Eusebius writes (*H.E.* iii. 24. 5): "Matthew for some years preached the Gospel to the Hebrews in Palestine; when he finally decided to go to others for this purpose, he left his Gospel in writing in his mother tongue,

so that even in his absence he might remain their teacher." Of this strictly speaking only half can be true. Only the occasion on which Matthew wrote his Gospel can be right. But this occasion was not that he had to write a *Hebrew* Gospel, but rather that he thought a Greek compilation to be required. That is: when he had preached for long enough to the Hebrews, he did not leave behind for the Hebrews his Gospel in Hebrew (among the Hebrews in Palestine there still remained many apostles whose oral instruction they could have at any moment), but for his future use, since he now intended to preach the Gospel to others who did not understand Hebrew, he made from the Hebrew *Gospel of the Apostles* a selection in the language understood by the majority.

30. Fourthly, the entire controversy concerning the original language of Matthew is settled in a way which can satisfy both parties: both those who, following the unanimous testimony of the Church Fathers, assert that the original language of Matthew's Gospel was Hebrew; and also the modern Protestant dogmatic theologians who have and must needs have their objections to this view.

31. Indeed, the original of Matthew was certainly Hebrew, but Matthew himself was not the actual author of this original. From him, as an apostle, many narratives in the Hebrew original may well derive. But he himself did not commit these narratives to writing. At his dictation others wrote them down in Hebrew and combined them with stories from the other apostles; and from this human collection he in his time made merely a connected selection in Greek. But because his selection, his translation, followed quickly on the original, because he himself could equally well have written in Hebrew, because in view of his personal circumstances it was more probable that he in fact wrote in Hebrew, it is not surprising that to some extent the original was confused with the translation.

32. And everyone will recognize how much may be gained from accepting this view by the modern divines who from the internal evidence of Matthew and for not inconsiderable dogmatic reasons think we must conclude that Matthew could not have written in any language other than that in which we now have him. Matthew wrote what he wrote in Greek; but he drew it from a Hebrew source.

33. If he made this selection in a better known language with all the diligence, with all the caution, of which such an enterprise is worthy, then indeed, to speak only humanly, a good spirit assisted him. And no one can object if one calls this good spirit the Holy Spirit. And in this way must Matthew have gone to work; such a good spirit must have guided and supported him. For his selection or his translation not only attached rapidly to canonical rank among the Christians generally, but even among the Nazarenes themselves the name of the Greek translator henceforth became attached to the Hebrew original, and this itself was given out to be a work of Matthew. The Gospel *secundum Apostolos* came in time to be called by most people the Gospel *juxta Matthaeum,* as Jerome expressly says.

34. That I have not drawn a false conclusion here is shown by the long threads that do not snap, which I am in a position to unwind from a very tangled ball. That is: from this suggestion of mine I can explain twenty things which remain insoluble problems if one or other of the usual assertions about the original language of Matthew is maintained. I mention the most important, because in critical matters, as is well known, the new solutions which a fresh hypothesis provides, are equal to proofs of its truth....

36. Likewise, who can answer the following? If Matthew wrote originally in Greek, how does it come about that the Church Fathers unanimously assert that his Gospel was composed in Hebrew? And if he wrote his Gospel originally in Hebrew, how could his original Hebrew text be allowed to become lost? Who, I ask, can give so satisfactory an answer to this as I? The Church Fathers found a Hebrew Gospel which contained everything in Matthew and more. They thus believed it to be Matthew's own work. But this Hebrew text, supposed to be Matthew's, was in fact as regards its historical content the source of Matthew. But only the Greek selection was the actual work of the apostle, who wrote under higher oversight. Why then did it happen that the material he used was lost, after it had been used in the most authoritative way?...

41. Have we not already seen that Matthew was not a mere translator of anything and everything which he found in the Gospel of the Nazarenes? He left much which was not familiar to him, though it had good authority. There were stories which originated from all eleven apostles; many of them were quite true but were not sufficiently useful for the later Christian world. There

were stories which originated only from Christ's women associates, of which it was in part doubtful whether they had always understood correctly the wonder-man whom they so loved. There were stories which could only have come from his mother, from people who had known him in his childhood at the house of his parents; and however reliable they were, what help could they be to the world, which had had enough to learn of what he did and said after entering upon his teaching office?

42. What was thus more natural? Since Matthew's translation could not be stamped with any unmistakable sign of divinity, and since it only attained canonical status through examination and comparison, and so was confirmed by the Church and preserved — what was more natural than that several others who either did not know or did not entirely approve of Matthew's work, because they wished it contained this or that story, or because they would have preferred this or that story to be told differently, should undertake the same work, and should carry it out as each individual's powers enabled him?

43. And thus we stand here at the source from which flowed forth both the better Gospels that are still extant and the less good ones which on that account fell out of use and so were finally lost? . . .

65. And now I would only have to explain how it came about that the Gospel of the flesh was proclaimed by three evangelists if I had not already explained it. For to speak more precisely, I would only have to explain why among many other Greek Gospels which originated from the Nazarene document, the Church only preserved Mark and Luke in addition to Matthew; for the reason given by Augustine for this is scarcely satisfactory.

66. I will give my opinion briefly. Mark and Luke were preserved by the church in addition to Matthew because in many respects they filled so to speak the gap between Matthew and John; and the one was a pupil of Peter and the other a pupil of Paul.

67. That, I say, is my opinion which provides an adequate reason why the four evangelists were put together in almost all ancient copies without variation. For it has not been shown that they must have been written in precise chronological order one after another.

68. But here I cannot produce the argument supporting this opinion because I must proceed by induction, and I have been un-

able to put enough examples together to give this induction the probability of demonstration.

Translated by Henry Chadwick

"The Christianity of Reason"

1. The one most perfect Being has from eternity been able to be concerned only with the consideration of what is the most perfect thing.

2. The most perfect thing is himself; and thus from eternity God has only been able to contemplate himself.

3. To conceive, to will, and to create are one with God. One can therefore say that anything which God conceives he also creates.

4. God can think only in two ways: either he thinks of all his perfections at once, and of himself as inclusive of them all, or he thinks of his perfections individually, one separated from another, and each one by itself in its own grade.

5. God contemplated himself from eternity in all his perfection; that is, God created from eternity a being lacking no perfection which he himself possessed.

6. This being is called in Scripture the Son of God, or, which would be still better, the Son-God. A God because he lacks none of the attributes which belong to God. A Son because according to our ideas that which conceives a thing has a certain priority to the conception.

7. This being is God himself and is not to be distinguished from God because one thinks of it as soon as one thinks of God, and one cannot think of it without God; that is, because one cannot think of God without God, or because that would be no God at all from whom one would take away his own conception.

8. This being one can call an image of God, indeed an identical image.

9. The more two things have in common with one another, the greater is the harmony between them. Therefore the greatest harmony must exist between two things which have everything in common with each other, that is, between the things which together are only one.

10. Two such things are God and the Son-God, or the identical image of God; and the harmony which exists between them is called by Scripture *the Spirit which proceeds from the Father and Son.*

11. In this harmony is everything that is in the Father and also therefore everything that is in the Son; this harmony is therefore God.

12. But this harmony is God in such a way that it would not be God if the Father were not God and the Son were not God, and that both could not be God unless this harmony existed; that is, *all three are one.*

13. God contemplated his perfections individually, that is, he created beings each one of which has something of his perfections; for, to repeat it once again, every thought is a creation with God.

14. All these beings together are called the World.

15. God could think of his perfections divided in an indefinite variety of ways. There could therefore be an indefinite number of possible worlds were it not that God thinks always of the most perfect, and thus among all these thought the most perfect of worlds, and so made it real.

16. The most perfect way of thinking of his perfections individually is that of thinking of them individually in infinite grades of greater and less, which so follow on one another that there is never a jump or a gap between them.

17. Therefore the beings in this world must be ordered in such grades. They must form a series in which every member contains everything that the lower members have, and something more; but this something never reaches the final limit.

18. Such a series must be an infinite series, and in this sense the infinity of the world is incontestable.

19. God creates only simple things, and the complex is a secondary consequence of his creation.

20. Since each of these simple beings has something which the others have, and none can have anything which the others have not, there must be a harmony among these simple beings; and from this harmony everything may be explained that happens among them, that is, in the world.

21. To this point at some future time a fortunate Christian will extend the sphere of natural philosophy, but only after long centuries when explanations have been found for all phenomena in

nature so that there is nothing left to do except trace them to their true origin.

22. Since these simple beings are, as it were, limited gods, their perfections also must be similar to the perfections of God, related as parts to the whole.

23. To God's perfections belong also the consciousness of his perfection and the power to act according to his perfections; both are, as it were, the seal of his perfections.

24. With the various grades of his perfections must therefore be connected various grades of the consciousness of these perfections and the power to act in accordance with them.

25. Beings which have perfections, which are conscious of their perfections, and which have the power to act in accordance with them, are called moral beings, that is beings which can follow a law.

26. This law is derived from their own nature, and can be none other than: *Act according to your individual perfections.*

27. Since in the series of beings there cannot possibly be a jump, there must also exist beings which are not sufficiently clearly conscious of their perfections....

Translated by Henry Chadwick

"On the Reality of Things outside God"

However I may seek to explain the reality of things outside God, I must confess that I can form no idea of it.

If it is called "the complement of possibility," I ask: Is there in God an idea of this complement of possibility or not? Who will assert that there is not? But if the idea of it is in him, then the thing itself is in him: all things are real in him.

But, it will be said, the idea which God has of the reality of a thing does not do away with the reality of this thing outside him. Does it not? This reality outside him must have something which distinguishes it from the reality in his idea. That is: in the reality outside him there must be something of which God has no idea. An absurdity! But if there is nothing of the sort; if in the idea which God has of the reality of a thing everything is present that is to be found in the reality outside him, then both realties are one, and everything which is supposed to exist outside God exists in God.

Or it may be said: The reality of a thing is the sum of all possible deletions that may be applied to it. Must not this sum also be in the idea possessed by God? What definition has the reality outside him if the ideal is not present in God? Consequently this ideal is the thing itself, and to say that the thing also exists outside this ideal means that this ideal is duplicated in a way both unnecessary and absurd.

I believe that when philosophers say they affirm the reality of a thing outside God, they mean nothing more than the mere assertion that this thing is different from God, and its reality is to be explained in another way from the necessary reality of God.

But if this is all they mean, why should we not say that the ideas which God has of real things are those real things themselves? They are still sufficiently distinct from God, and their reality becomes in no sense necessary because they are real in him. For must not the contingency which they must have outside him also correspond to an image in his idea? And this image is merely their contingency itself. What is contingent outside God is also contingent in God, or God could not have any idea of the contingent outside him. I use this phrase "outside him" as it is commonly used, to show from the way I apply it that it ought not to be used.

But people will cry out in horror: Contingencies in the immutable being of God! Why? Am I the only one who does this? You yourselves must ascribe to God ideas of contingent things. Has it never occurred to you that ideas of contingent things are contingent ideas?

Translated by Henry Chadwick

"On the Origin of Revealed Religion"

1. To acknowledge one God, to seek to form the ideas most worthy of him, to take account of these most worthy ideas in all our actions and thoughts, is the most complete summary of all religion.

2. To this natural religion every man, according to the capacity of his powers, is committed and bound.

3. But since this capacity differs with every man, and accordingly each man's natural religion will be different, it has been thought necessary to guard against the disadvantages which this difference can cause not in the state of man's natural freedom but in the state of his social connection with other people.

4. That is: as soon as it is recognized as a good thing to make religion a concern for the community, people must be united about certain things and ideas, and to attribute to these conventional things and ideas precisely the importance and necessity which the acknowledged truths of natural religion possess in their own right.

5. That is: out of the religion of nature, which was not capable of being universally practiced by all men alike, a positive religion had to be constructed, just as out of the law of nature, for the same cause, a positive law has been constructed.

6. This positive religion received its sanction through the distinction of its founder, who claimed that the conventional elements in it came from God, only mediated through him, just as certainly as the essential elements in it were immediately derived from God though each individual's reason.

7. The indispensability of a positive religion, because of which the natural religion is modified in each State according to its natural and accidental conditions, I call its inner truth, and this inner truth is as great in one as in another.

8. Consequently all positive and revealed religions are equally true and equally false.

9. Equally true: insofar as it has everywhere been necessary to come to an agreement over various things in order to get uniformity and unity in public religion.

10. Equally false: in that the matters on which agreement is reached not only stand beside what is essential but also weaken and supplant it.

11. The best revealed or positive religion is that which contains the fewest conventional additions to natural religion, and least hinders the good effects of natural religion....

Translated by Henry Chadwick

"The Religion of Christ, 1780"

"For the Father also seeketh those who thus worship him."
ST. JOHN

1. It is a question whether Christ was more than a mere man. That he was a real man if he was a man at all, and that he never ceased to be a man, is not in dispute.

2. It follows that the religion of Christ and the Christian religion are two quite different things.

3. The former, the religion of Christ, is that religion which as a man he himself recognized and practiced; which every man has in common with him; which every man must so much the more desire to have in common with him, the more exalted and admirable the character which he attributes to Christ as a mere man.

4. The latter, the Christian religion, is that religion which accepts it as true that he was more than a man, and makes Christ himself, as such, the object of its worship.

5. How these two religions, the religion of Christ and the Christian religion, can exist in Christ in one and the same person, is inconceivable.

6. The doctrines and tenets of both could hardly be found in one and the same book. At least it is obvious that the former, that is the religion of Christ, is contained in the evangelists quite differently from the Christian religion.

7. The religion of Christ is therein contained in the clearest and most lucid language.

8. On the other hand, the Christian religion is so uncertain and ambiguous, that there is scarcely a single passage which, in all the history of the world, has been interpreted in the same way by two men.

Translated by Henry Chadwick

Johann Wolfgang von Goethe

Johann Goethe (1749–1832) is the most protean figure in German literature, and perhaps in all of world literature. Nothing failed to come into the purview of his Promethean curiosity, from metallurgy and mining to art criticism and philosophical speculation. Perhaps the last "Renaissance man" to grace the stage of European history, Goethe has only one peer in the sheer range of his accomplishments — Leonardo da Vinci; but unlike da Vinci, whose scientific speculations are treated with respect by historians of science, Goethe still remains somewhat the neglected genius, especially in scientific matters.

This is due above all to his lifelong resistance to Newtonian physics, which he felt was robbing the world of all that made it a home: color, resonance, and spirit. For him, as he said, "Measurements, numbers and signs do not constitute a phenomenon."[1] Virtually the whole of his professional life was spent trying to fight off the implications of Newtonianism, whether in his theory of colors, in his botanical researches, or even in his poetry. So consistent was this polemic against Newton and so high is the repute of Newton in the history of the Western mind that Goethe's consistent rebellion against Newtonian science has caused considerable embarrassment among his advocates and interpreters, who generally relegate his scientific activities to the charming and edifying spectacle of an amusing hobby indulged in by a genius whose real talents lay in other directions.

So embedded is this view that it has become something of a cliché that can be overcome only with effort. In an important testimonial, T. S. Eliot once described how much this same spell

---

1. Goethe, *Dünndruckausgabe,* ed. G. Ipsen, 2:678.

had influenced his thinking: "For most of my life I had taken it for granted that Goethe's scientific theories...were no more than the amiable eccentricities of a man of abounding curiosity who had strayed into regions for which he was not equipped."[2] This same essay describes in fascinating detail how Eliot came to suspect he might be wrong, a journey that he felt had proven to be liberating ("And antipathy overcome, when it is antipathy to any figure so great as that of Goethe, is an important liberation from a limitation of one's own mind").[3] What made Eliot especially suspicious of his prejudices was the sheer unanimous weight with which conventional wisdom had rendered its verdict on Goethe's scientific efforts: "It was, first, the unanimity of ridicule and the ease with which the learned in these matters appear to dismiss Goethe's views, [that] impelled me to wonder whether Goethe may not have been right, or at least whether his critics might not be wrong."[4]

What makes Goethe's religious views important in this regard is not just his thoroughgoing anti-Newtonianism but also his refusal to countenance a naïve optimism, even utopianism, that has characterized so much of German religious (and in the case of Feuerbach and Marx, antireligious) thought. This comes out most clearly in the essay selected for this Reader, Goethe's "Epochs of the Spirit — according to Hermann's Latest Theories," an essay little known even in Germany and whose translation, to the best of my knowledge, appears here in English for the first time.

In this essay, Goethe posits four ages of man: the age of poetry, the age of the holy (or theology), the age of philosophy (rationalism or enlightenment, the period in which Goethe was living), and finally the prosaic age, the age to come. This distinction is in some way reminiscent of Auguste Comte's later division of human history into the age of theology, the age of metaphysics, and the

---

2. T. S. Eliot, "Goethe as the Sage," in *On Poetry and Poets* (London: Faber and Faber, 1957), 214.

3. Ibid., 210.

4. Ibid., 215. Another important scholar of the German mind puts it similarly: "It may have become clear by now that Goethe's physics, though anti-Newtonian in motivation, is in fact not anti-mathematical, but as it were amathematical, which is as much as to say that it is not physics at all — at least not in the now accepted sense of the word. Newton's and Goethe's theories never meet, except at some points of confusion on Goethe's part" (Erich Heller, *The Disinherited Mind: Essays in Modern German Literature and Thought* [London: Bowes and Bowes, 1975/1952], 24).

age of science, but again Goethe's reserve toward science as it was understood by the Newtonians of his day (ancestors to today's positivism) means that there is nothing of the fatuous optimism about his predictions of the future that so marks the positivistic spirit.

"Epochs of the Spirit — according to Hermann's Latest Theories"

In the most primitive period in world history, nations and individuals were the same everywhere. Desolate emptiness at first encompassed everything. The spirit, however, was already brooding over a fluid and vivid scene. While the crowd of the autochthonous looked around in fear and astonishment, anxiously trying to satisfy the most indispensable needs, a favorable spirit gazed into the great phenomena of the world, saw what was happening, and, filled with presentiment, expressed what it saw as if it were emerging at that moment. And so in the farthest reaches of time we have: contemplation, philosophy, naming, and the poetry of nature — all in one.

Then the world became brighter: those dark and somber elements cleared up and sorted themselves out, and man seized on them so as to conquer them in a different way. A fresh, healthy sensibility looked about, serenely seeing in the past and present ... only itself. It bestowed new form to the old name and anthropomorphized (personified) the lifeless as something that had once been alive but had now died out. And thus it gave its own character to all creation. This was how popular belief lived and wove its stories.

But this faith sometimes freed itself too casually from everything abstruse that might have remained from the earlier primitive epoch. For the empire of poetry had thrived, and only he was a poet who possessed this popular faith or knew that he had to adapt himself to it. The character of this epoch was a free, virtuous, serious, and noble sensibility, exalted through its imaginative powers.

But since man knows no boundaries in his self, even when trying to be noble, and since even the clear region of human existence does not speak to him in all circumstances, he still strives to go back into the mystery and seeks a higher source for what appears before him. And just as poetry creates dryads and hamadryads over whom the higher gods exert their presence, so too does theology bring forth demons that it has been subordinating to itself for so long that they can finally be thought of as completely dependent on *one* God. We must call this epoch holy: it belongs in the highest sense of the word to reason. But reason cannot be maintained in its pure state for very long and must eventually be made subordinate (*verdächtig*) to the understanding, because it is still relying for this purpose on popular faith without being poetry and because it still gives expression to what is miraculous and ascribes to it an objective validity.

In its greatest energy and purity, the understanding honors its earliest beginnings and rejoices in the poetic faith of the people, highly esteeming this noble need of man to recognize a highest realm. Only, the man of understanding strives to appropriate everything thinkable to terms of his clarity and to dissolve even the most mysterious of phenomena. This in no way means that the faith of the people and the priests has been rejected, but behind that same faith what the man of understanding assumes is something conceivable, commendable, useful. He seeks for the meaning and transforms the unique into the general, deriving from all things national, provincial, and even individual something that can pertain to mankind in general. One cannot deny to this epoch a noble, pure, and clever striving, but it suits much better the individual of talent than the people as a whole.

Now as this way of looking on things spreads out, the last epoch arrives, which we must call the prosaic, since it does not humanize, for example, the content of the earlier ages, trying to adapt human understanding and household customs to each other, but drags out the most venerable of customs and forces them into the glare of everyday life, thereby completely destroying the primitive feelings and faith of the people and priests — in fact even destroying the faith of the understanding, which had previously assumed that behind the strange there was still a laudable context.

This epoch cannot last that long. Man's need, activated by the world fates, leaps backward and bursts the bonds of the understanding's tutelage, mixes together the faith of primeval times, that of the people and of the priests, clinging now to this tradition, now to that one, sinking into mysteries and putting fairytales in place of poetry and elevating them to articles of faith. Instead of instructing their age with their understanding and serenely sinking their roots into the past, the people of this age randomly strew good seed and bad in all directions. There is no center of gravity anymore from which perspective can be gained. Every individual steps forth and sets up shop as teacher and leader and purveys the most utter nonsense as the most rounded perfection of the whole.

In this way, then, even the value of each individual mystery has been destroyed and the faith of the people desecrated. Elements that used to develop out of each other in the most natural of ways now clash like war factions and work against each other. *Tohu we Bohu* (primeval chaos) returns. But not the first, fruitful, life-beating primeval chaos, but a chaos that chokes off life, one that leads to corruption and decomposition, from which the Spirit of God can scarcely create once more a world worthy of Himself.

We may schematize these four epochs in the following manner:

Earliest Beginnings:
Penetratingly Examined, Skillfully Named

AGE	RULING MODE	VIRTUE	FACULTY
1. Poetry	Popular belief	Hard-working	Imagination
2. Theology	Elevation to the Idea	Holy	Reason
3. Philosophy	Explanation by derivation	Clever	Understanding
4. Prose	Dissolution into everyday life	Vulgar	Sensuality

Translated by Edward T. Oakes, S.J.

Johann Gottlieb Fichte

Johann Fichte (1762–1814) was born into a large family as the eldest son of a ribbon-maker in Saxony, whose genteel poverty would no doubt have kept his son from getting much of an education (indeed young Johann herded geese as a child) but for the fortuitous accident of the report of his remarkably retentive mind reaching the ears of a local baron, who had arrived one Sunday to church too late to hear the sermon; someone suggested to him that little Fichte could reproduce the sermon verbatim. The child did this so well that the baron decided to informally adopt him and assume the responsibility for his further education, which Fichte eventually pursued, after secondary schooling at Pforta, at the Universities of Jena, Wittenberg, and Leipzig. The baron, however, died while neglecting to provide for his charge, so that Fichte was thrown upon his own resources, often bringing him throughout his life to the brink of poverty.

Nor did he help matters with his rather belligerent and provocative ways. For example, at Jena he had antagonized students with his program for reforming student societies and offended religious leaders by scheduling some of his lectures for Sunday morning. And finally a charge of atheism was leveled against him for an article of his that identified God with the moral order of the universe, the article appearing in a journal of which he was the editor. When he threatened to resign if he were censured, the government (with Goethe's concurrence) took this as an actual letter of resignation, and he was fired.

Amidst this "storm and stress," however, this "linkage" (for "identification" is too strong a term in this case) between God and the moral order provides the clue to Fichte's subsequent development. Indeed, it provides the avenue by which he can be seen primarily as a religious philosopher. That became especially clear when he went to Berlin in 1799. At first he made common cause with the Schlegels and other Romantics, but a falling out soon occurred at the publication of Fichte's *The Destiny of Man* (1800), which showed how strong his moral and religious convictions were. What especially upset the Romantics was Fichte's strong separation of man's moral essence from the nature so beloved in the Romantic sensibility, a point that comes out especially clearly in the following selection from this work.

From The Destiny of Man

Faith

This then is my true nature, my whole sublime destination. I am a member of two orders; of one purely spiritual, in which I rule merely by pure will, and of a sensuous one, in which my act alone avails. The whole aim of reason is its own activity, independent, unconditional, and having no need of any organ beyond itself. The will is the living principle of the rational soul, is indeed itself reason, when purely and simply apprehended. That reason is itself active, means, that the pure will, as such, rules and is effectual. The infinite reason alone lies immediately and entirely in the purely spiritual order. The finite being lives necessarily at the same time in a sensuous order; that is to say, in one which presents to him other objects than those of pure reason; a material object, to be advanced by instruments and powers, standing indeed under the immediate command of the will, but whose efficacy is conditional also on its own natural laws. Yet as certainly as reason is reason, must the will operate absolutely by itself, and independently of all the natural laws which determine the action, and therefore does the sensuous life of every finite being point toward a higher, into which the will itself shall lead him, and of which it shall procure him possession, a possession which indeed will be again sensually present as a state, and by no means as a mere will.

These two orders, the purely spiritual, and the sensuous, the latter consisting of an immeasurable succession of states, have existed in me from the first moment of the development of my active reason, and proceed parallel to each other. The latter producing phenomena cognizable by myself and by other beings similar to myself; the former alone bestowing on them significance, purpose, and value. I am immortal, imperishable, eternal, as soon as I form the resolution to obey the laws of eternal reason; I am not merely destined to become so. The transcendental world is no future world, it is now present; it can at no period of finite existence be more present than at another; not more after the lapse of myriads of ages than at this moment. My future sensuous existence may be liable to various modifications, but these are just as little true life, as those of the present. By that resolution of the will I lay hold on eternity, and rise high above all transitory states of existence. My will itself becomes for me a spring of eternal life, when it becomes a source of moral goodness. Without view to any further object, without inquiry as to whether my will may or may not have any result, it shall be brought into harmony with the moral law. My will shall stand alone, apart from all that is not itself, and be a world to itself, not merely as not proceeding from any thing gone before, but as not giving birth to any thing following, by which its efficacy might be brought under the operation of a foreign law. Did any second effect proceed from it, and from this again a third, in any conceivable sensuous world, opposed to that of spirit, its strength would be broken by the resistance it would encounter, the mode of its operation would no longer exactly correspond to the idea of volition, and the will would not remain free, but be limited by the peculiar laws of its heterogeneous sphere of action.

Thus indeed must I regard the will, in the present material world, the only one known to me. I am indeed compelled to believe, or to act as if I believed, that by my mere volition, my tongue, my hand, my foot, could be set in motion; but how an impulse of intelligence, a mere thought, can be the principle of motion to a heavy material mass, is not only not conceivable, but, to the mere understanding, an absurdity. To the understanding, the movements of matter can only be explained by the supposition of forces existing in matter itself....

What, then, is this law of the spiritual world which I conceive? I believe it to be this; that my will, absolutely of itself, and without the intervention of any instrument that might weaken its effect, shall act in a sphere perfectly congenial — reason upon reason, spirit upon spirit; in a sphere to which it does not give the laws of life, of activity, of progress, but which has them in itself, therefore, upon self-active reason. But spontaneous, self-active reason is will. The law of the transcendental world must, there, be a Will. A Will which operates purely as will of itself, without other instrumentality or sensual material for its operation, which is, at the same time, will and act, with whom to will is to do — to command is to execute. A Will, which is itself law; liable to no accident or caprice, nor requiring previous thought and hesitation — eternal, unchangeable, on which we may infallibly reckon as the mortal counts securely on the laws of his material world. That sublime Omnipotent Will does not dwell apart. There exists between him and all his rational creatures a spiritual bond, and he himself is this spiritual bond of the rational universe. Let me will, purely and decidedly, my duty, and in the spiritual world, at least, I shall not fail of success. Every virtuous resolution of a finite being influences the Omnipotent Will (if I may be allowed to use such an expression), not in consequence of a momentary approval, but of an everlasting law of his being. With surprising clearness does this thought now come before my soul, which hitherto was surrounded by darkness; the thought that my will, as such merely, and of itself, could have any consequences.

It has these consequences because it is immediately and infallibly perceived by another Will to which it bears affinity, which is at the same time will and act, and the only living principle of the spiritual world; its first results are in him, and, through him, on the world, which is but the product of the Infinite Will.

Thus — (for the mortal must speak in his own language,) — thus do I communicate with that Infinite Will; and through the voice of conscience in my heart, which proclaims to me what I have to do in every situation of my life, does he again communicate with me. That voice, sensualized and translated into my language, is the oracle of the Eternal, which announces to me what is to be my part in the order of the spiritual world, or in the Infinite Will, who himself makes that order. I cannot, indeed, see through, or over, that spiritual order, and I need not to do so. I am but a link in the chain, and can no more judge of the whole, than a single tone can judge of an entire harmony. But what I, myself, shall be in this harmony of spirits I must know, and this is revealed to me. Thus am I connected with the Infinite One, and there is nothing real, lasting, imperishable in me, but the voice of conscience, and my free obedience to it. By the first, the spiritual world bows down to me, and embraces me as one of its members; by the second I raise myself into it; and the Infinite Will unites me with it, and is the source of it, and of me. This only is the true and imperishable, for which my soul has yearned. All else is but phenomenon — phantasm, which vanishes, and returns in a new form.

*　　*　　*

The Infinite Will unites me with himself, and with all finite beings such as myself. The great mystery of the invisible world, and its fundamental law, inasmuch as it is a world or system of many individual wills, is the union, and reciprocal action, of many self-active and independent wills; a mystery, which lies in the present life, obvious to all, without any deeming it matter for wonder. The voice of conscience, which imposes on each his particular duty, is the ray proceeding from the Infinite One to each individual, the true constituent and basis of his life. The absolute freedom of the will, which we derive from the Infinite, and bring with us into the world of time, is the principle of this our life. I act, and the sensual perception by which alone I become a personal intelligence being supposed, it is easy to conceive that I must know of this my action, and that it must appear as a fact in a sensual world, and that inversely by the same sensualization, the in-itself purely spiritual law of duty should appear as the command to such or such an action. It is conceivable that a world should appear to me as the condition of this action, and in part the consequence and product of it. Thus far I remain on my own territory; all this has developed itself purely out of myself; I contemplate only my own state of being. But in this, my world, I admit, also, the operations of other beings independent of me, and self-active like myself. That they should know of their own operations, as I of mine, is conceivable. But how I should know of them is entirely inconceivable, as it is that they should have the knowledge of my existence, and its manifestations which I ascribe to them. How do they enter my world, or I theirs — since the principle by which we become conscious of ourselves and our operations, finds here no application? How have free spirits knowledge of free spirits, since we know that free spirits are the only reality, and that a substantial external world of matter, through which they might act on each other, is not to be thought of? Or shall we still say, we perceive our rational fellow beings by the changes they produce in the material world? In this case it may be asked again, how we perceive these changes? I comprehend very well that we should perceive changes brought about by the mechanism of nature; for the law of this mechanism is no other than the law of our own thought. But the changes of which we speak are not brought about by the mechanism of nature, but by a free will raised above all nature; and only inasmuch as we thus regard them, do we infer the existence of beings like ourselves. By what law in ourselves, then, could we discover the manifestations of other beings absolutely independent of us? In short, this mutual recognition and reciprocal action of free beings in this world, is perfectly inexplicable by the laws of nature, or of thought, and can only be explained by the supposition of their being all united in the one Infinite Will, supporting each in his sphere. The knowledge which we have of each other does not flow immediately from you to me, and from me to you, for we are separated by an insurmountable barrier; but we recognize each other in him who is the common source of our being. My conscience commands me to respect in a fellow creature the image of freedom upon the earth. Again, — whence come our feelings, our sensual perceptions, our discursive laws of thought, on which is founded the external world which we behold, in which we believe we influence each other? With respect to the two last, it is no answer to say, these are the laws of reason in itself. For us, indeed, it may be impossible to conceive any other law of reason than that under which we stand, but the actual law of reason in itself is the law of the transcendental world, or of that sublime Will, whence comes the universal agreement in feelings, which, nevertheless, are something positive, immediate, inexplicable. From this agreement, however, in feeling, perception, and in the laws of thought, proceeds our agreement in that sensual world which we all behold.

This unanimity concerning the external world, which we all receive as the sphere of our duty, is, when closely looked into, just as incomprehensible as our unanimity concerning the products of our reciprocal free agency. This is the result of the one Everlasting Infinite Will. Our faith in duty, of which we have spoken, is faith in him, in his reason, in his truth. The only pure and absolute truth which we admit in the external world is that our faithful and impartial performance of our duty in it will open to us a way to an everlasting life of moral freedom.

If this be, then indeed is there truth in this present world, and the only truth possible for finite beings: and it must be, for this world is the result of the Eternal Will in us, and this Will can have no other purpose with respect to finite beings than that which we have seen. The Eternal Will is therefore the Creator of the World, as he is the Creator of the finite reason. Those who will have that a world must have been created out of a mass of inert matter, which must always remain inert and lifeless, like a vessel made by human hands, know neither the world nor him. Reason alone truly exists. The Infinite in himself, — the finite in him; and in our minds alone has he created a world, or at least that by which and through which we unfold it. It is in his light that we behold the light, and all that it reveals to us. In our minds he continues the creation of the world, and acts on them by the call to duty. In our minds he upholds the world and the finite existence of which alone we are capable, by causing one state to arise perpetually from another. When he shall have sufficiently proved us for our further destination, and we sufficiently cultivated ourselves, by that which we call death, will he annihilate for us this life, and awaken us to the new life wrought out for us by our virtuous actions. Our life is his life. We are in his hands, and remain in them, and no one can tear us from them.

Great living Will! whom no words can name, and no conception embrace, well may I lift my thoughts to thee, for I can think only in thee. In thee, the incomprehensible, does my own existence, and that of the world, become comprehensible to me; all the problems of being are solved, and the most perfect harmony reigns. Thou art best divined by humble, child-like simplicity; thou knowest her heart, and art the always-present witness of all its dispositions, and though they should be mistaken by all the world, thou wilt not mistake them. Thou art her father, who lookest ever kindly on her, and all for her good. To thy decrees does she resign herself, body and soul. "Do with me what thou writ," she says; "I know that it will be good for me, as surely as I know that it is thou who dost it."

I veil my face before thee, and lay my finger on my lips. What thou art in thyself, or how thou appearest to thyself, I can never know. After living through a thousand lives, I shall comprehend Thee as little as I do now in this mansion of clay. What I can comprehend, becomes finite by my mere comprehension, and this can never, by perpetual ascent, be transformed into the infinite, for it does not differ from it in degree merely, but in kind. By that ascent we may find a greater and greater man, but never a God, who is capable of no measurement. I have and can imagine only this discursive, progressive consciousness, and how could I ascribe this to thee? In the idea of personality is included limitation, and I cannot ascribe to thee one without the other. I will not attempt what is impossible to my finite nature; I will not seek to understand thy nature in itself; but thy relations to me, the finite creature, and to all finite creatures, lie open before my eyes. Let me only become what I ought to become, and they will appear to me more brightly, more clearly, than my consciousness of my own existence. Thou hast wrought in me the recognition of my duty, and of my destination in the rank of reasonable beings; — how, I know not and I need not to know. Thou knowest what I think and will; how thou canst know it, by what act thou canst attain this consciousness, I know not, — nay, I know that the idea of an act, and an especial act of consciousness, belongs to me, the finite, and not to thee, the infinite. Thou willest, for thou hast willed that my free voluntary obedience should have consequences through all eternity....

*   *   *

Oh, how have I wandered in darkness during the past days of my life, how have I heaped error upon error, and deemed myself wise! Now first do I understand the doctrine which seemed so strange to me; for now first do I comprehend it in its whole compass, in its deepest foundations, and through all its consequences.

Man is not the mere product of the sensual world, and the whole aim of his existence cannot be attained in it. His high destiny passes time and space, and all that is sensual. What he is, and what he is to make himself, he must know; as his destiny is a lofty one, he must be able to raise his thoughts above all sensual limits; where his true home is, thither must his thoughts necessarily fly, and his real humanity, in which his whole mental power is displayed, appears most when he raises himself above those limits, and all that belongs to the senses vanishes in a mere reflection to mortal eyes, of what is transcendent and immortal.

Many have raised themselves to this view without any course of intellectual inquiry, merely by nobleness of heart and pure moral instinct. They have denied in practice the reality of the sensual world, and made it of no account in their resolutions and their conduct, although they might never have entertained the question of its real existence, far less have come to any conclusion in the negative. Those who are entitled to say, "Our citizenship is in heaven, we have here no abiding place, we seek it in a world to come," those whose chief principle it was to die to the world, to be born again, and already here below to enter on the kingdom of God, certainly set no value on what is merely sensual, and were, to use the scholastic expression, "transcendental Idealists."

Others, who, with the natural tendency to sensuality common to us all, have strengthened themselves in it by the adoption of a system of thought leading in the same direction, can only rise above it by a thorough and persevering course of investigation; with the purest moral intentions they would be liable to be perpetually drawn down again by their intellectual mistakes, and their whole nature would be involved in inextricable contradiction.

For such as these will the philosophy, which I now first truly understand, be the first power that can enable the imprisoned Psyche to break from the chrysalis and unfold her wings; poised on which, she casts a glance on her abandoned cell, before springing upward to live and move in a higher sphere.

Blessed be the hour in which I was first led to inquire into my own spiritual nature and destination! All my doubts are removed; I know what I can know, and have no fears for what I cannot know. I am satisfied; perfect clearness and harmony reign in my soul, and a new and more glorious existence begins for me.

My entire destiny I cannot comprehend; what I am to become, exceeds my present power of conception. A part, which is concealed from me, is visible to the father of spirits. I know only that it is secure, everlasting, and glorious. That part of it which is confided to me I know, for it is the root of all my other knowledge.

I know at every moment of my life what I have to do, and this is the aim of my existence as far as it depends on myself. Since my knowledge does not reach beyond this, I am not required to go further. On this central point I take my stand. To this shall all my thoughts and endeavors tend, and my whole power be directed — my whole existence be woven around it.

It is my duty to cultivate my understanding and to acquire knowledge, as much as I can, but purely with the intention of enlarging my sphere of duty; I shall desire to gain much, that much may be required of me. It is my duty to exercise my powers and talents in every direction, but merely in order to render myself a more convenient and better qualified instrument for the work I am called to do; for until the law of God in my heart shall have been fulfilled in practice, I am answerable for it to my conscience. It is my duty to represent in my person, as far as I am able, the most complete and perfect humanity; not for its own sake, but in order that in the form of humanity may be represented the highest perfection of virtue. I shall regard myself, and all that in me is, merely as the means to the fulfillment of duty; and shall have no other anxiety than that I may be able, as far as possible, to fulfil it.

Translated by Mrs. Percy Sinnett

Friedrich Daniel Ernst Schleiermacher

It would be hard indeed to overestimate the importance of Friedrich Schleiermacher (1768–1834) in the course of German religious thought, and indeed on Protestant thought throughout the world. Born in the city of Breslau in Silesia, he was the son of an army chaplain in the Reformed Church; but his parents converted to the Herrnhuter Brethren, a branch of the Moravian Brethren, a dissident sect of Pietist Christians who tended to look suspiciously at doctrinal formulas (at their services they would usually recite the Easter Litany instead of the Athanasian Creed common in most mainline churches since the Council of Nicea in A.D. 325), stressing instead the role of feeling and emotion. And indeed it was while on a walk with his father on their way to a meeting of the Brethren in April 1783 that Schleiermacher experienced "the first stirrings of the religious" within his breast. But while still an adolescent he came to find even the loosely held dogmas of the Herrnhuter Brethren too confining and broke with their orthodoxy, thereby provoking a deeply painful rupture in his relationship with his clerical father that was not healed until just before the elder Schleiermacher's death.

At the time of the rupture he left the confining schooling of the Brethren and enrolled at the University of Halle in 1787, where he advanced rapidly in Greek and the study of Kant and Aristotle particularly. In 1790 he accepted a position as a tutor to a noble family in Prussia and was later ordained (1794) to the ministry in the Reformed Church in Berlin, where he came into close contact with representatives of the Romantic movement. It was at that point that he discovered the hostility of the cultured elite to religion and yet the deep affinities to the religious sensibility that Romanticism represented. This gave him the idea for one of his most important works, *Speeches on Religion to Its Cultured Despisers* (1799), a work in which he drew from the standard Enlightenment contrast between natural and "positive" religion, with the former representing both the *terminus a quo* and the *terminus ad quem* of positive religion (that is, that all positive religions come from natural religion and are authentic insofar as they can be referred back to it). Unlike Kant, Schleiermacher refused to interpret this putative natural religion in terms of morality and duty but rather, true to his Pietistic background, saw it in terms of intuition and feeling (*Anschauung und Gefühl*), above all the feeling of "absolute dependence" (*schlechthinige Abhängigkeit*).

Based on the fame of this book, Schleiermacher became professor of theology at Halle but left in 1807, after the defeat of Prussia by Napoleon. He then went to Berlin where he was eventually appointed (in 1810) dean of the theological faculty at the newly created University of Berlin. And there he published his most famous work, *The Christian Faith* (1821–22), which interpreted Christianity not as a positive religion in opposition or in contrast to natural religion but as its culmination: since religion is best interpreted as the social expression of man's feeling of absolute dependence, Jesus' divinity means that he knew to the fullest extent his dependence on his Father, and this was expressed in the Christian doctrine, and Jesus was fully God and man. For Schleiermacher, this no longer stood in opposition to the dictates of reason but could be interpreted in terms of his general understanding of religion.

The selection that follows comes from his *Speeches on Religion*.

From Speeches on Religion

The Multiplicity of Religion

Divisions of the church and differences of religion almost always come together. Where there are as many creeds and confessions as churches or religious communions the two seem inseparably bound together. When you look at the present state of affairs, therefore, you might easily suppose that my judgment on the multiplicity of churches implies a similar judgment on the multiplicity of religions. But this would be to mistake my meaning entirely. I have condemned the multiplicity of churches, but my whole discussion has presupposed that the multiplicity of religions and the most distinct differences between them are both necessary and unavoidable. This became clear as I pointed out that from the very nature of the matter all strict lines of division in the church should fall away, all distinct partitions disappear....

Why should the true inner church be one? Isn't it so that each person may perceive and share the religion of others? Isn't it so that each person may have a share in expressions of religion he cannot perceive as his own because their elements emerge in quite a different way? And why should the external "church" attain unity as well, since it is only to be called this in a derivative way? Surely it is so that each person may seek out religion within the church in a form best fitted to nurture the inchoate seed of religion within him. If that seed is to grow it must have some specific form, and whatever agency serves to nurture it must have the same form.

It stands to reason, therefore, that these various manifestations of religion cannot be interpreted as mere component parts, differing only in number and size. They cannot be interpreted as the kind of parts that would not form a complete whole unless they were brought into some uniform order. If that were the case, then in the natural course of his development each person would simply attain on his own whatever it is that others have. Whatever religion another person might communicate to him would forthwith change into his own, becoming identical with it. The church would simply be an interim arrangement. The more it made its proper effect as an institution the more quickly that institution would disappear. Never have I wished even to conceive of such a view of the church, much less to present it! In the view I have given, the church is regarded as being indispensable to every religious man, since it comprises his fellowship with all the faithful. On the other hand, I certainty have presupposed the multiplicity of religions, for I find that multiplicity embedded in the very nature of religion.

Diversity, the Essence of Religious Community

Anybody can see this far into the matter: that no one can possess all religion completely in himself. While a man is always determined in some particular way, religion is determinable with endless variety. But it must be equally obvious to you that religion is not haphazardly parceled out among men depending on how each person can grasp it. No, the point must be that religion organizes itself into manifestations which resemble or differ from each other in varying degrees. Do you recall the several stages of religion to which I drew your attention earlier? I noted that the religion of a person to whom the world reveals itself as a living whole cannot be a mere continuation of the outlook of one who only perceives the world in its apparently contrasting elements. I further indicated that no vantage point surveying the whole can be attained by a person for whom the notion of a universe is still chaotic and confused. You may call these differences either types or degrees of religion. In either case you will have to admit that wherever such differences exist — that is, wherever an infinite force becomes divided or separated apart as it presents itself — these differences are ordinarily revealed in distinctive and diverse forms.

On this account, then, the multiplicity of religions is quite different from that of the churches. The essential intention of the church is to be a community. Its boundaries, therefore, cannot be set according to some uniformity among religious persons, since diversity itself is part and parcel of the making of community. If you think that in actuality the church can never become completely and uniformly united, you are perfectly right. But the only reason for this is that the community which actually exists in time and space is by its very nature limited, so that as it makes immense gains in breadth it necessarily loses too much in inner depth. On the other hand, religion presupposes the greatest possible unity of the church in its very multiplicity; it does so precisely in the fact that religion seeks to be cultivated within the church in the most definite fashion — and this move toward greater definiteness is no less important for the community than for its individual members. This definiteness and multiplicity are also necessary, moreover, for the complete manifestation of religion itself.

Religion must contain an individualizing principle within it; otherwise it could neither have existence nor be perceived. Hence we must postulate, and expect to discover, an unending quantity of definite forms in which religion reveals itself. Where we find something claiming special importance, as every particular religion does, we must see whether it actually corresponds to the individualizing principle it proclaims. We must then ascertain what causes it to be a special religion and to present itself as such — even though that may be hidden under disguises alien to its true nature. We must ascertain this essence no matter how distorted it may be either by the unavoidable influences of this transitory existence to which the imperishable has condescended or by the tainted hand of sacrilegious men.

To be satisfied with a general concept of religion would be unworthy of you because it would be so incomplete. If you wish to understand religion as it actually appears, to apprehend it from a religious perspective as an endlessly progressive work of the Spirit which is revealed in all human history, then you must abandon the senseless desire that there should be only one religion. You must lay aside your opposition to its multiplicity. As impartially as possible you must look closely at everything among the changing shapes of humanity which could possibly have sprung from that eternally fertile source of spiritual life as humanity has advanced.

Positive versus Natural Religion

These various historical manifestations of religion you call "positive religions." Under this name you have long made them the special object of scorn while you have always borne more patiently with what you call "natural religion" in contrast, despite your opposition to religion generally. You have even spoken of "natural religion" with some respect. I do not hesitate to express my deep feeling about this attitude. In a word: for my part I completely reject this weighted comparison between positive and natural religion. For anyone who has religion at all and professes to love it, to concede the comparison would be the grossest inconsistency, throwing him into the most patent self-contradiction. Indeed, for my own part I would consider all my efforts wasted if I had been no more successful than to make this so-called natural religion commendable to you.

On the other hand, since religion is generally offensive to you, I have always considered it quite natural for you to make this distinction — and in a way suitable to your own outlook. Ordinarily, so-called natural religion has worn so thin, and has such a metaphysical and moral style to it, that little of the distinctive character of religion is allowed to shine through. It knows how to live "the reserved life" very well, how to restrain and accommodate itself so that it can be tolerated anywhere. In contrast, every positive religion bears certain strong traits, has a very clearly marked physiognomy, so that every move it makes, even if one throws only a fleeting glance at it, offers an unfailing reminder of what it actually is.

Is this the true inner basis of your aversion? So it seems. For it is the only reason given which actually touches the matter itself. If this is true, then you must rid yourselves of it now. That done, I shall have no real quarrel against you left. If you see that a special and noble human disposition underlies religion, one which must take form wherever it shows itself, then it can no longer be offensive to you to view religion in the definite forms in which it has actually appeared to date. Instead you must grant these forms your consideration all the more willingly as the distinctively different character of religion takes shape within each one.

But you may not admit the truth of this explanation. You might now apply all those reproaches you are accustomed to make against religion to the particular religions as well, asserting that what continually occasions and justifies those reproaches lies precisely in what you call the "positive" element in religion. You might also claim that in consequence these religions cannot possibly be the natural manifestations of true religion as I have tried to indicate. You might point out to me that all these religions, without exception, are full of what I have expressly denied belongs to the nature of religion and that a principle of corruption must therefore lie deeply lodged within their very constitution. You might remind me that each declares itself alone to be the true religion, claiming that its distinctive character makes it the very highest form. They would seem, you might say, to be distinguished from each other not by essentials but by incidentals they should get rid of. Or you might indicate that, quite against the nature of true religion, they are always demonstrating, refuting, and contending, either with the weapons of art and intellect or with instruments still more foreign and unworthy. You might add that precisely in proportion as you esteem religion and acknowledge its importance you are drawn to take a lively interest in its enjoying the greatest possible freedom, the freedom to cultivate itself on all sides and in the most manifold fashion. But you might also suppose that you are therefore forced to despise those particular forms all the more keenly which hold their adherents to the same form and the same word which refuse them the freedom to follow their own nature and force them into molds against their nature. In contrast, you might then strenuously acclaim the superiority of natural over positive religion in all these respects.

Externals: Necessary and Misleading

Once again I attest that I do not wish to ignore the misinterpretations and distortions present in all religions. The repugnance they arouse in you is not at all objectionable to me. Indeed, I recognize this much-bewailed degeneration, this detouring into foreign territory, in them all. The greater the divine quality of a religion the less I would be inclined to cover up its corruption or admiringly to look after its maverick expressions. But forget this one-sided view for once and let me conduct you to another outlook on the matter. Consider how much of this corruption is due to those who have dragged religion from the inner sanctuary of the heart out into the civil arena. And note that much of this corruption becomes unavoidable as soon as the infinite has put on an imperfect and limited frame, descending into the sphere of time and submitting to the general influence of finite things. However deeply rooted this corruption may be within such people, moreover, and however greatly the religions may have suffered from it, consider at least this as well. Suppose I am right. Suppose this is the genuinely religious view of things: that every trace of the divine, the true, and the eternal is to be sought out wherever it can be found, even if it is in what to us appears common and lowly, and that even the faintest vestige is to be revered. Then your investigations can dispense least of all with these "petty" evidences, because they actually have more valid claims to be judged religiously than anything else.

Nevertheless, you would find more than remote traces of the deity here. I invite you to study every faith professed by man, every religion to which you can assign a definite name and character. Suppose it had degenerated into a vacuous heap of rituals long ago, or into a vacant system of abstract theories and concepts. Wouldn't you discover, in examining its original ingredients at their source, that all this dead dross was once the molten outpourings of an inner fire? Wouldn't you learn that in all religions there is something, more or less, of the true nature of religion as I have depicted it to you? Wouldn't you see, accordingly, that each religion has been one of those special forms which mankind has necessarily to assume somewhere within the various regions of the earth, somewhere along the various stages of its spiritual development?

I must forgo trying to compass the whole field for you in any fully systematic way. That would be the study of a lifetime, not the business of a single discourse. Yet you should also be protected against the dangers of wandering about aimlessly within this endless chaos, against being misled by false concepts because they happen to be prominent today. You should be helped to estimate the genuine essence of particular religions and their true contents by an appropriate standard. By using a definite and secure procedure, you should thus be able to distinguish the inner from the outer factors, the genuine from the borrowed and extraneous, the sacred from the profane. As a beginning, forget all the particular religions and the attributes characteristically assigned to them. Try first to obtain a general view from the inside out, to see how the essence of a positive religion is actually to be apprehended and defined. You will immediately discover that the positive religions are actually those specific forms in which religion must present itself. You will discover that your so-called natural religion cannot lay claim to anything like this. It cannot, because it is nothing more than a paltry, imprecise thought to which nothing can correspond in reality. You will further discover that a true individual cultivation of religious capacity is possible only in the positive religions, and that in their essence they do nothing to impede the freedom of their adherents.

Religious Plurality

Why have I assumed that religion can only come to be fully given through a great multiplicity of forms, all as thoroughly definite as possible? Only on grounds that naturally follow from what I have said about the essence of religion. That is, the whole of religion is nothing other than the totality of all man's relations to the deity. It is this totality of relations as apprehended in all the possible ways through which man can be aware of the deity as his immediate life. In this sense there certainly is a single universal religion, for it really would be a poor and crippled life were all man's basic relations to the deity not included wherever religion is found. These relations cannot possibly come to be apprehended all in the same way, however. Each is quite differently grasped. Why? Precisely because the diverse relations alone can be immediately felt, and only because these relations are immediately felt can they be depicted; but the actual composition of all the differences is simply a product of thought. You are mistaken, therefore, when you speak of your "single universal religion" as though it were natural to all, for no one will have his true and proper religion if it is to be the same for all.

We all exist "somewhere." Therefore these relations of man to the whole have varying degrees of proximity to each other, and because of this difference in overall relationship each feeling is bound to arise differently in the life of each person. We all exist as "someone." Therefore each person has a greater receptivity for some religious perceptions and feelings than for others. In this manner every person's experience is different. Obviously, then, no single relationship can do justice to every feeling. This can only be done through all of these relationships together, so that the whole of religion cannot be present until all these differently arising views of each relationship are actually given. But this further condition can only be fulfilled through an endless quantity of different forms, each of which sufficiently determines what the other forms are according to the distinctly different principle of relationship operative within it. The same religious element is distinctively modified in each of these forms. Taken together, the elements of each form thus constitute a truly distinct religion.

Now what determines and distinguishes these individual forms is already evident in what I have said. What is common to their component parts and holds them together — that is, the principle of adhesion which they follow and which must therefore be used to judge to which kind of religion each religious datum belongs — has also been made clear. But some people claim that the religions we know of historically — which are the only ones available for testing this view — are not actually situated or interrelated in this way. We must look into this assertion.

The Quantum Theory of Religion

First of all, a given form of religion is not distinct merely because it contains a certain quantity of religious matter. It is a complete misunderstanding of the nature of particular religions to think so, even though the error is frequently propagated among their own adherents. And it can only give rise to variously infectious false beliefs. For example, those who hold this view suppose that since so many men have adopted the same religion as they have, they all must share exactly the same body of religious views and feelings as they have — the same faith, the same opinions. This commonality they take to be the essence of their religion. It is very hard to learn what is distinctively characteristic or individual in a religion by adding up the particulars like this. This is, moreover, about the least successful method for deriving the concept of a religion, no matter how general the concept. Do you really think the positive religions demand a specific, exclusive sum of religious perspectives and feelings, thus deterring the individual's freedom to cultivate religion for himself? If so, you are simply mistaken. Individual perceptions and feelings are, as you know, the basic elements of religion. We cannot possibly begin to understand the character of a religion by viewing these elements as a mere quantitative heap, taking no regard for their respective roles or status.

I have already tried to show you that religion has to be variously formed because various views may apply to each relationship depending on how that relationship, or circumstance, relates to the rest. If this is true, such an exclusive composition of some of these relationships would not help us at all, since the composite result would not enable us to determine any of the possible views applied to them. If the positive religions were only distinguishable by means of such an excluding process, they could certainly not be the special manifestations we seek. But this is not their character, which can be seen in the fact that it is impossible to gain a definite concept of the positive religions from this point of view. Such a concept must be possible to form, however, since they persist in existing apart. Only what merges in fact is inseparable in concept.

It is clear that the various perceptions and feelings are not in any determinate way dependent on or aroused by each other. Each one exists for itself. By various combinations each one can lead to every other. Hence, if the different religions were only distinguished in this fashion they could not continue side by side for long; each would soon adapt itself to the point of achieving uniformity with all the rest. Even in the religion of an individual person nothing is more accidental as it develops through his life's course than the sum of religious matter that comes to consciousness within him. He may remain opaque to some views while others shine right through to him. In this respect his religion is in constant flux. Now if these boundaries shift so in the lives of individual persons, then this is all the more reason why they cannot be identical with what is permanent and essential in the religion several persons hold in common. It must be a highly accidental and unusual occurrence indeed for several men to remain together even for awhile in precisely the same circle of perceptions and to share exactly the same feelings.

Translated by Terrence N. Tice

Georg Wilhelm Friedrich Hegel

No one in the history of philosophy has made greater claims for philosophy vis-à-vis its competitor, religion, yet has gone further to make philosophy a quasi-religious activity than G. W. F. Hegel (1770–1831). We can capture something of Hegel's style as well as of his daring boldness in appropriating, in a rather Promethean way, the religious attitude into his philosophy from the following remark: "I raise myself in thought to the Absolute,... thus being infinite consciousness. Yet at the same time I am finite consciousness.... Both aspects seek each other out and yet flee from each other.... I am the struggle between them."[1]

But how the "I" manages this struggle depends crucially on the historical situation wherein this "I" is situated. In an important adumbration of Feuerbach's theory of alienation and Marx's historical critique of religion, Hegel will insist that the outcome of the eternal struggle in man between finite and infinite consciousness depends on the dialectical movement in history between freedom and tyranny:

> Thus the despotism of the Roman emperors had chased the human spirit from the earth and spread a misery which compelled men to seek and expect happiness in heaven; robbed of freedom, their spirit, their eternal and absolute element, was forced to take flight to the deity. [The doctrine of] God's objectivity is a counterpart to the corruption and slavery of man, and it is strictly only a revelation, only a manifestation of the spirit of the age.... The spirit of the age was revealed

---

1. Hegel, *Philosophie der Religion*, 11:64, in *Werke: Vollständige Ausgabe durch eine Verein von Freunden des Verewigten*, 2d ed. (Berlin: Duncker and Humbolt, 1840–47).

in its objective conception of God when He was no longer regarded as like ourselves, though infinitely greater, but was put into another world in whose confines we had no part, to which we contributed nothing by our activity, but into which, at best, we could beg or conjure our way.[2]

As we have already noted, Hegel saw his way clear to the healing of this historically induced alienation through the absorption (*Aufhebung*) of religion into philosophy, specifically his own. The project was made possible because of his identification of eternal mind (or Spirit) with itself in the positing of finite minds. And once philosophy realized this insight, the way was open to the philosophical healing of religion's alienating effects. The Hegel selection is drawn from his lectures on the philosophy of religion delivered in 1827.

From Lectures on the Philosophy of Religion

The Relationship of the Science of Religion to the Needs of Our Time

Although it follows upon a period when the antipathy became once more a presupposition, the present day seems again to be more propitious for the linkage of philosophy and theology. In support of this view two circumstances must be underlined. The first concerns the content, the second the form. With reference to the *content,* the reproach has usually been brought against philosophy that by it the content of the doctrine of the revealed, positive religion is suppressed, that through it Christianity is destroyed. Only a so-called natural religion and theology has been admitted in philosophy, i.e., a content that the natural light of reason could supply regarding God; but it was invariably considered as standing opposed to Christianity. At present this reproach that philosophy is destructive of dogma has been removed, and in fact the theology

---

2. Hegel, *The Positivity of the Christian Religion*, 2.2, in *Early Theological Writings,* trans. T. M. Knox and R. Kroner (Chicago: University of Chicago Press, 1948), 162–63.

of our time, i.e., of the last thirty to fifty years, has on its own part effected this removal.

In recent theology very few of the dogmas of the earlier system of ecclesiastical confessions have survived or at least retained the importance previously attributed to them, and others have not been set in their place. One could easily arrive at the view that a widespread, nearly universal indifference toward the doctrines of faith formerly regarded as essential has entered into the general religiousness of the public. For though Christ as reconciler and savior is still constantly made the focus of faith, nevertheless what formerly was called in orthodox dogmatics the work of salvation has taken on a significance so strongly psychological and so very prosaic that only the semblance of the ancient doctrine of the church remains. In lieu of the former dogmas we now behold in Christ merely "great energy of character and constancy of conviction, for the sake of which Christ deemed his life of no account." This is now the universal object of faith. Thus Christ is dragged down to the level of human affairs, not to the level of the commonplace but still to that of the human, into the sphere of a mode of action of which pagans such as Socrates have also been capable. And so, although Christ has remained the focal point of faith for many people who are religious and also more profound in outlook, it must still seem that the most weighty doctrines have lost much of their interest, faith in the Trinity, for example, or the miracles in the Old and New Testaments, etc.

If a large part of the educated public, even many theologians, had to declare with hand on heart whether they hold those doctrines of faith to be indispensable for eternal blessedness, or whether not believing in them would have eternal damnation as its consequence, there can surely be no doubt what the answer would be. "Eternal damnation" and "eternal blessedness" are themselves phrases that may not be used in so-called polite company; such expressions count as *arrēta* (inexpressible). Even though one does not disavow them, one still would be embarrassed to have to declare oneself about them. And if one has read the books of dogmatics, of edification and sermons of our day, in which the basic doctrines of Christianity ought to be expounded or at any rate taken as fundamental, and one were obliged to pass judgment on whether in the greater part of current theological literature those doctrines are expressed in an orthodox sense and without ambiguity or escape hatches, then again there is no question what the answer would be. If now theology no longer places such importance on the positive doctrines of Christianity, or for that matter if through their interpretation these doctrines are enveloped in such a fog, then one impediment to the philosophical comprehension of dogmas drops away, which used to arise from the fact that philosophy was considered to be an opponent of the teachings of the church. If those doctrines have declined so sharply in their interest, then philosophy can operate without constraint in regard to them.

The most important sign that these positive dogmas have lost much of their importance is that in the main these doctrines are treated *historically*. As far as this historical procedure is concerned, it deals with thoughts and representations that were had, introduced, and fought over by others, with convictions that belong to others, with histories that do not take place within our spirit, do not engage the needs of our spirit. What is of interest is rather how these things have come about in the case of others, the contingent way in which they were formed. The absolute way in which these doctrines were formed — out of the depths of spirit — is forgotten, and so their necessity and truth is forgotten, too, and the question what one holds as one's own conviction meets with astonishment. The historical procedure is very busy with these doctrines, though not with their content but rather with the external features of the controversies about them, with the passions that have attached themselves to them, etc. For this reason philosophy no longer has to face the reproach that it devalues the dogmas. Instead it suffers the reproach of containing within itself too much of the teachings of the church, more than the generally prevailing theology of our time.

The other circumstance that seems to favor the renewed linkage of theology and philosophy concerns the *form*. Here indeed it is a question of the conviction of the age that God is revealed immediately in the consciousness of human beings, that religion amounts just to this point, that the human being *knows God immediately*. This immediate knowing is called "religion," but also "reason" and "faith," too, though faith in a sense different from that of the church. All conviction *that* God is, and regarding *what* God is, rests, so it is surmised, upon this immediate revealedness in the human being, upon this faith. This general representation is now an established preconception. It implies that the highest or

religious content discloses itself to the human being in the spirit itself, that spirit manifests itself in spirit, *in this my own spirit,* that
faith has its root in the inner self or in what is most my own, that
my inmost core is inseparable from it. This is the general principle, the way in which religious faith is defined in recent times as
immediate intuition, as knowledge within me that absolutely does
not come from without. Its effect is utterly to remove all external
authority, all alien confirmation. What is to be valid for me must
have its confirmation in my own spirit. The impetus can certainly
come from without, but the external origin is unimportant. *That* I
believe is due to *the witness of my own spirit.*

Now this being-present or manifesting of that content is the
simple principle of philosophical cognition itself: namely, that our
consciousness has immediate knowledge of God, that we have
an absolutely certain knowledge of God's being. Not only does
philosophy not repudiate this proposition, but it forms a basic
determination within philosophy itself. In this way it is to be
regarded as a gain, as a kind of good fortune, that basic principles of philosophy itself are active as general preconceptions in
the universal [i.e., popular] mode of representation, so that the
philosophical principle can more easily gain general assent among
educated people.

[However, in the first place,] in regard to this immediate knowledge it is noteworthy that the principle does not stand still at
this simple determinacy, this naïve content. It does not express
itself merely affirmatively. Instead the naïve knowledge proceeds
polemically against cognition and is especially directed against the
cognition or conceptual comprehension of God. What it demands
is not merely that one should believe, should know immediately.
What it maintains is not simply that consciousness of God is con-
joined with self-consciousness, but rather that the relationship to
God is only and exclusively an immediate one. The immediacy
of the connectedness is taken as precluding the alternative determination of mediation, and because it is a mediated knowledge
philosophy is disparaged on the grounds that it is only a finite
knowledge of the finite.

More precisely, the *immediacy* of this knowledge is supposed to
reside above all in the fact that one knows *that* God is, *not what*
God is. The expansion, the content, the fulfillment of the representation of God is thus negated. But what we call "cognition"

involves knowing not only *that* an object is but *also what* it is; and knowing what it is, not just in a general way or having a certain acquaintance with it, some certitude about it, but knowing what its determinations are, what its content is, so that our knowing is a fulfilled and verified knowledge in which we are aware of the necessary connectedness of these determinations.

It is claimed that God cannot be cognized at all, but that we are only aware that God *is;* this we [supposedly] *found* in our consciousness. If we first set aside the polemical orientation of this claim and consider only just what is involved in the assertion of immediate knowledge, it is this: that on the one hand it is our spirit itself that bears witness to this content, that the content does not come from without or only through instruction. On the contrary, our conviction about it rests on the assent of our own spirit, on our consciousness, that spirit finds this content within itself. On the other hand, consciousness also relates itself to this content, so that this consciousness and this content, God, are inseparable. In fact it is *this connection* in general, this knowledge of God and the inseparability of consciousness from this content, that we call *religion in general.* But at the same time the implication in this assertion of immediate knowledge is that we ought to stop short with the consideration of religion as such — more precisely, with the consideration of this connection with God. There is to be no progressing to the cognitive knowledge of God, to the divine content as this content would be divinely, or essentially, in God himself. In this sense it is further declared that we can know only our relation to God, not what God himself is. "Only our relation" falls within what is meant by religion generally. That is why it is that nowadays we merely hear religion talked about but find no investigations into God's nature or what God might be within himself, how God's nature must be defined. God as such is not made the object [of inquiry] himself; God is not before us as an object of cognition, and knowledge does not spread out within this sphere. Only our relation to God, or religion as such, is an object [of inquiry] for us. Our discussion concerns religion as such and does not, or at least not very much, concern God. Expositions of God's nature have become ever fewer. What is said is only that human beings ought to have religion. The connection religion has with philosophy and the state is discussed, but not God.

But if we elucidate what is implied in the thesis of immediate knowledge, what is immediately declared by it, then God himself is expressed in relation to consciousness in such a way that this relation is something inseparable or that we must consider both sides together, and this is the essential object of our consideration. This is itself the philosophical idea, and is not opposed to the philosophical concept. According to the philosophical concept God is *spirit,* concrete; and if we inquire more precisely what spirit is, it turns out that the basic concept of spirit is the one whose development constitutes the entire doctrine of religion. If we ask our consciousness for a provisional account of what spirit is, the answer is that spirit is a self-manifesting, a being for spirit. *Spirit is for spirit* and of course not merely in an external, contingent manner. Instead it *is* spirit only insofar as it is *for* spirit. This is what constitutes the concept of spirit itself. Or, to put the point more theologically, God's spirit is [present] essentially in his community; God *is* spirit only insofar as God is in his *community.*

Because the inseparable unity of consciousness with God is affirmed in what immediate knowledge contains, this inseparability therefore contains what is implied in the *concept of spirit:* [namely,] that spirit is for spirit itself, that the treatment cannot be one-sided or merely treatment of the subject according to its finitude, i.e., according to its contingent life; instead it [must be] considered under the aspect in which it has the infinite absolute content as its object. When the subject is considered by itself (the subjective individual as such) it is considered in its finite knowing, its knowledge of the finite. By the same token it is also maintained regarding the other side of the relation that God is not to be considered in isolation, for that is not possible. One knows of God only in connection with consciousness.

What has been stated are the basic characteristics that we can regard as immediate impressions and unmediated convictions of the age relating expressly to religion, to knowledge of God. Therefore only what are basic elements or fundamental concepts of philosophy of religion can be linked up with this foundation. This also provides us with an external justification for forging a path to our science without having to be polemical toward the views that supposedly stand in the way of philosophy. Certainly these contentions do oppose themselves to philosophical cognition, for there is no limit to that lack of awareness about the knowledge of God which is opposed to philosophy. But exactly those contentions, which for this reason maintain that they are contradicting philosophy, that they are contesting it and are most sharply opposed to it — if we look at their content, the determinate view they express, then we see that in themselves they exhibit agreement with that which they assail.

The result of the study of philosophy is that those walls of division, which are supposed to separate absolutely, become transparent; or that when we get to the bottom of things we discover absolute agreement where we thought there was the most extreme antithesis.

More specifically, these contemporary impressions are polemical against the amplification of the inherent content. We are to believe in God, but in general are not to know what God is, are not to have any determinate knowledge of God. The possession of determinate knowledge is what is meant by "cognition." On this basis theology as such has been reduced to a minimum of dogma. Its content has become extremely sparse although much talking, scholarship, and argumentation go on. This tendency is principally directed against the mode of amplification called dogmatics. We can compare this shift in attitude to what was done for the purpose of the Reformation. Then the amplification of the system of hierarchy was contested, and the leading of Christianity back to the simplicity of the first Christian era was offered as the defining goal. Similarly, it is basically characteristic of the modern period that the doctrines of the Protestant church have been brought back to a minimum. But despite theology's reduction of its knowledge to a minimum it still needs to know many things of different sorts, such as the ethical order and human relationships. Moreover, its subject matter is becoming more extensive; the learning displayed in its manifold historical eloquence is highly accomplished. Thus one is engaged not with one's own cognition but with cognition of other people's representations. We can compare this bustling about of theology with the work of the countinghouse clerk or cashier, because all the active bustle is concerned with the alien truths of others. It will become plain in our treatment of the science of religion that it is the peculiar concern of reason to form itself into an all-embracing intellectual realm. The main thing about this intellectual formation is that it occurs *rationally*, according to the necessity of the subject matter, of the content itself, not according to caprice and chance.

Because it has thus contracted exclusively into the knowledge *that* God is, theology has extended its object to embrace ethical life and morality; and because this extension itself is not supposed to occur via cognition, it takes place *arbitrarily,* rather than according to necessity. This argumentative thinking makes some assumption or other, and proceeds according to the relationships of the understanding [employed in the kind] of reflection that we have developed within us through our education, without any criticism of these relationships. That approach is gaining ground in this science [theology]. In contrast, development by means of the concept admits of no contingency. That is just why it is so fervently denounced, because it chains us down to proceeding according to the necessity of the thing rather than according to fancies and opinions.

That argumentative method involves assumptions, which themselves can in turn be called in question. Yet the argumentative theology of the Christian church pretends nevertheless to possess a firm footing, asserting, "For us the firm footing is the Bible, it is the words of the Bible." But against this one can quote the essential sense of the text, "the letter kills," etc. One does not take the words [of the Bible] as they stand, because what is understood by the biblical "word" is not words or letters as such but the spirit with which they are grasped. For we know historically that quite opposite dogmas have been derived from these words, that the most contrasting viewpoints have been elicited from the letter of the text because the spirit did not grasp it. In these instances appeal was to the letter, but the genuine ground is the spirit.

The words of the Bible constitute an unsystematic account; they are Christianity as it appeared in the beginning. It is *spirit* that grasps the content, that spells it out. How it is done depends on how spirit is disposed, on whether it is the right and true spirit that grasps the words. This true spirit can only be the one that proceeds within itself according to necessity, not according to assumptions. This spirit that interprets must legitimate itself on its own account, and its proper legitimation is the subject matter itself, the content, that which the concept substantiates.

Hence the authority of the canonical faith of the church has been in part degraded, in part removed. The *symbolum* or *regula fidei* itself is no longer regarded as something totally binding but instead as something that has to be interpreted and explained from the Bible. But the interpretation depends on the spirit that explains. The absolute footing is just the concept. To the contrary, by means of exegesis such basic doctrines of Christianity have been partly set aside and partly explained in quite lukewarm fashion. Dogmas such as those of the Trinity and the miracles have been put in the shadows by theology itself. Their justification and true affirmation can occur only by means of the cognizing spirit, and for this reason much more of dogmatics has been preserved in philosophy than in dogmatics or in theology itself as such.

We should note in the second place the consequence of imposing upon philosophy, in particular upon philosophy of religion, the demand that before we embark upon cognitive knowing we must investigate the nature of the cognitive faculty itself; only this investigation of the instrument would show for certain whether we can rightfully try for cognition of God. We wanted just to proceed to the thing itself without turning to further preliminaries. But this question lies so close to our concern that it must be attended to. It seems to be a fair demand that one should test one's powers and examine one's instrument before setting to work. But plausible as this demand may appear, it proves to be no less unjustified and empty. With such analogies it is often the case that forms that suit one context do not suit another. How should reason be investigated? Doubtless rationally. Therefore this investigation is itself a rational cognizing. For the investigation of cognition there is no way open save that of cognition. We are supposed to cognize reason, and what we want to do is still supposed to be a rational cognizing. So we are imposing a requirement that annuls itself. This is the same demand as the one in the familiar anecdote in which a Scholastic declares that he won't go into the water until he has learned to swim.

Besides, in philosophy of religion we have as our object God himself, *absolute reason*. Since we know God [who is] absolute reason, and investigate this reason, we cognize it, we behave cognitively. Absolute spirit is knowledge, the determinate rational knowledge of its own self. Therefore when we occupy ourselves with this object it is immediately the case that we are dealing with and investigating rational cognition, and this cognition is itself rational conceptual inquiry and knowledge. So the [critical] requirement proves to be completely empty. Our *scientific cognition is itself the required investigation* of cognitive knowing.

The second circumstance requiring discussion at this point is the following observation. We should recall here what we said by way of introduction, that on the whole religion is the highest or ultimate sphere of human consciousness, whether as feeling, volition, representation, knowledge, or cognition. It is the absolute result, the region into which the human being passes over as that of absolute truth. In order to meet this universal definition, consciousness must already have elevated itself into this sphere transcending the finite generally, transcending finite existence, conditions, purposes, and interests — in particular, transcending all finite thoughts and finite relationships of every sort. In order to be within the sphere of religion one must have set aside these things, forgotten them. In contrast with these basic specifications, however, it very frequently happens when philosophy in general and philosophizing about God in particular are criticized, that finite thoughts, relationships of limitedness, and categories and forms of the finite are introduced in the service of this discourse. Opposition that draws upon such finite forms is directed against philosophy generally and especially against the highest kind, the philosophy of religion in particular. Belonging to such finite forms is the immediacy of knowing or the "fact of consciousness." Examples of such categories include the antitheses of finite and infinite and of subject and object, abstract forms that are no longer in place in that absolute abundance of content that religion is. They must of course occur in our science, for they are moments of the essential relationship that lies at the basis of religion. But the main thing is that their nature must have been investigated and cognized long beforehand. If we are dealing with religion scientifically, this primarily logical cognition must lie behind us. We must long since have finished with such categories. The usual practice, however, is to base oneself on them in order to oppose the concept, the idea, rational cognition. These categories are employed entirely uncritically, in a wholly artless fashion, just as if Kant's *Critique of Pure Reason* were nonexistent, a book that put them to the test and arrived in its own way at the result that they can serve only for the cognition of phenomena and not of the truth. In religion, however, one is not dealing with phenomena but with the absolute content. How totally improper, indeed tasteless, it is that categories of this kind are adduced against philosophy, as if one could say something novel to philosophy or to any educated person in this way, as if anyone who has not totally neglected his education would not know that the finite is not the infinite, that subject is different from object, immediacy different from mediation. Yet this sort of cleverness is brought forward triumphantly and without a blush, as if here one has made a discovery.

That these forms are different everyone knows; but that these determinations are still at the same time inseparable is another matter. There is reluctance to ascribe to the concept this power, though it can be encountered even in physical phenomena. We know that in the magnet the south pole is quite distinct from the north pole, and yet they are inseparable. We also say of two things, for example, that they are as different as heaven and earth. It is correct that these two are plainly different, but they are inseparable. We cannot point out earth apart from the heavens, and vice versa. Immediate and mediated knowledge are *distinct* from one another, and yet only a very modest investigation is needed in order to see that they are *inseparable*. Hence, before one is ready to proceed to philosophy of religion, one must be done with such one-sided forms. From these considerations it can easily be seen how difficult it is for a philosopher to engage in discussion with those who oppose philosophy of religion in this fashion; for they display too great an ignorance and are totally unfamiliar with the forms and categories in which they launch their attack and deliver their verdict upon philosophy. Being unfamiliar with the inner spirit of the concepts, they bluntly declare that immediacy is surely something different from mediation. They utter such platitudes as something novel, but in so doing they also assert that immediate knowledge exists in isolation, on its own account, wholly unaffected, without having reflected upon these subjects, without having paid attention to their outer nature or inner spirit to see how these determinations are present in them. This kind of opposition to philosophy has the tedious consequence that in order to show people that their contentions are self-contradictory one must first go back to the alphabet of philosophy itself. But the thinking spirit must be beyond such forms of reflection. It must be acquainted with their nature, with the true relationship that obtains within them, namely the infinite relationship, in which their finitude is sublated.

Only slight experience is needed to see that where there is immediate knowledge there is also mediated knowledge, and vice versa. Immediate knowledge, like mediated knowledge, is by itself completely one-sided. *The true* is their unity, *an immediate knowledge that likewise mediates,* a mediated knowledge that is at the same time internally simple, or is immediate reference to itself. That one-sidedness makes these determinations finite. Inasmuch as it is suspended through such a connection, it is a relationship of infinity. It is the same with object and subject. In a subject that is internally objective the one-sidedness disappears; the difference emphatically does not disappear, for it belongs to the pulse of its vitality, to the impetus, motion, and restlessness of spiritual as well as of natural life. Here is a unification in which the difference is not extinguished, but all the same it is sublated.

Translated by Peter C. Hodgson et al.

Arthur Schopenhauer

Arthur Schopenhauer (1788–1860) is notorious for being a philosopher of "pessimism," but the reputation can be misleading if not properly understood. Though often truculent and even paranoid in his personal dealings (he often slept with a loaded pistol near him) and compulsively obsessed with the possibility of disease, he nonetheless could be a lively and much sought-after guest at dinner parties, for he was renowned for his satirical wit. And his obsession with disease was not all that irrational: he left Berlin during the cholera epidemic in 1831; Hegel did not, and that cost him his life — an ironic ending to probably the most famous grudge-match in the history of philosophy. No term of abuse, if wittily phrased and devastatingly accurate, was foreign to Schopenhauer: windbag, charlatan, the Caliban of philosophy, the terms and invective pile up without measure. Richard Taylor attributes this aversion to the happy accident that Schopenhauer was partly educated in England, "and forever exhibited some of the intellectual habits characteristic of British thought, particularly clarity of style."[1]

This clarity of style, Schopenhauer knew, was not merely a matter of embellishment but had a direct bearing on the quality of thought: only a man whose thoughts are trite and vapid, he said,

---

1. Richard Taylor, "Schopenhauer," in *A Critical History of Philosophy*, ed. D. J. O'Connor (New York: Free Press, 1964), 365. It should also be mentioned that Schopenhauer contemplated translating Kant's *Critique of Pure Reason* into English as well as Hume's *Dialogue concerning Natural Religion* into German, a twofold challenge that Patrick Gardiner holds to have been fully within his powers: "There can be little doubt that he would have performed both of these tasks well, for his knowledge of English was excellent; but unfortunately nothing came of either project" (Patrick Gardiner, "Schopenhauer," in *Encyclopedia of Philosophy*, ed. Paul Edwards [New York: Free Press, 1967], 7:326.

feels the need to wrap them in an obfuscating and preposterous style, just as an ugly person resorts to cosmetics. And this he found to be the central disease of all the German Idealists, including Kant, whom he admired:

> Kant's style bears throughout the stamp of a preeminent mind, genuine strong individuality, and quite exceptional powers of thought.... Nevertheless Kant's language is often indistinct, indefinite, inadequate, and sometimes obscure. ...He who is himself clear to the bottom and knows with perfect distinctness what he thinks and wishes, will never write indistinctly, will never set up wavering and indefinite conceptions.... The most injurious result of Kant's occasionally obscure language is that it acted as *exemplar vitiis imitabile;* indeed, it was misconstrued as a pernicious authorization. The public was compelled to see that what is obscure is not always without significance; consequently, *what was without significance took refuge behind obscure language.* Fichte was the first to seize this new privilege and use it vigorously; Schelling at least equaled him; and a host of hungry scribblers, without talent and without honesty, soon outbade them both. But the height of audacity, in serving up pure nonsense, in stringing together senseless and extravagant mazes of words, such as had previously only been heard in madhouses, was finally reached in Hegel, and became the instrument of the most barefaced general mystification that has ever taken place, with a result which will appear fabulous to posterity, and will remain henceforth as a monument of German stupidity.[2]

And this uncomfortably accurate stylistic diagnosis goes far to explain Schopenhauer's alleged "pessimism." For what most annoyed Schopenhauer about Hegel was his presumption in assuming that his own philosophy had absorbed and superseded all that came before it, representing the culmination of a process of inevitable improvement and progressive divinization of human history.[3] Against this kind of fatuous optimism, Schopenhauer

---

2. Arthur Schopenhauer, *The World as Will and Representation,* trans. R. B. Haldane and J. Kemp (London: Kegan Paul, 1891), 2:20–22.

3. For example, when Napoleon marched into Jena in October 1806, Hegel was there, feverishly trying to put the finishing touches on his first great work,

set himself to do battle with full force, usually not by stressing such "grim" topics as death and disease (though he by no means shies away from these either) but simply by pointing out what most philosophers like to ignore, such as noise, sex, and animal behavior.[4]

The Phenomenology of Spirit. The night Jena burned, Hegel's flat was ransacked, and he lost nearly everything, underwear included. But as Charles Larmore explains, "Far from being frightened or angry, he was beside himself with delight. The conclusion of his book had proclaimed that philosophy should aspire not to rise above history, but to be one with it, in 'the Golgotha of the Absolute Spirit.' And now...who should ride through town but History personified, Napoleon himself. 'I saw the Emperor, that World Soul,' he exclaimed to a friend. Napoleon took no notice of Hegel, of course; but this, too, was as it should be: Philosophy had called upon History, and History had returned the favor, though naturally without knowing that it was doing so" (Charles Larmore, "Where There's a Will," *New Republic,* March 4, 1991, 38).

4. Taylor gives a brilliant summation of Schopenhauer's realism about sex: "[He] found displayed in all living things, in their response to the sexual impulse, a bondage to something quite unknown to them, and it seemed obvious to him that human beings were no exception at all. We view with amused fascination the behavior of adolescents as these desires begin to be uncomprehendingly but nonetheless compellingly felt. Sexual desire, in all its numberless expressions, has been the primary ingredient of poetry, song, and humor since these began. Any allusion to it, however vague and dimly hinted, is always instantly recognized and always raises a smile, just because of the consciousness all men have both of its ineluctable appeal to the will and its absurdity to the intellect. Animals battle rain, cold, and every obstacle to gain the goal of procreation, having no real conception of what it is and usually no knowledge whatever of what constrains them so — something which, moreover, could only appear to them, from the standpoint of their own interest, as trivial in comparison to its cost. It appeared to Schopenhauer no different on the level of man, except that men have a clear intellectual comprehension of what they take to be the goal, namely the act of procreation itself — which is, however, not the goal at all, but only a means. They represent it to themselves as something quite sublime and deserving of all the effort it claims. Men even suppose that, unlike lower creatures, they first perceive sexual union as an inestimable good and then direct their wills to the attainment of it, as though the opposite were not perfectly obvious. No man ever chooses the goal, or selects the impulse to be driven toward it. Sexual desire expresses itself, even in men, before there is any clear knowledge at all of the means to its gratification. The perniciousness of this was considered by Schopenhauer to be appalling beyond human reckoning. The highest claims of duty, as in famines and wars, subside in its presence. Things that men have learned should have an absolute claim on their conduct — such as honor, veracity, and justice — are almost casually jettisoned in favor of this prior claim laid upon them by nature, the moment a chance for its fulfillment is seen or even hinted at. Thrones have been abandoned to it, fortunes squandered, and few men can think without shame upon how their own petty affairs are ceaselessly muddled by it. Cupid finds ways, Schopenhauer noted, of slipping locks of hair even into the manuscripts of philosophers and into the portfolios of cabinet ministers" (Taylor, "Schopenhauer," 374–75).

And among those often unnoticed realities, Schopenhauer pointed out how religion achieves its greatness when it unsparingly points out the bleakness of the human condition; indeed for him, the great founders such as the Buddha and Jesus penetrate beyond all wishful thinking and ceaselessly insist that the world is infected with suffering and evil. After all, the very symbol of Christianity is an instrument of torture, degradation, and capital punishment. Our selection from Schopenhauer is an illustration of these views.

From The World as Will and Representation

If we compare life to a circular path of red-hot coals having a few cool places, a path that we have to run over incessantly, then the man entangled in delusion is comforted by the cool place on which he is just now standing, or which he sees near him, and sets out to run over the path. But the man who sees through the *principium individuationis,* and recognizes the true nature of things-in-themselves, and thus the whole, is no longer susceptible of such consolation; he sees himself in all places simultaneously, and withdraws. His will turns about; it no longer affirms its own inner nature, mirrored in the phenomenon, but denies it. The phenomenon by which this becomes manifest is the transition from virtue to *asceticism.* In other words, it is no longer enough for him to love others like himself, and to do as much for them as for himself, but there arises in him a strong aversion to the inner nature whose expression is his own phenomenon, to the will-to-live, the kernel and essence of that world recognized as full of misery. He therefore renounces precisely this inner nature, which appears in him and is expressed already by his body, and his action gives the lie to his phenomenon, and appears in open contradiction thereto. Essentially nothing but a phenomenon of the will, he ceases to will anything, guards against attaching his will to anything, tries to establish firmly in himself the greatest indifference to all things. His body, healthy and strong, expresses the sexual impulse through the genitals, but he denies the will, and gives the lie to the body; he desires no sexual satisfaction on any condition. Voluntary and complete chastity is the first step in asceticism or the denial of the will-to-live. It thereby denies the affirmation of the will which goes beyond the individual life, and thus announces that the will, whose phenomenon is the body, ceases with the life of this body. Nature, always true and naïve, asserts that, if this maxim became universal, the human race would die out; and after what was said in the second book about the connection of all phenomena of will, I think I can assume that, with the highest phenomenon of will, the weaker reflection of it, namely the animal world, would also be abolished, just as the half-shades vanish with the full light of day. With the complete abolition of knowledge the rest of the world would of itself also vanish into nothing, for there can be no object without a subject. Here I would like to refer to a passage in the *Veda* where it says: "As in this world hungry children press round their mother, so do all beings await the holy oblation." Sacrifice signifies resignation generally, and the rest of nature has to expect its salvation from man who is at the same time priest and sacrifice. In fact, it is worth mentioning as extremely remarkable that this thought has also been expressed by the admirable and immeasurably profound Angelus Silesius in the little poem entitled "Man Brings All to God"; it runs:

> Man! all love you; great is the throng around you:
> All flock to you that they may attain to God.

But an even greater mystic, Meister Eckhart, whose wonderful writings have at last (1857) become accessible to us through the edition of Franz Pfeiffer, says wholly in the sense here discussed: "I confirm this with Christ, for he says: 'I, if I be lifted up from...the earth, will draw all things [men] unto me' (John xii, 32). So shall the good man draw all things up to God, to the source whence they first came. The masters certify to us that all creatures are made for the sake of man. This is proved in all creatures by the fact that one creature makes use of another; the ox makes use of the grass, the fish of the water, the bird of the air, the animals of the forest. Thus all creatures come to the profit of the good man. A good man bears to God one creature in the other." He means that because, in and with himself, man also saves the animals, he makes use of them in this life. It seems to me indeed that that difficult passage in the Bible, Rom. viii, 21–24, is to be interpreted in this sense.

Even in Buddhism there is no lack of expressions of this matter; for example, when the Buddha, while still a Bodhisattva, has his horse saddled for the last time, for the flight from his father's house into the wilderness, he says to the horse in verse: "Long have you existed in life and in death, but now you shall cease to carry and to draw. Bear me away from here just this once, O Kantakana, and when I have attained the Law (have become Buddha), I shall not forget you."

Asceticism shows itself further in voluntary and intentional poverty, which arises not only *per accidens,* since property is given away to alleviate the sufferings of others, but which is here an end in itself; it is to serve as a constant mortification of the will, so that satisfaction of desires, the sweets of life, may not again stir the will, of which self-knowledge has conceived a horror. He who has reached this point still always feels, as living body, as concrete phenomenon of will, the natural tendency to every kind of willing; but he deliberately suppresses it, since he compels himself to refrain from doing all that he would like to do, and on the other hand to do all that he would not like to do, even if this has no further purpose than that of serving to mortify the will. As he himself denies the will that appears in his own person, he will not resist when another does the same thing, in other words, inflicts wrong on him. Therefore, every suffering that comes to him from outside through chance or the wickedness of others is welcome to him; every injury, every ignominy, every outrage. He gladly accepts them as the opportunity for giving himself the certainty that he no longer affirms the will, but gladly sides with every enemy of the will's phenomenon that is his own person. He therefore endures such ignominy and suffering with inexhaustible patience and gentleness, returns good for all evil without ostentation, and allows the fire of anger to rise again within him as little as he does the fire of desires. Just as he mortifies the will itself, so does he mortify its visibility, its objectivity, the body. He nourishes it sparingly, lest its vigorous flourishing and thriving should animate afresh and excite more strongly the will, of which it is the mere expression and mirror. Thus he resorts to fasting, and even to self-castigation and self-torture, in order that, by constant privation and suffering, he may more and more break down and kill the will that he recognizes and abhors as the source of his own suffering existence and of the world's. Finally, if death comes, which breaks up the phenomenon of this will, the essence of such will having long since expired through free denial of itself except for the feeble residue which appears as the vitality of this body, then it is most welcome, and is cheerfully accepted as a longed-for deliverance. It is not merely the phenomenon, as in the case of others, that comes to an end with death, but the inner being itself that is abolished; this had a feeble existence merely in the phenomenon. This last slender bond is now severed; for him who ends thus, the world has at the same time ended.

And what I have described here with feeble tongue, and only in general terms, is not some philosophical fable, invented by myself and only of today. No, it was the enviable life of so many saints and great souls among the Christians, and even more among the Hindus and Buddhists, and also among the believers of other religions. Different as were the dogmas that were impressed on their faculty of reason, the inner, direct, and intuitive knowledge from which alone all virtue and holiness can come is nevertheless expressed in precisely the same way in the conduct of life. For here also is seen the great distinction between intuitive and abstract knowledge, a distinction of such importance and of general application in the whole of our discussion, and one which hitherto has received too little notice. Between the two is a wide gulf; and, in regard to knowledge of the inner nature of the world, this gulf can be crossed only by philosophy. Intuitively, or *in concreto,* every man is really conscious of all philosophical truths; but to bring them into his abstract knowledge, into reflection, is the business of the philosopher, who neither ought to nor can do more than this.

Thus it may be that the inner nature of holiness, of self-renunciation, of mortification of one's own will, of asceticism, is here for the first time expressed in abstract terms and free from everything mythical, as *denial of the will-to-live,* which appears after the complete knowledge of its own inner being has become for it the quieter of all willing. On the other hand, it has been known directly and expressed in deed by all those saints and ascetics who, in spite of the same inner knowledge, used very different language according to the dogmas which their faculty of reason had accepted, and in consequence of which an Indian, a Christian, or a Lamaist saint must each give a very different account of his own conduct; but this is of no importance at all as regards the fact. A saint may be full of the most absurd superstition, or, on the other hand, may be a philosopher; it is all the same. His conduct alone is evidence that he is a saint; for, in a moral regard, it springs not from abstract knowledge, but from intuitively apprehended, immediate knowledge of the world and of its inner nature, and is expressed by him through some dogma only for the satisfaction of his faculty of reason. It is therefore just as little necessary for the saint to be a philosopher as for the philosopher to be a saint; just as it is not necessary for a perfectly beautiful person to be a great sculptor, or for a great sculptor to be himself a beautiful person. In general, it is a strange demand on a moralist that he should commend no other virtue than that which he himself possesses. To repeat abstractly, universally, and distinctly in concepts the whole inner nature of the world, and thus to deposit it as a reflected image in permanent concepts always ready for the faculty of reason, this and nothing else is philosophy....

But my description, given above, of the denial of the will-to-live, or of the conduct of a beautiful soul, of a resigned and voluntarily expiating saint, is only abstract and general, and therefore cold. As the knowledge from which results the denial of the will is intuitive and not abstract, it finds its complete expression not in abstract concepts, but only in the deed and in conduct. Therefore, in order to understand more fully what we express philosophically as denial of the will-to-live, we have to learn to know examples from experience and reality. Naturally we shall not come across them in daily experience: *nam omnia praeclara tam difficilia quam rara sunt* [For all that is excellent and eminent is as difficult as it is rare], as Spinoza admirably says. Therefore, unless we are made eyewitnesses by a specially favorable fate, we shall have to content ourselves with the biographies of such persons. Indian literature, as we see from the little that is so far known to us through translations, is very rich in descriptions of the lives of saints, penitents, Samanas, Sannyasis, and so on. Even the well-known *Mythologie des Indous* of Madame de Polier, although by no means praiseworthy in every respect, contains many excellent examples of this kind (especially in vol. 2, chap. 13). Among Christians there is also no lack of examples affording us the illustrations that we have in mind. Let us see the biographies, often badly written, of those persons sometimes called saintly souls, sometimes pietists, quietists, pious enthusiasts, and so on. Collections of such biographies have been made at various times, such as Tersteegen's *Leben heiliger Seefen,* Reiz's *Geschichte der Wiedergeborenen* in our own day, a collection by Kanne which, with much that is bad, yet contains some good, especially the *Leben der Beata Sturmin*. To this category very properly belongs the life of St. Francis of Assisi, that true personification of asceticism and prototype of all mendicant friars. His life, described by his younger contemporary St. Bonaventure, also famous as a scholastic, has recently been republished: *Vita S. Francisci a S. Bonaventura concinnata* (Soest, 1847), shortly after the appearance in France of an accurate and detailed biography which utilizes all the sources: *Histoire de S. François d'Assise*, by Chavin de Mallan (1845). As an oriental parallel to these monastic writings, we have the book of Spence Hardy: *Eastern Monachism, An Account of the Order of Mendicants founded by Gotama Budha* (1850), which is very well worth reading. It shows us the same thing under a different cloak. We also see how immaterial it is whether it proceeds from a theistic or from an atheistic religion. But as a special and extremely full example and actual illustration of the conceptions I advance, I can particularly recommend the *Autobiography* of Madame de Guyon. To become acquainted with that great and beautiful soul, whose remembrance always fills me with reverence, and to do justice to the excellence of her disposition while making allowances for the superstition of her faculty of reason, must be gratifying to every person of the better sort, just as with common thinkers, in other words the majority, that book will always stand in bad repute. For everyone, always and everywhere, can appreciate only that which is to some extent analogous to him, and for which he has at any rate a feeble gift; this holds good of the ethical as well as of the intellectual. To a certain extent we might regard even the well-known French biography of Spinoza as a case in point, if we use as the key to it that excellent introduction to his very inadequate essay, *De Emendatione Intellectus*. At the same time, I can recommend this passage as the most effective means known to me of stilling the storm of the passions. Finally, even the great Goethe, Greek as he was, did not regard it as beneath his dignity to show us this most beautiful side of humanity in the elucidating mirror of the poetic art, since he presented to us in an idealized form the life of Fräulein Klettenberg in the *Confessions of a Beautiful Soul,* and later, in his own biography, gave us also a historical account of it. Besides this, he twice narrated the life of St. Philip Neri. The history of the world will, and indeed must, always keep silence about the persons whose conduct is the best and only adequate illustration of this important point of our investigation. For the material of world-history is quite different therefrom, and indeed opposed to it; thus it is not the denial and giving up of the will-to-live, but its affirmation and manifestation in innumerable individuals in which its dissension with itself at the highest point of its objectification appears with perfect distinctness, and brings before our eyes, now the superior strength of the individual through his shrewdness, now the might of the many through their mass, now the ascendancy of chance personified as fate, always the vanity and futility of the whole striving and effort. But we do not follow here the thread of phenomena in time, but, as philosophers, try to investigate the ethical significance of actions, and take this as the only criterion of what is significant and important for us. No fear of the always permanent majority of vulgarity and shallowness will prevent us from acknowledging that the greatest, the most important, and the most significant phenomenon that the world can show is not the conqueror of the world, but the overcomer of the world, and so really nothing but the quiet and unobserved conduct in the life of such a man. On this man has dawned the knowledge in consequence of which he gives up and denies that will-to-live that fills everything, and strives and strains in all. The freedom of this will first appears here in him alone, and by it his actions now become the very opposite of the ordinary. For the philosopher, therefore, in this respect those accounts of the lives of saintly, self-denying persons, badly written as they generally are, and mixed up with superstition and nonsense, are through the importance of the material incomparably more instructive and important than even Plutarch and Livy....

I wish to add only a little more to the general description of their state. We saw above that the wicked man, by the vehemence of his willing, suffers constant, consuming, inner torment, and finally that, when all the objects of willing are exhausted, he quenches the fiery thirst of his willfulness by the sight of others' pain. On the other hand, the man in whom the denial of the will-to-live has dawned, however poor, cheerless, and full of privation his state may be when looked at from outside, is full of inner cheerfulness and true heavenly peace. It is not the restless and turbulent pressure of life, the jubilant delight that has keen suffering as its preceding or succeeding condition, such as constitute the conduct of the man attached to life, but it is an unshakable peace, a deep calm and inward serenity, a state that we cannot behold without

the greatest longing, when it is brought before our eyes or imagination, since we at once recognize it as that which alone is right,
infinitely outweighing everything else, at which our better spirit
cries to us the great *sapere aude*. We then feel that every fulfillment of our wishes won from the world is only like the alms that
keep the beggar alive today so that he may starve again tomorrow.
Resignation, on the other hand, is like the inherited estate; it frees
its owner from all care and anxiety for ever....

By the expression *asceticism*, which I have already used so often,
I understand in the narrower sense this *deliberate* breaking of the
will by refusing the agreeable and looking for the disagreeable, the
voluntarily chosen way of life of penance and self-chastisement, for
the constant mortification of the will.

Now, if we see this practiced by persons who have already attained to denial of the will, in order that they may keep to it,
then suffering in general, as it is inflicted by fate, is also a second way of attaining to that denial. Indeed, we may assume that
most men can reach it only in this way, and that it is the suffering
personally felt, not the suffering merely known, which most frequently produces complete resignation, often only at the approach
of death. For only in the case of a few is mere knowledge sufficient
to bring about the denial of the will, the knowledge namely that
sees through the *principium individuationis*, first producing perfect goodness of disposition and universal love of mankind, and
finally enabling them to recognize as their own all the sufferings
of the world. Even in the case of the individual who approaches
this point, the tolerable condition of his own person, the flattery
of the moment, the allurement of hope, and the satisfaction of the
will offering itself again and again, i.e., the satisfaction of desire,
are almost invariably a constant obstacle to the denial of the will,
and a constant temptation to a renewed affirmation of it. For this
reason, all those allurements have in this respect been personified
as the devil. Therefore in most cases the will must be broken by
the greatest personal suffering before its self-denial appears. We
then see the man suddenly retire into himself, after he is brought
to the verge of despair through all the stages of increasing affliction
with the most violent resistance. We see him know himself and the
world, change his whole nature, rise above himself and above all
suffering, as if purified and sanctified by it, in inviolable peace,
bliss, and sublimity, willingly renounce everything he formerly de-

sired with the greatest vehemence, and gladly welcome death. It is the gleam of silver that suddenly appears from the purifying flame of suffering, the gleam of the denial of the will-to-live, of salvation. Occasionally we see even those who were very wicked purified to this degree by the deepest grief and sorrow; they have become different, and are completely converted. Therefore, their previous misdeeds no longer trouble their consciences, yet they gladly pay for such misdeeds with death, and willingly see the end of the phenomenon of that will that is now foreign to and abhorred by them. The great Goethe has given us a distinct and visible description of this denial of the will, brought about by great misfortune and by the despair of all deliverance, in his immortal masterpiece *Faust,* in the story of the sufferings of Gretchen. I know of no other description in poetry. It is a perfect specimen of the second path, which leads to the denial of the will not, like the first, through the mere knowledge of the suffering of a whole world which one acquires voluntarily, but through the excessive pain felt in one's own person. It is true that very many tragedies bring their violently willing heroes ultimately to this point of complete resignation, and then the will-to-live and its phenomenon usually end at the same time. But no description known to me brings to us the essential point of that conversion so distinctly and so free from everything extraneous as the one mentioned in *Faust.*

In real life we see those unfortunate persons who have to drink to the dregs the greatest measure of suffering, face a shameful, violent, and often painful death on the scaffold with complete mental vigor, after they are deprived of all hope; and very often we see them converted in this way. We should not, of course, assume that there is so great a difference between their character and that of most men as their fate seems to suggest; we have to ascribe the latter for the most part to circumstances; yet they are guilty and, to a considerable degree, bad. But we see many of them converted in the way mentioned, after the appearance of complete hopelessness. They now show actual goodness and purity of disposition, true abhorrence of committing any deed in the least degree wicked or uncharitable. They forgive their enemies, even those through whom they innocently suffered; and not merely in words and from a kind of hypocritical fear of the judges of the nether world, but in reality and with inward earnestness, and with no wish for revenge. Indeed, their suffering and dying in the end become agreeable to them, for the denial of the will-to-live has made its appearance. They often decline the deliverance offered them, and die willingly, peacefully, and blissfully. The last secret of life has revealed itself to them in the excess of pain, the secret, namely, that evil and wickedness, suffering and hatred, the tormented and the tormentor, different as they may appear to knowledge that follows the principle of sufficient reason, are in themselves one phenomenon of the one will-to-live that objectifies its conflict with itself by means of the *principium individuationis*. They have learned to know both sides in full measure, the wickedness and the evil; and since they ultimately see the identity of the two, they reject them both at the same time; they deny the will-to-live. As we have said, it is a matter of complete indifference by what myths and dogmas they account to their faculty of reason for this intuitive and immediate knowledge, and for their conversion. . . .

However, a knowledge of the above-mentioned kind of the nature of this existence may depart again simultaneously with its occasion, and the will-to-live, and with it the previous character, may reappear. . . . For every case of suffering, a will can be conceived which surpasses it in intensity, and is unconquered by it. Therefore, Plato speaks in the *Phaedo* [116 E] of persons who, up to the moment of their execution, feast, carouse, drink, indulge in sexual pleasures, affirming life right up to the death. Shakespeare in Cardinal Beaufortos presents to us the fearful end of a wicked ruffian who dies full of despair, since no suffering or death can break his will that is vehement to the extreme point of wickedness.

The more intense the will, the more glaring the phenomenon of its conflict, and hence the greater the suffering. A world that was the phenomenon of an incomparably more intense will-to-live than the present one is, would exhibit so much the greater suffering; thus it would be a *hell*.

Translated by E. F. J. Payne

Ludwig Andreas Feuerbach

It would scarcely be possible to overestimate the importance of Ludwig Feuerbach (1804–1872) to the history of modern thought on religion. For it is his theory of projection that provides the indispensable foundation for the later theories of Marx, Nietzsche, and Freud, the three most important thinkers in Germany who took this idea and made it central to all subsequent modern theorizing on religion — whether in support or opposition. No less a figure than Karl Barth, in fact, could say:

> No one among the modern philosophers has been so intensively, so exclusively and precisely occupied with the problem of theology as Feuerbach — although his love was an unhappy one.... In his writings, at least in those on the Bible, the Church Fathers, and especially on Luther, his theological skill places him above most modern philosophers. No philosopher of his time penetrated the contemporary theological situation as effectually as he, and few spoke with such relevance.[1]

It is true that Feuerbach tends to be a bit of a "one-note Johnny" who can vary his central insight that theology is really anthropology in different formulations but who never goes beyond that one insight the way Marx, Nietzsche, and Freud all did, with their much greater mental powers. But Feuerbach was the first to raise the challenge that everything that has to do with religion — the idea of God, the dogma in Christianity of the divinity of Christ, images of Father-God and Mother of God — is an outgrowth

---

1. Karl Barth, *Die Theologie und die Kirche* (Zurich: Evangelischer Verlag, 1928), 2:212.

of the human mind that, unbeknownst to itself, has "projected" its own internal experiences and images onto the "blank screen" of the universe and made these images seem externally real by divinizing them in the hypostasis of a projected Godhead.

Feuerbach was born in Landshut in 1804, his father a criminologist who later became a judge. He began his university studies in theology at Heidelberg, but in 1824 he went to Berlin where, by attending Hegel's lectures, he came under his direct personal sway and decided to change his field from theology to philosophy. In 1828 he became a lecturer in philosophy at the University of Erlangen but resigned his post in 1832 because it had just been discovered that he was the author of the anonymously published tract *Gedanken über Tod und Unsterblichkeit,* which had enjoyed for a brief time a *succès de scandale* for its interpretation of Christianity as a selfish and inhumane religion. He never held a public post after that, living off a moderate pension from the Bavarian government, income from his writings, and revenue accruing to his wife's holdings in a pottery factory. In 1841 he published his most famous work, *Das Wesen des Christentums*, which was soon (1854) translated into English by the renowned novelist George Eliot, who herself shared some of the notoriety of the book.

Feuerbach's claim in this book that he was not attacking Christianity but only interpreting it receives at least a measure of support from his refusal to collaborate with Karl Marx and from his sneering contempt for what he called "obtuse materialism," under which he subsumed Newtonian science, empiricism, and positivism. Nonetheless, his critique of Hegelianism served as the starting point for the rest of left-wing Hegelianism, of whom Marx is by far the most important and influential representative.

From The Essence of Christianity

Preface

. . . Religion is the dream of the human mind. But even in dreams we do not find ourselves in emptiness or in heaven, but on earth, in the realm of reality; we only see real things in the entrancing splendor of imagination and caprice, instead of in the simple daylight of reality and necessity. Hence I do nothing more to religion — and to speculative philosophy and theology also — than to open its eyes, or rather to turn its gaze from the internal toward the external, i.e., I change the object as it is in the imagination into the object as it is in reality.

But certainly for the present age, which prefers the sign to the thing signified, the copy to the original, fancy to reality, the appearance to the essence, this change, inasmuch as it does away with illusion, is an absolute annihilation, or at least a reckless profanation; for in these days *illusion* only is *sacred, truth profane.* Nay, sacredness is held to be enhanced in proportion as truth decreases and illusion increases, so that the highest degree of illusion comes to be the highest degree of sacredness. Religion has disappeared, and for it has been substituted, even among Protestants, the *appearance* of religion — the Church — in order at least that "the faith" may be imparted to the ignorant and indiscriminating multitude; *that* faith being still the Christian, because the Christian churches stand now as they did a thousand years ago, and now, as formerly, the *eternal signs* of the faith are in vogue. That which has no longer any existence in faith (the faith of the modern world is only an ostensible faith, a faith which does not believe what it fancies that it believes, and is only an undecided, pusillanimous unbelief) is still to pass current as *opinion:* that which is no longer sacred in itself and in truth is still at least to *seem* sacred. Hence the simulated religious indignation of the present age, the age of shows and illusion, concerning my analysis, especially of the Sacraments. But let it not be demanded of an author who proposes to himself as his goal not the favor of his contemporaries, but only the truth, the unveiled, naked truth, that he should have or feign respect toward an empty appearance, especially as the object which underlies this appearance is in itself the culminating point of religion, i.e., the point at which the religious slides into the irreligious. Thus much in justification, not in excuse, of my analysis of the Sacraments....

Chapter 1: Introduction

The Essential Nature of Man

Religion has its basis in the essential difference between man and the brute — the brutes have no religion. It is true that the old uncritical writers on natural history attributed to the elephant, among other laudable qualities, the virtue of religiousness; but the religion of elephants belongs to the realm of fable. Cuvier, one of the greatest authorities on the animal kingdom, assigns, on the strength of his personal observations, no higher grade of intelligence to the elephant than to the dog.

But what is this essential difference between man and the brute? The most simple, general, and also the most popular answer to this question is — consciousness: — but consciousness in the strict sense; for the consciousness implied in the feeling of self as an individual, in discrimination by the senses, in the perception and even judgment of outward things according to definite sensible signs, cannot be denied to the brutes. Consciousness in the strictest sense is present only in a being to whom his species, his essential nature, is an object of thought. The brute is indeed conscious of himself as an individual — and he has accordingly the feeling of self as the common center of successive sensations — but not as a species: hence, he is without that consciousness which in its nature, as in its name, is akin to science. Where there is this higher consciousness there is a capability of science. Science is the cognizance of species. In practical life we have to do with individuals; in science, with species. But only a being to whom his own species, his own nature, is an object of thought, can make the essential nature of other things or beings an object of thought.

Hence the brute has only a simple, man a twofold life: in the brute, the inner life is one with the outer; man has both an inner and an outer life. The inner life of man is the life which has relation to his species, to his general, as distinguished from his individual, nature. Man thinks — that is, he converses with himself. The brute can exercise no function which has relation to its species without another individual external to itself; but man can perform the functions of thought and speech, which strictly imply such a relation, apart from another individual. Man is himself at once I and thou; he can put himself in the place of another, for this reason, that to him his species, his essential nature, and not merely his individuality, is an object of thought.

Religion being identical with the distinctive characteristic of man, is then identical with self-consciousness — with the consciousness which man has of his nature. But religion, expressed generally, is consciousness of the infinite; thus it is and can be nothing else than the consciousness which man has of his own — not finite and limited, but infinite nature. A really finite being has not even the faintest adumbration, still less consciousness, of an infinite being, for the limit of the nature is also the limit of the consciousness. The "consciousness" of the caterpillar, whose life is confined to a particular species of plant, does not extend itself beyond this narrow domain. It does, indeed, discriminate between this plant and other plants, but more it knows not. A consciousness so limited, but on account of that very limitation so infallible, we do not call consciousness, but instinct. Consciousness, in the strict or proper sense, is identical with consciousness of the infinite; a limited consciousness is no consciousness; consciousness is essentially infinite in its nature. The consciousness of the infinite is nothing else than the consciousness of the infinity of the consciousness; or, in the consciousness of the infinite, the conscious subject has for his object the infinity of his own nature....

Wherever, therefore, the denial of the sensual delights is made a special offering, a sacrifice well-pleasing to God, there the highest value is attached to the senses, and the sensuality which has been renounced is unconsciously restored, in the fact that God takes the place of the material delights which have been renounced. The nun weds herself to God; she has a heavenly bridegroom, the monk a heavenly bride. But the heavenly virgin is only a sensible presentation of a general truth, having relation to the essence of religion. Man denies as to himself only what he attributes to God. Religion abstracts from man, from the world; but it can only abstract from the limitations, from the phenomena; in short, from the negative, not from the essence, the positive, of the world and humanity: hence, in the very abstraction and negation it must recover that from which it abstracts, or believes itself to abstract. And thus, in reality, whatever religion consciously denies — always supposing that what is denied by it is something essential, true, and consequently incapable of being ultimately denied — it unconsciously restores in God. Thus, in religion man denies his reason; of himself he knows nothing of God, his thoughts are only worldly, earthly; he can only believe what God reveals to him. But on this account the thoughts of God are human, earthly thoughts: like man, he has plans in his mind, he accommodates himself to circumstances and grades of intelligence, like a tutor with his pupils; he calculates closely the effect of his gifts and revelations; he observes man in all his doings; he knows all things, even the most earthly, the commonest, the most trivial. In brief, man in relation to God denies his own knowledge, his own thoughts, that he may place them in God. Man gives up his personality; but in return, God, the Almighty, infinite, unlimited being, is a person; he denies human dignity, the human *ego;* but in return God is to him a selfish, egoistical being, who in all things seeks only himself, his own honor, his own ends; he represents God as simply seeking the satisfaction of his own selfishness, while yet he frowns on that of every other being; his God is the very luxury of egoism. Religion further denies goodness as a quality of human nature; man is wicked, corrupt, incapable of good; but, on the other hand, God is only good — the Good Being. Man's nature demands as an object goodness, personified as God; but is it not hereby declared that goodness is an essential tendency of man? If my heart is wicked, my understanding perverted, how can I perceive and feel the holy to be holy, the good to be good? Could I perceive the beauty of a fine picture if my mind were aesthetically an absolute piece of perversion? Though I may not be a painter, though I may not have the power of producing what is beautiful myself, I must yet have aesthetic feeling, aesthetic comprehension, since I perceive the beauty that is presented to me externally. Either goodness does not exist at all for man, or, if it does exist, therein is revealed to the individual man the holiness and goodness of human nature. That which is absolutely opposed to my nature, to which I am united by no bond of sympathy, is not even conceivable or perceptible by me. The holy is in opposition to me only as regards the modifications of my personality, but as regards my fundamental nature it is in unity with me. The holy is a reproach to my sinfulness; in it I recognize myself as a sinner; but in so doing, while I blame myself, I acknowledge what I am not, but ought to be, and what, for that very reason, I, according to my destination, can be; for an *"ought"* which has no corresponding capability does not affect me, is a ludicrous chimera without any true relation to my mental constitution. But when I acknowledge goodness as my destination, as my law, I acknowledge it, whether consciously or unconsciously, as my own nature. Another nature than my own, one different in quality, cannot touch me. I can perceive sin as sin, only when I perceive it to be a contradiction of myself with myself — that is, of my personality with my fundamental nature. As a contradiction of the absolute, considered as another being, the feeling of sin is inexplicable, unmeaning. . . .

Man — this is the mystery of religion — projects his being into objectivity, and then again makes himself an object to this projected image of himself thus converted into a subject; he thinks of himself as an object to himself, but as the object of an object, of another being than himself. Thus here. Man is an object to God. That man is good or evil is not indifferent to God; no! He has a lively, profound interest in man's being good; he wills that man should be good, happy — for without goodness there is no happiness. Thus the religious man virtually retracts the nothingness of human activity, by making his dispositions and actions an object to God, by making man the end of God — for that which is an object to the mind is an end in action; by making the divine activity a means of human salvation. God acts, that man may be good and happy. Thus man, while he is apparently humiliated to the lowest degree, is in truth exalted to the highest. Thus, in and through God, man has in view himself alone. It is true that man places the aim of his action in God, but God has no other aim of action than the moral and eternal salvation of man: thus man has in fact no other aim than himself. The divine activity is not distinct from the human.

How could the divine activity work on me as its object, nay, work in me, if it were essentially different from me; how could it have a human aim, the aim of ameliorating and blessing man, if it were not itself human? Does not the purpose determine the nature of the act? When man makes his moral improvement an aim to himself, he has divine resolutions, divine projects; but also, when God seeks the salvation of man, he has human ends and a human mode of activity corresponding to these ends. Thus in God man has only his own activity as an object. But for the very reason that he regards his own activity as objective, goodness only as an object, he necessarily receives the impulse, the motive not from himself, but from this object. He contemplates his nature as external to himself, and this nature as goodness; thus it is self-evident, it is mere tautology to say that the impulse to good comes only from thence where he places the good.

God is the highest subjectivity of man abstracted from himself; hence man can do nothing of himself, all goodness comes from God. The more subjective God is, the more completely does man divest himself of his subjectivity, because God is, *per se,* his relinquished self, the possession of which he however again vindicates to himself. As the action of the arteries drives the blood into the extremities, and the action of the veins brings it back again, as life in general consists in a perpetual systole and diastole; so is it in religion. In the religious systole man propels his own nature from himself, he throws himself outward; in the religious diastole he receives the rejected nature into his heart again. God alone is the being who acts of himself, — this is the force of repulsion in religion; God is the being who acts in me, with me, through me, upon me, for me, is the principle of my salvation, of my good dispositions and actions, consequently my own good principle and nature, — this is the force of attraction in religion.

The course of religious development which has been generally indicated consists specifically in this, that man abstracts more and more from God, and attributes more and more to himself. This is especially apparent in the belief in revelation. That which to a later age or a cultured people is given by nature or reason, is to an earlier age, or to a yet uncultured people, given by God. Every tendency of man, however natural — even the impulse to cleanliness, was conceived by the Israelites as a positive divine ordinance. From this example we again see that God is lowered, is conceived more entirely on the type of ordinary humanity, in proportion as man detracts from himself. How can the self-humiliation of man go further than when he disclaims the capability of fulfilling spontaneously the requirements of common decency? The Christian religion, on the other hand, distinguished the impulses and passions of man according to their quality, their character; it represented only good emotions, good dispositions, good thoughts, as revelations, operations — that is, as dispositions, feelings, thoughts, — of God; for what God reveals is a quality of God himself: that of which the heart is full overflows the lips; as is the effect such is the cause; as the revelation, such the being who reveals himself. A God who reveals himself in good dispositions is a God whose essential attribute is only moral perfection.

The Christian religion distinguishes inward moral purity from external physical purity; the Israelites identified the two. In relation to the Israelitish religion, the Christian religion is one of criticism and freedom. The Israelite trusted himself to do nothing except what was commanded by God; he was without will even in external things; the authority of religion extended itself even to his food. The Christian religion, on the other hand, in all these external things made man dependent on himself, i.e., placed in man what the Israelite placed out of himself in God. Israel is the most complete presentation of Positivism in religion. In relation to the Israelite, the Christian is an *esprit fort,* a free-thinker. Thus do things change. What yesterday was still religion is no longer such today; and what today is atheism, tomorrow will be religion.

Translated by George Eliot

Karl Marx

Karl Marx (1818–83) once said that it used to be that "philosophers only interpreted the world in various ways; [but] the point is to change it."[1] Judged by that norm, he must be viewed as probably the most influential philosopher in the history of the world. But in his discussions of religion he is surprisingly derivative, as the following selection from his "Contribution to the Critique of Hegel's *Philosophy of Right*" makes clear. His great difference from Feuerbach is his explicit, and indeed crucial, affirmation of materialism. This adds a new dimension to Feuerbach's critique, which tended to hold that theology is *illusory* anthropology that a correct (Idealist) philosophy will discover. But Marx adds that theology is also thereby *alienating* anthropology. This has given to Marx's philosophy of religion a programmatic dynamic that is an aspect of his whole philosophical project.

Marx is original in one other area of religion: his identification of Judaism not just with capitalism (for this had long been a staple of conservative philosophies hostile to the corrosive and tradition-threatening dynamic of liquid capital) but also with bourgeois rights. Not only did he see the natural-law rights defended by the Enlightenment (freedom of speech, thought, press, religion, etc.) as but the superstructure of the latest development in industrial society, he more crucially counterposed those rights to what he regarded as the more fundamental economic rights to food, clothing, shelter, and employment. And in a twist that would later prove fateful indeed, he identified the Jews with those rights most of all.

---

1. Karl Marx, *The German Ideology* (Moscow: International House, 1968), 662.

From "Contribution to the Critique of Hegel's *Philosophy of Right*"

For Germany, the *criticism of religion* has been largely completed; and the criticism of religion is the premise of all criticism.

The *profane* existence of error is compromised once its *celestial oratio pro aris et focis* has been refuted. Man, who has found in the fantastic reality of heaven, where he sought a supernatural being, only his own reflection, will no longer be tempted to find only the *semblance* of himself — a non-human being — where he seeks and must seek his true reality.

The basis of irreligious criticism is this: *man makes religion; religion does not make man.* Religion is indeed man's self-consciousness and self-awareness so long as he has not found himself or has lost himself again. But man is not an abstract being, squatting outside the world. Man is the human world, the state, society. This state, this society, produce religion which is an *inverted world consciousness,* because they are an inverted world. Religion is the general theory of this world, its encyclopedic compendium, its logic in popular form, its spiritual *point d'honneur,* its enthusiasm, its moral sanction, its solemn complement, its general basis of consolation and justification. It is *the fantastic realization* of the human being inasmuch as the human being possesses no true reality. The struggle against religion is, therefore, indirectly a struggle against that world whose spiritual *aroma* is religion.

Religious suffering is at the same time an expression of real suffering and a *protest* against real suffering. Religion is the sigh of the oppressed creature, the sentiment of a heartless world, and the soul of soulless conditions. It is the *opium* of the people.

The abolition of religion as the illusory happiness of men, is a demand for their real happiness. The call to abandon their illusions about their condition is a *call to abandon a condition which requires illusions.* The criticism of religion is, therefore, *the embryonic criticism of this vale of tears* of which religion is the halo.

Criticism has plucked the imaginary flowers from the chain, not in order that man shall bear the chain without caprice or consolation but so that he shall cast off the chain and pluck the living flower. The criticism of religion disillusions man so that he will think, act, and fashion his reality as a man who has lost his illusions and regained his reason; so that he will revolve about himself as his own true sun. Religion is only the illusory sun about which man revolves so long as he does not revolve about himself.

It is the task of history, therefore, once the other-world of truth has vanished, to establish the truth of this world. The immediate task of philosophy, which is in the service of history, is to unmask human self-alienation in its secular form now that it has been unmasked in its sacred form. Thus the criticism of heaven is transformed into the criticism of earth, the criticism of religion into the criticism of law, and the criticism of theology into the criticism of politics.

Translator unknown

From "On the Jewish Question"

1. Bruno Bauer, *Die Judenfrage*

The German Jews seek emancipation. What kind of emancipation do they want? *Civic, political* emancipation.

Bruno Bauer replies to them: In Germany no one is politically emancipated. We ourselves are not free. How then could we liberate you? You Jews are egoists if you demand for yourselves, as Jews, a special emancipation. You should work, as Germans, for the political emancipation of Germany, and as men, for the emancipation of mankind. You should feel the particular kind of oppression and shame which you suffer, not as an exception to the rule but rather as a confirmation of the rule.

Or do the Jews want to be placed on a footing of equality with the Christian subjects? If they recognize the Christian state as legally established they also recognize the regime of general enslavement. Why should their particular yoke be irksome when they accept the general yoke? Why should the German be interested in the liberation of the Jew, if the Jew is not interested in the liberation of the German?

The Christian state recognizes nothing but *privileges*. The Jew himself, in this state, has the privilege of being a Jew. As a Jew he possesses rights which the Christians do not have. Why does he want rights which he does not have but which the Christians enjoy?

In demanding his emancipation from the Christian state he asks the Christian state to abandon its *religious* prejudice. But does he, the Jew, give up his religious prejudice? Has he then the right to insist that someone else should forswear his religion?

The Christian state, *by its very nature,* is incapable of emancipating the Jew. But, adds Bauer, the Jew, by his very nature, cannot be emancipated. As long as the state remains Christian, and as long as the Jew remains a Jew, they are equally incapable, the one of conferring emancipation, the other of receiving it.

With respect to the Jews the Christian state can only adopt the attitude of a Christian state. That is, it can permit the Jew, as a matter of privilege, to isolate himself from its other subjects; but it must then allow the pressures of all the other spheres of society to bear upon the Jew, and all the more heavily since he is in *religious* opposition to the dominant religion. But the Jew likewise can only adopt a Jewish attitude, i.e., that of a foreigner, toward the state, since he opposes his illusory nationality to actual nationality, his illusory law to actual law. He considers it his right to separate himself from the rest of humanity; as a matter of principle he takes no part in the historical movement and looks to a future which has nothing in common with the future of mankind as a whole. He regards himself as a member of the Jewish people, and the Jewish people as the chosen people.

On what grounds, then, do you Jews demand emancipation? On account of your religion? But it is the mortal enemy of the state religion. As citizens? But there are no citizens in Germany. As men? But you are not men any more than are those to whom you appeal.

Bauer, after criticizing earlier approaches and solutions, formulates the question of Jewish emancipation in a new way. What, he asks, is the nature of the Jew who is to be emancipated, and the *nature* of the Christian state which is to emancipate him? He replies by a critique of the Jewish religion, analyzes the religious opposition between Judaism and Christianity, explains the essence of the Christian state; and does all this with dash, clarity, wit, and profundity, in a style which is as precise as it is pithy and vigorous.

How then does Bauer resolve the Jewish question? What is the result? To formulate a question is to resolve it. The critical study of the Jewish question is the answer to the Jewish question. Here it is in brief: we have to emancipate ourselves before we can emancipate others.

The most stubborn form of the opposition between Jew and Christian is the *religious* opposition. How is an opposition resolved? By making it impossible. And how is religious opposition made impossible? By abolishing religion. As soon as Jew and Christian come to see in their respective religions nothing more than *stages in the development of the human mind* — snake skins which have been cast off by history, and man as the snake who clothed himself in them — they will no longer find themselves in religious opposition, but in a purely critical, *scientific,* and human relationship. *Science* will then constitute their unity. But scientific oppositions are resolved by science itself.

The *German* Jew, in particular, suffers from the general lack of political freedom and the pronounced Christianity of the state. But in Bauer's sense the Jewish question has a general significance, independent of the specifically German conditions. It is the question of the relations between religion and the state, of the *contradiction between religious prejudice and political emancipation.* Emancipation from religion is posited as a condition, both for the Jew who wants political emancipation, and for the state which should emancipate him and itself be emancipated.

"Very well, it may be said (and the Jew himself says it), but the Jew should not be emancipated because he is a Jew, because he has such an excellent and universal moral creed; the Jew should take second place to the citizen, and he will be a citizen although he is and desires to remain a Jew. In other words, he is and remains a *Jew,* even though he is a *citizen* and as such lives in a universal human condition; his restricted Jewish nature always finally triumphs over his human and political obligations. The bias persists even though it is overcome by general principles. But if it persists, it would be truer to say that it overcomes all the rest." "It is only in a sophistical and superficial sense that the Jew could remain a Jew in political life. Consequently, if he wanted to remain a Jew, this would mean that the superficial became the essential and thus triumphed. In other words, his life *in the state* would be only a semblance, or a momentary exception to the essential and normal."

Let us see also how Bauer establishes the role of the state.

"France," he says, "has provided us recently, in connection with the Jewish question (and for that matter all other *political* questions), with the spectacle of a life which is free but which revokes its freedom by law and so declares it to be merely an appearance; and which, on the other hand, denies its free laws by its acts."

"In France, universal liberty is not yet established by law, nor is the *Jewish question as yet resolved,* because legal liberty, i.e., the equality of all citizens, is restricted in actual life, which is still dominated and fragmented by religious privileges, and because the lack of liberty in actual life influences law in its turn and obliges it to sanction the division of citizens who are by nature free into oppressors and oppressed."

When, therefore, would the Jewish question be resolved in France?

"The Jew would really have ceased to be Jewish, for example, if he did not allow his religious code to prevent his fulfillment of his duties toward the state and his fellow citizens; if he attended and took part in the public business of the Chamber of Deputies on the sabbath. It would be necessary, further, to abolish all *religious privilege,* including the monopoly of a privileged church. If, thereafter, some or many or *even the overwhelming majority felt obliged to fulfil their religious duties,* such practices should be left *to them as an absolutely* private matter." "There is no longer any religion when there is no longer a privileged religion. Take away from religion its power to excommunicate and it will no longer exist." "Mr. Martin du Nord has seen, in the suggestion to omit any mention of Sunday in the law, a proposal to declare that Christianity has ceased to exist. With equal right (and the right is well founded) the declaration that the law of the sabbath is no longer binding upon the Jew would amount to proclaiming the end of Judaism."

Thus Bauer demands, on the one hand, that the Jew should renounce Judaism, and in general that man should renounce religion, in order to be emancipated as a citizen. On the other hand, he considers, and this follows logically, that the political abolition of religion is the abolition of all religion. The state which presupposes religion is not yet a true or actual state. "Clearly, the religious idea gives some assurances to the state. But to what state? *To what kind of state?*"

At this point we see that the Jewish question is considered only from one aspect.

It was by no means sufficient to ask: Who should emancipate? Who should be emancipated? The critic should ask a third question: *What kind of emancipation* is involved? What are the essential conditions of the emancipation which is demanded? The criticism of *political emancipation* itself was only the final criticism of the Jewish question and its genuine resolution into the "general question the age."

Bauer, since he does not formulate the problem at this level, falls into contradictions. He establishes conditions which are not based upon the nature of *political* emancipation. He raises questions which are irrelevant to his problem, and he resolves problems which leave his question unanswered. When Bauer says of the opponents of Jewish emancipation that "Their error was simply to assume that the Christian state was the only true one, and not to subject it to the same criticism as Judaism," we see his own error in the fact that he subjects *only* the "Christian state," and not the "state as such" to criticism, that he does not examine *the relation between political emancipation and human emancipation,* and that he, therefore, poses conditions which are only explicable by his lack of critical sense in confusing political emancipation and universal human emancipation. Bauer asks the Jews: Have you, from your standpoint, the right to demand *political emancipation?* We ask the converse question: From the standpoint of *political* emancipation can the Jew be required to abolish Judaism, or man be asked to abolish religion?

The Jewish question presents itself differently according to the state in which the Jew resides. In Germany, where there is no political state, no state as such, the Jewish question is purely *theological.* The Jew finds himself in *religious* opposition to the state, which proclaims Christianity as its foundation. This state is a theologian *ex professo.* Criticism here is criticism of theology; a double-edged criticism, of Christian and of Jewish theology. And so we move always in the domain of theology, however *critically* we may move therein.

In France, which is a *constitutional* state, the Jewish question is a question of constitutionalism, of the incompleteness of *political emancipation.* Since the semblance of a state religion is maintained here, if only in the insignificant and self-contradictory formula of a *religion of the majority,* the relation of the Jews to the state also retains a semblance of religious, theological opposition.

It is only in the free states of North America, or at least in some of them, that the Jewish question loses its *theological* significance and becomes a truly *secular* question. Only where the state exists in its completely developed form can the relation of the Jew, and of the religious man in general, to the political state appear in a pure form, with its own characteristics. The criticism of this relation ceases to be theological criticism when the state ceases to maintain a *theological* attitude toward religion, that is, when it adopts the attitude of a state, i.e., a *political* attitude. Criticism then becomes *criticism of the political state.* And at this point, where the question ceases to be theological, Bauer's criticism ceases to be critical.

"There is not, in the United States, either a state religion or a religion declared to be that of a majority, or a predominance of one religion over another. The state remains aloof from all religions." There are even some states in North America in which "the constitution does not impose any religious belief or practice as a condition of political rights." And yet, "no one in the United States believes that a man without religion can be an honest man." And North America is pre-eminently the country of religiosity, as Beaumont, Tocqueville, and the Englishman, Hamilton, assure us in unison. However, the states of North America only serve as an example. The question is: What is the relation between *complete* political emancipation and religion? If we find in the country which has attained full political emancipation, that religion not only continues to exist but is fresh and vigorous, this is proof the existence of religion is not at all opposed to the perfection of the state. But since the existence of religion is the existence of a defect, the source of this defect must be sought in the *nature* of the state itself. Religion no longer appears as the basis, but as the *manifestation* of secular narrowness. That is why we explain the religious constraints upon the free citizens by the secular constraints upon them. We do not claim that they must transcend their religious narrowness in order to get rid of their secular limitations. We claim that they will transcend their religious narrowness once they have overcome their secular limitations. We do not turn secular questions into theological questions; we turn theological questions into secular ones. History has for long enough been resolved into superstition; but we now resolve superstition into history. The question of the relation between *political emancipation and religion* becomes for us a question of the relation between *political emancipation and human emancipation.* We criticize the religious failings of the political state by criticizing the political state in its secular form, disregarding its religious failings. We express in human terms the contradiction between the state and a particular religion, for example *Judaism,* by showing the contradiction between the state and particular secular elements, between the state and religion in general, and between the state and its general presuppositions.

The *political* emancipation of the Jew or the Christian — of the *religious* man in general — is the emancipation of the state from Judaism, Christianity, and religion in general. The state emancipates itself from religion in its own particular way, in the mode which corresponds to its nature, by emancipating itself from the state religion; that is to say, by giving recognition to no religion and affirming itself purely and simply as a state. To be politically emancipated from religion is not to be finally and completely emancipated from religion, because political emancipation is not the final and absolute form of human emancipation.

The limits of political emancipation appear at once in the fact that the state can liberate itself from a constraint without man himself being really liberated; that a state may be a *free state* without man himself being a *free man.* Bauer himself tacitly admits this when he makes political emancipation depend upon the following condition —

"It would be necessary, moreover, to abolish all religious privileges, including the monopoly of a privileged church. If some people, or even the *immense majority, still felt obliged to fulfil their religious duties,* this practice should be left to them as a *completely private matter."* Thus the state may have emancipated itself from religion, even though the immense majority of people continue to be religious. And the immense majority do not cease to be religious by virtue of being religious in private.

The attitude of the state, especially the free state, toward religion is only the attitude toward religion of the individuals who compose the state. It follows that man frees himself from a constraint in a *political* way, through the state, when he transcends his limitations, in contradiction with himself, and in an *abstract, narrow,* and partial way. Furthermore, by emancipating himself politically, man emancipates himself in a *devious way*, through an intermediary, however necessary this intermediary may be. Finally, even when he proclaims himself an atheist through the intermediary of the state, that is, when he declares the state to be an atheist, he is still engrossed in religion, because he only recognizes himself as an atheist in a roundabout way, through an intermediary. Religion is simply the recognition of man in a roundabout fashion; that is, through an intermediary. The state is the intermediary between man and human liberty. Just as Christ is the intermediary to whom man attributes all his own divinity and all his religious *bonds,* so the state is the intermediary to which man confides all his non-divinity and all his *human freedom.*

The political elevation of man above religion shares the weaknesses and merits of all such political measures. For example, the state as a state abolishes *private property* (i.e., man decrees by political means the abolition of private property) when it abolishes the property qualification for electors and representatives, as has been done in many of the North American states. Hamilton interprets this phenomenon quite correctly from the political standpoint: *The masses have gained a victory over property owners and financial wealth.* Is not private property ideally abolished when the non-owner comes to legislate for the owner of property? The property qualification is the last *political* form in which private property is recognized.

But the political suppression of private property not only does not abolish private property; it actually presupposes its existence. The state abolishes, after its fashion, the distinctions established by birth, social rank, education, occupation, when it decrees that birth, social rank, education, occupation are *non-political* distinctions; when it proclaims, without regard to these distinctions, that every member of society is an *equal* partner in popular sovereignty, and treats all the elements which compose the real life of the nation from the standpoint of the state. But the state, nonetheless, allows private property, education, occupation, to *act* after their own fashion, namely as private property, education, occupation, and to manifest their *particular* nature. Far from abolishing these effective differences, it only exists so far as they are presupposed; it is conscious of being a political state and it manifests its universality only in opposition to these elements. Hegel, therefore, defines the relation of the political state to religion quite correctly when he says: "In order for the state to come into existence as the *self-knowing* ethical actuality of spirit, it is essential that it should be distinct from the forms of authority and of faith. But this distinction emerges only insofar as divisions occur within the ecclesiastical sphere itself. It is only in this way that the state, above the *particular* churches, has attained to the universality of thought — its formal principle — and is bringing this universality into existence." To be sure! Only in this manner, *above* the *particular* elements, can the state constitute itself as universality.

The perfected political state is, by its nature, the *species-life* of man as opposed to his material life. All the presuppositions of this egoistic life continue to exist in civil society *outside* the political sphere, as qualities of civil society. Where the political state has attained to its full development, man leads, not only in thought, consciousness, but in *reality*, in *life*, a double existence — celestial and terrestrial. He lives in the *political community*, where he regards himself as a *communal being*, and in *civil society*, where he acts simply as a *private individual*, treats other men as means, degrades himself to the role of a mere means, and becomes the plaything of alien powers. The political state, in relation to civil society, is just as spiritual as is heaven in relation to earth. It stands in the same opposition to civil society, and overcomes it in the same manner as religion overcomes the narrowness of the profane world; i.e., it has always to acknowledge it again, re-establish it, and allow itself to be dominated by it. Man, in his *most intimate* reality, in civil society, is a profane being. Here, where he appears both to himself and to others as a real individual he is an *illusory* phenomenon. In the state, on the contrary, where he is regarded as a species-being, man is the imaginary member of an imaginary sovereignty, divested of his real, individual life, and infused with an unreal universality.

The conflict in which the individual, as the professor of a *particular* religion, finds himself involved with his own quality of citizenship and with other men as members of the community, may be resolved into the *secular* schism between the political state and civil society. For man as a bourgeois, "Life in the state is only an appearance or a fleeting exception to the normal and essential." It is true that the bourgeois, like the Jew, participates in political life only in a sophistical way, just as the *citoyen* is a Jew or a bourgeois only in a sophistical way. But this sophistry is not personal. It is the *sophistry of the political state* itself. The difference between the religious man and the citizen is the same as that between the shopkeeper and the citizens, between the day-laborer and the citizen, between the landed proprietor and the citizen, between the *living individual* and the *citizen.* The contradiction in which the religious man finds himself with the political man, is the same contradiction in which the bourgeois finds himself with the citizen, and the member of civil society with his *political lion's skin.*

This secular opposition, to which the Jewish question reduces itself — the relation between the political state and its presuppositions, whether the latter are material elements such as private property, etc., or spiritual elements such as culture or religion, the conflict between the general interest and private interest, the schism between the political state and civil society — these profane contradictions, Bauer leaves intact, while he directs his polemic against their *religious* expression. "It is precisely this basis — that is, the needs which assure the existence of *civil society* and *guarantee its necessity* — which exposes its existence to continual danger, maintains an element of uncertainty in civil society, produces this continually changing compound of wealth and poverty, of prosperity and distress, and above all generates change." Compare the whole section entitled "Civil Society," which follows closely the distinctive features of Hegel's philosophy of right. Civil society, in its opposition to this political state, is recognized as necessary because the political state is recognized as necessary.

Political emancipation certainly represents a great progress. It is not, indeed, the final form of human emancipation, but it is the final form of human emancipation *within* the framework of the prevailing social order. It goes without saying that we are speaking here of real, practical emancipation.

Man emancipates himself politically from religion by expelling it from the sphere of public law to that of private law. Religion is no longer the spirit of the *state,* in which man behaves, albeit in a specific and limited way and in a particular sphere, as a species-being, in community with other men. It has become the spirit of *civil society,* of the sphere of egoism and of the *bellum omnium contra omnes.* It is no longer the essence of *community,* but the essence of *differentiation.* It has become what it was at the beginning, an expression of the fact that man is separated from the community, from himself and from other men. It is now only the abstract avowal of an individual folly, a private whim or caprice. The infinite fragmentation of religion in North America, for example, already gives it the *external* form of a strictly private affair. It has been relegated among the numerous private interests and exiled from the life of the community as such. But one should have no illusions about the scope of political emancipation. The division of man into the public person and the private person, the displacement of religion from the state to civil society — all this is not a stage in political emancipation but its consummation. Thus political emancipation does not abolish, and does not even strive to abolish, man's *real* religiosity.

The decomposition of man into Jew and citizen, Protestant and citizen, religious man and citizen, is not a deception practiced *against* the political system nor yet an evasion of political emancipation. It is *political emancipation itself,* the *political* mode of emancipation from religion. Certainly, in periods when the political state as such comes violently to birth in civil society, and when men strive to liberate themselves through political emancipation, the state can, and must, proceed to *abolish and destroy religion;* but only in the same way as it proceeds to abolish private property, by declaring a maximum, by confiscation, or by progressive taxation, or in the same way as it proceeds to abolish life, by the guillotine. At those times when the state is most aware of itself, political life seeks to stifle its own prerequisites — civil society and its elements — and to establish itself as the genuine and harmonious species-life of man. But it can only achieve this end by setting itself in *violent* contradiction with its own conditions of existence, by declaring a *permanent* revolution. Thus the political drama ends necessarily with the restoration of religion, of private property, of all the elements of civil society, just as war ends with the conclusion of peace.

Translator unknown

Friedrich Nietzsche

If Marx has proved to be, at least on the grand scale, the most influential German philosopher of religion, Friedrich Nietzsche (1844–1900) is the most difficult to interpret. Influential he has definitely been, but has that influence come from the real Nietzsche? Paradoxically enough, this problem in a way stems not from any inherent difficulty in his thought, and still less from any obscurity of style, but on the contrary, from the very brilliance of his work. As one of his premier interpreters says, "There are philosophers who can write and philosophers who cannot. Most of the great philosophers belong to the first group. There are also, much more rarely, philosophers who can write too well for their own good — as philosophers. Plato wrote so dramatically that we shall never know for sure what precisely he himself thought about any number of questions. And Nietzsche furnishes a more recent and no less striking example."[1]

This not only makes describing his philosophy of religion extraordinarily difficult but also makes the task of choosing one of his essays on religion almost inevitably an exercise in futility: so protean was his mind, so fiery was his rhetoric, so contradictory were his statements (at least at first glance) that it would seem to be impossible not to distort his thought without presenting it in its entirety. And this danger is especially vivid in the history of the reception of his work, as the example of his sister anointing him the philosopher of the Nazi movement only too clearly attests. But other examples abound as well, as Félix Bertaux, a historian of German thought, has noted:

---

1. Walter Kaufmann, introduction to *The Portable Nietzsche* (New York: Penguin, 1954), 1.

Nietzsche is ordinarily considered a difficult and dangerous writer. Yet so far as difficulty is concerned, his work is not difficult in form — he rightly prided himself on having done as much for the language of Goethe as Goethe had done for the language of Martin Luther, and he wrote a German as beautiful and as clear as any ever written — but in substance his ideas, at first glance changing and inconsistent, actually correspond to the unity of life, whose mingled order and complexity he was attempting to grasp. As for being dangerous, Nietzsche is dangerous only to those who read him in haphazard fashion, selecting what flatters their own passionate desires and thus doing violence to a tissue of living thought so delicate that it can only be appreciated if it is approached dispassionately.... His work is such that it must be studied as a whole, approached with the care and disinterestedness of the scientist, and, if necessary, read antagonistically.[2]

To "solve" this problem, which is actually insoluble, I have chosen, undoubtedly *faute de mieux*, passages from Nietzsche's book *Human, All Too Human,* a work published in 1878, about midway through his career and well before his collapse into insanity in 1890. I have made this choice because I think Bertaux is right: unless one approaches Nietzsche dispassionately, he will be misunderstood; and the best way of approaching him disinterestedly in a Reader such as this one is to draw his remarks on religion from a work that is not as heated or as shrill as some of his later writings (where he will give his chapters such embarrassing titles as "Why I Write Such Great Books" or "Why I am So Clever"). But in *Human, All Too Human,* Nietzsche manages to speak of both religion in general and Christianity in particular; while highly critical and skeptical, he presents his argument in a way that the

---

2. Félix Bertaux, *A Panorama of German Literature: From 1871–1931,* trans. John J. Trounstine (New York: Cooper Square, 1970), 48. This is a judgment with which Hans Urs von Balthasar (whom we shall meet at the end of this volume) agrees in its essentials: "Few know who Nietzsche was. To Christians he is the 'anti-Christ,' to the new pagans a welcome quarry of polemical programs and slogans, to psychologists and psychiatrists a strange 'case,' to adolescents a stimulating poison. Yet his silent summit continues to tower over all simple 'solutions' and interpretations" (Hans Urs von Balthasar, afterword to *Vergeblichkeit,* ed. Hans Werner [Basel: Benno Schwabe Verlag, 1942], 93).

reader can take him at face value without wondering, because of the enormity of the emotional investment, what he is really trying to say.

From Human, All Too Human

The Religious Life

111

The Origin of the Religious Cult. — If we go back to the times in which the religious life flourished to the greatest extent, we find a fundamental conviction, which we now no longer share, and whereby the doors leading to a religious life are closed to us once for all, — it concerns Nature and intercourse with her. In those times people knew nothing of natural laws; neither for earth nor for heaven is there a "must"; a season, the sunshine, the rain may come or may not come. In short, every idea of natural causality is lacking. When one rows, it is not the rowing that moves the boat, but rowing is only a magical ceremony by which one compels a *daemon* to move the boat. All maladies, even death itself, are the result of magical influences. Illness and death never happen naturally; the whole conception of "natural sequence" is lacking, — it dawned first among the older Greeks, that is, in a very late phase of humanity, in the conception of *Moira,* enthroned above the gods. When a man shoots with a bow, there is still always present an irrational hand and strength; if the wells suddenly dry up, men think first of subterranean *daemons* and their tricks; it must be the arrow of a god beneath whose invisible blow a man suddenly sinks down. In India (says Lubbock) a carpenter is accustomed to offer sacrifice to his hammer, his hatchet, and the rest of his tools; in the same way a Brahmin treats the pen with which he writes, a soldier the weapons he requires in the field of battle, a mason his trowel, a laborer his plough. In the imagination of religious people all nature is a summary of the actions of conscious and voluntary creatures, an enormous complex or *arbitrariness.* No conclusion may be drawn with regard to everything that is outside of us, that anything will *be* so and so, *must* be so and so; the approximately sure, reliable are *we*, — man is the *rule*, nature is *irregularity*, — this theory contains the fundamental conviction which obtains in rude, religiously productive primitive civilizations. We latter-day men feel just the contrary, — the richer man now feels himself inwardly, the more polyphonous is the music and the noise of his soul, the more powerfully the symmetry of nature works upon him. We all recognize with Goethe the great means in nature for the appeasing of the modern soul; we listen to the pendulum swing of this greatest of clocks with a longing for rest, for home and tranquillity, as if we could absorb this symmetry into ourselves and could only thereby arrive at the enjoyment of ourselves. Formerly it was otherwise; if we consider the rude, early condition of nations, or contemplate present-day savages at close quarters, we find them most strongly influenced by *law* and by *tradition:* the individual is almost automatically bound to them, and moves with the uniformity of a pendulum. To him Nature — uncomprehended, terrible, mysterious Nature — must appear as the *sphere of liberty*, of voluntariness, of the higher power, even as a superhuman degree of existence, as God. In those times and conditions, however, every individual felt that his existence, his happiness, and that of the family and the State, and the success of all undertakings, depended on those spontaneities of nature; certain natural events must appear at the right time, others be absent at the right time. How can one have any influence on these terrible unknown things, how can one bind the sphere of liberty? Thus he asks himself, thus he inquires anxiously; — is there, then, no means of making those powers as regular through tradition and law as you are yourself? The aim of those who believe in magic and miracles is to *impost a law on nature*, — and, briefly, the religious cult is a result of this aim. The problem which those people have set themselves is closely related to this: how can the *weaker* race dictate laws to the *stronger*, rule it, and guide its actions (in relation to the weaker)? One would first remember the most harmless sort of compulsion, that compulsion which one exercises when one has gained any one's affection. By imploring and praying, by submission, by the obligation of regular taxes and gifts, by flattering glorifications, it is also possible to exercise an influence upon the powers of nature, inasmuch as one gains the affections; love binds and becomes bound. Then one can make compacts by which one is mutually bound to a certain behavior, where one gives pledges and exchanges vows. But far more important is a species of more forcible compulsion, by magic and witchcraft. As with the sorcerer's help man is able to injure a more powerful enemy and keep him in fear, as the love-charm works at a distance, so the weaker man believes he can influence the mightier spirits of nature. The principal thing in all witchcraft is that we must get into our possession something that belongs to some one, hair, nails, food from their table, even their portrait, their name. With such apparatuses we can then practice sorcery; for the fundamental rule is, to everything spiritual there belongs something corporeal; with the help of this we are able to bind the spirit, to injure it, and destroy it; the corporeal furnishes the handles with which we can grasp the spiritual. As man controls man, so he controls some natural spirit or other; for this has also its corporeal part by which it may be grasped. The tree and, compared with it, the seed from which it sprang, — this enigmatical contrast seems to prove that the same spirit embodied itself in both forms, now small, now large. A stone that begins to roll suddenly is the body in which a spirit operates; if there is an enormous rock lying on a lonely heath it seems impossible to conceive human strength sufficient to have brought it there, consequently the stone must have moved there by itself, that is, it must be possessed by a spirit. Everything that has a body is susceptible to witchcraft, therefore also the natural spirits. If a god is bound to his image we can use the most direct compulsion against him (through refusal of sacrificial food, scourging, binding in fetters, and so on). In order to obtain by force the missing favor of their god, the lower classes in China wind cords round the image of the one who has left them in the lurch, pull it down and drag it through the streets in the dust and the dirt: "You dog of a spirit," they say, "we gave you a magnificent temple to live in, we gilded you prettily, we fed you well, we offered you sacrifice, and yet you are so ungrateful." Similar forcible measures against pictures of the Saints and Virgin when they refused to do their duty in pestilence or drought, have been witnessed even during the present century in Catholic countries. Through all these magic relations to nature, countless ceremonies have been called into life; and at last, when the confusion has grown too great, an endeavor has been made to order and systematize them, in order that the favorable course of the whole progress of nature, i.e., of the great succession of the seasons, may seem to be guaranteed by a corresponding course of a system of procedure. The essence of the religious cult is to determine and confine nature to human advantage, *to impress it with a legality, therefore, which it did not originally possess;* while at the present time we wish to recognize the legality of nature in order to adapt ourselves to it. In short, then, the religious cult is based upon the representations of sorcery between man and man, — and the sorcerer is older than the priest. But it is likewise based upon other and nobler representations; it premises the sympathetic relation of man to man, the presence of goodwill, gratitude, the hearing of pleaders, of treaties between enemies, the granting of pledges, and the claim to the protection of property. In very low stages of civilization man does not stand in the relation of helpless slave to nature, he is *not* necessarily its involuntary bondsman. In the *Greek* grade of religion, particularly in relation to the Olympian gods, there may even be imagined a common life between two castes, a nobler and more powerful one, and one less noble; but in their origin both belong to each other somehow, and are of one kind; they need not be ashamed of each other. That is the nobility of the Greek religion.

112

At the Sight of Certain Antique Sacrificial Implements. — The fact of how many feelings are lost to us may be seen, for instance, in the mingling of the *droll,* even of the *obscene,* with the religious feeling. The sensation of the possibility of this mixture vanishes, we only comprehend historically that it existed in the feasts of Demeter and Dionysus, in the Christian Easter-plays and Mysteries. But we also know that which is noble in alliance with burlesque and such like, the touching mingled with the laughable, which perhaps a latter age will not be able to understand.

113

Christianity as Antiquity. — When on a Sunday morning we hear the old bells ring out, we ask ourselves, "Is it possible! This is done on account of a Jew crucified two thousand years ago who said he was the Son of God. The proof of such an assertion is wanting." Certainly in our times the Christian religion is an antiquity that dates from very early ages, and the fact that its assertions are still believed, when otherwise all claims are subjected to such strict examination, is perhaps the oldest part of this heritage. A God who creates a son from a mortal woman; a sage who requires that man should no longer work, no longer judge, but should pay attention to the signs of the approaching end of the world; a justice that accepts an innocent being as a substitute in sacrifice; one who commands his disciples to drink his blood; prayers for miraculous intervention; sins committed against a God and atoned for through a God; the fear of a future to which death is the portal; the form of the cross in an age which no longer knows the signification and the shame of the cross, how terrible all this appears to us, as if risen from the grave of the ancient past! Is it credible that such things are still believed?

114

What Is Un-Greek in Christianity. — The Greeks did not regard the Homeric gods as raised above them like masters, nor themselves as being under them like servants, as the Jews did. They only saw, as in a mirror, the most perfect examples of their own caste; an ideal, therefore, and not an opposite of their own nature. There is a feeling of relationship, a mutual interest arises, a kind of symmachy. Man thinks highly of himself when he gives himself such gods, and places himself in a relation like that of the lower nobility toward the higher; while the Italian nations hold a genuine peasant-faith, with perpetual fear of evil and mischievous powers and tormenting spirits. Wherever the Olympian gods retreated into the background, Greek life was more somber and more anxious. Christianity, on the contrary, oppressed man and cursed him utterly, sinking him as if in deep mire; then into the feeling of absolute depravity it suddenly threw the light of divine mercy, so that the surprised man, dazzled by forgiveness, gave a cry of joy and for a moment believed that he bore all heaven within himself. All psychological feelings of Christianity work upon this unhealthy excess of sentiment, and upon the deep corruption of head and heart it necessitates; it desires to destroy, break, stupefy, confuse, — only one thing it does not desire, namely *moderation,* and therefore it is in the deepest sense barbaric, Asiatic, ignoble, and un-Greek.

115

To Be Religions with Advantage. — There are sober and industrious people on whom religion is embroidered like a hem of higher humanity; these do well to remain religious, it beautifies them. All people who do not understand some kind of trade in weapons — tongue and pen included as weapons — become servile; for such the Christian religion is very useful, for then servility assumes the appearance of Christian virtues and is surprisingly beatified. People to whom their daily life appears too empty and monotonous easily grow religious; this is comprehensible and excusable, only they have no right to demand religious sentiments from those whose daily life is not empty and monotonous.

116

The Commonplace Christian. — If Christianity were right, with its theories of an avenging God, of general sinfulness, of redemption, and the danger of eternal damnation, it would be a sign of weak intellect and lack of character *not* to become a priest, apostle, or hermit, and to work only with fear and trembling for one's own salvation; it would be senseless thus to neglect eternal benefits for temporary comfort. Taking it for granted that there *is belief,* the commonplace Christian is a miserable figure, a man that really cannot add two and two together, and who, moreover, just because of his mental incapacity for responsibility, did not deserve to be so severely punished as Christianity has decreed.

117

Of the Wisdom of Christianity. — It is a clever stroke on the part of Christianity to teach the utter unworthiness, sinfulness, and despicableness of mankind so loudly that the disdain of their fellow-men is no longer possible. "He may sin as much as he likes, he is not essentially different from me, — it is I who am unworthy and despicable in every way," says the Christian to himself. But even this feeling has lost its sharpest sting, because the Christian no longer believes in his individual despicableness; he is bad as men are generally, and comforts himself a little with the axiom, "We are all of one kind."

118

Change of Front. — As soon as a religion triumphs it has for its enemies all those who would have been its first disciples.

119

The Fate of Christianity. — Christianity arose for the purpose of lightening the heart; but now it must first make the heart heavy in order afterward to lighten it. Consequently it will perish.

120

The Proof of Pleasure. — The agreeable opinion is accepted as true, — this is the proof of the pleasure (or, as the Church says, the proof of the strength), of which all religions are so proud when they ought to be ashamed of it. If Faith did not make blessed it would not be believed in; of how little value must it be, then!

121

A Dangerous Game. — Whoever now allows scope to his religious feelings must also let them increase, he cannot do otherwise. His nature then gradually changes; it favors whatever is connected with and near to the religious element, the whole extent of judgment and feeling becomes clouded, overcast with religious shadows. Sensation cannot stand still; one must therefore take care.

122

The Blind Disciples. — So long as one knows well the strength and weakness of one's doctrine, one's art, one's religion, its power is still small. The disciple and apostle who has no eyes for the weaknesses of the doctrine, the religion, and so forth, dazzled by the aspect of the master and by his reverence for him, has on that account usually more power than the master himself. Without blind disciples the influence of a man and his work has never yet become great. To help a doctrine to victory often means only so to mix it with stupidity that the weight of the latter carries off also the victory for the former.

123

Church Disestablishment. — There is not enough religion in the world even to destroy religions.

124

The Sinlessness of Man. — If it is understood how "sin came into the world," namely through errors of reason by which men held each other, even the single individual held himself, to be much blacker and much worse than was actually the case, the whole sensation will be much lightened, and man and the world will appear in a blaze of innocence which it will do one good to contemplate. In the midst of nature man is always the child *per se*. This child sometimes has a heavy and terrifying dream, but when it opens its eyes it always finds itself back again in Paradise.

125

The Irreligiousness of Artists. — Homer is so much at home among his gods, and is so familiar with them as a poet, that he must have been deeply irreligious; that which the popular faith gave him — a meager, rude, partly terrible superstition — he treated as freely as the sculptor does his clay, with the same unconcern, therefore, which Aeschylus and Aristophanes possessed, and by which in later times the great artists of the Renaissance distinguished themselves, as also did Shakespeare and Goethe.

126

The Art and Power of False Interpretations. — All the visions, terrors, torpors, and ecstasies of saints are well-known forms of disease, which are only, by reason of deep-rooted religious and psychological errors, differently *explained* by him, namely not as diseases. Thus, perhaps, the *Daimanian* of Socrates was only an affection of the ear, which he, in accordance with his ruling moral mode of thought, *expounded* differently from what would be the case now. It is the same thing with the madness and ravings of the prophets and soothsayers; it is always the degree of knowledge, fantasy, effort, morality in the head and heart of the *interpreters* which has *made* so much of it. For the greatest achievements of the people who are called geniuses and saints it is necessary that they should secure interpreters by force, who *misunderstand* them for the good of mankind.

127

The Veneration of Insanity. — Because it was remarked that excitement frequently made the mind clearer and produced happy inspirations it was believed that the happiest inspirations and suggestions were called forth by the greatest excitement; and so the insane were revered as wise and oracular. This is based on a false conclusion.

128

The Promises of Science. — The aim of modern science is: as little pain as possible, as long a life as possible, — a kind of eternal blessedness therefore; but certainly a very modest one as compared with the promises of religion.

129

Forbidden Generosity. — There is not sufficient love and goodness in the world to permit us to give some of it away to imaginary beings.

Translated by Helen Zimmern

Sigmund Freud

Sigmund Freud's (1856–1939) influence on the modern attitude toward religion is probably second only to that of Karl Marx, and indeed is rooted in the same theology-as-anthropology theories of Feuerbach, but now transposed to the psychological and clinical level. Freud shares another similarity with Marx in his appropriation of Feuerbach: his rejection of Feuerbach's relatively "neutral" stance toward religion based on his Idealistic presuppositions, and his insistence on the pathology and not merely the illusoriness of religion.

Freud does, however, differ radically from Marx regarding the final result of all of this therapeutic intervention upon the symptom of religion. While Freud is pessimistic, Marx — because of his apparently sincerely held belief in the "scientific" nature of his socialist theories — seems really to have looked forward to a time in history when man's material needs would be taken care of and his supposedly "spiritual" needs would thereupon vanish.

Freud was too much a man of Schopenhauer's cloth to buy into that scheme.[1] Though he agreed with Feuerbach that religion was a projection entirely generated by man's mind and not from a response to a divinity in nature or to an alleged revelation from a transcendent deity, he did not find this insight liberating or use it as a basis for espousing a system of hope that he knew in advance was incapable of fulfillment.

---

1. Some of Freud's statements, indeed, seem to be derived directly from Schopenhauer, as in the following line from *Civilization and Its Discontents:* "An unrestricted satisfaction of every need presents itself as the most enticing method of conducting one's life, but it means putting enjoyment before caution, and soon brings its own punishment."

The following selection comes from his *Civilization and Its Discontents* and summarizes this ambivalence very succinctly.

From Civilization and Its Discontents

I had sent [a friend] my small book that treats religion as an illusion, and he answered that he entirely agreed with my judgment upon religion, but that he was sorry I had not properly appreciated the true source of religious sentiments. This, he says, consists in a peculiar feeling, which he himself is never without, which he finds confirmed by many others, and which he may suppose is present in millions of people. It is a feeling which he would like to call a sensation of "eternity," a feeling as of something limitless, unbounded — as it were, "oceanic." This feeling, he adds, is a purely subjective fact, not an article of faith; it brings with it no assurance of personal immortality, but it is the source of the religious energy which is seized upon by the various Churches and religious systems, directed by them into particular channels, and doubtless also exhausted by them. One may, he thinks, rightly call oneself religious on the ground of this oceanic feeling alone, even if one rejects every belief and every illusion.

The views expressed by the friend whom I so much honor, and who himself once praised the magic of illusion in a poem, caused me no small difficulty. I cannot discover this "oceanic" feeling in myself. It is not easy to deal scientifically with feelings. One can attempt to describe their physiological signs. Where this is not possible — and I am afraid that the oceanic feeling too will defy this kind of characterization — nothing remains but to fall back on the ideational content which is most readily associated with the feeling. If I have understood my friend rightly, he means the same thing by it as the consolation offered by an original and somewhat eccentric dramatist to his hero who is facing a self-inflicted death. "We cannot fall out of this world." That is to say, it is a feeling of an indissoluble bond, of being one with the external world as a whole. I may remark that to me this seems something rather in the nature of an intellectual perception, which is not, it is true, without an accompanying feeling-tone, but only such as would be present with any other act of thought of equal range. From my own experience I could not convince myself of the primary nature of such a feeling. But this gives me no right to deny that it does in fact occur in other people. The only question is whether it is being correctly interpreted and whether it ought to be regarded as the *fons et origo* of the whole need for religion.

I have nothing to suggest which could have a decisive influence on the solution of this problem. The idea of men's receiving an intimation of their connection with the world around them through an immediate feeling which is from the outset directed to that purpose sounds so strange and fits in so badly with the fabric of our psychology that one is justified in attempting to discover a psycho-analytic — that is, a genetic — explanation of such a feeling. The following line of thought suggests itself. Normally, there is nothing of which we are more certain than the feeling of our self, of our own ego. This ego appears to us as something autonomous and unitary, marked off distinctly from everything else. That such an appearance is deceptive, and that on the contrary the ego is continued inward, without any sharp delimitation, into an unconscious mental entity which we designate as the id and for which it serves as a kind of facade — this was a discovery first made by psycho-analytic research, which should still have much more to tell us about the relation of the ego to the id. But toward the outside, at any rate, the ego seems to maintain clear and sharp lines of demarcation. There is only one state — admittedly an unusual state, but not one that can be stigmatized as pathological — in which it does not do this. At the height of being in love the boundary between ego and object threatens to melt away. Against all the evidence of his senses, a man who is in love declares that "I" and "you" are one, and is prepared to behave as if it were a fact. What can be temporarily done away with by a physiological [i.e., normal] function must also, of course, be liable to be disturbed by pathological processes. Pathology has made us acquainted with a great number of states in which the boundary lines between the ego and the external world become uncertain or in which they are actually drawn incorrectly. There are cases in which parts of a person's own body, even portions of his own mental life — his perceptions, thoughts and feelings — , appear alien to him and as not belonging to his ego; there are other cases in which he ascribes to the external world things that clearly originate in his own ego and that ought to be acknowledged by it. Thus even the feeling of our own ego is subject to disturbances and the boundaries of the ego are not constant....

In this way, then, the ego detaches itself from the external world. Or, to put it more correctly, originally the ego includes everything, later it separates off an external world from itself. Our present ego-feeling is, therefore, only shrunken residue of a much more inclusive — indeed, an all-embracing — feeling which corresponded to a more intimate bond between the ego and the world about it. If we may assume that there are many people in whose mental life this primary ego-feeling has persisted to a greater or less degree, it would exist in them side by side with the narrower and more sharply demarcated ego-feeling of maturity, like a kind of counterpart to it. In that case, the ideational contents appropriate to it would be precisely those of limitlessness and of a bond with the universe — the same ideas with which my friend elucidated the "oceanic" feeling....

In spite of the incompleteness [of my remarks] I will venture on a few remarks as a conclusion to our inquiry. The program of becoming happy, which the pleasure principle imposes on us, cannot be fulfilled; yet we must not — indeed, we cannot — give up our efforts to bring it nearer to fulfillment by some means or other. Very different paths may be taken in that direction, and we may give priority either to the positive aspect of the aim, that of gaining pleasure, or to its negative one, that of avoiding unpleasure. By none of these paths can we attain all that we desire. Happiness, in the reduced sense in which we recognize it as possible, is a problem of economics of the individual's libido. There is no golden rule which applies to everyone: every man must find out for himself in what particular fashion he can be saved....

Religion restricts this play of choice and adaptation, since it imposes equally on everyone its own path to the acquisition of happiness and protection from suffering. Its technique consists in depressing the value of life and distorting the picture of the real world in a delusional manner — which presupposes an intimidation of the intelligence. At this price, by forcibly fixing them in a state of psychical infantilism and by drawing them into a mass-delusion, religion succeeds in sparing many people an individual neurosis. But hardly anything more. There are, as we have said, many paths which may lead to such happiness as is attainable by men, but there is none which does so for certain. Even religion cannot keep its promise. If the believer finally sees himself obliged to speak of God's "inscrutable decrees," he is admitting that all that is left to him as a last possible consolation and source of pleasure in his suffering is an unconditional submission. And if he is prepared for that, he could probably have spared himself the *détour* he has made.

Translated by James Strachey

Ernst Troeltsch

Ernst Troeltsch (1865–1923) is best understood as the intersection of two, perhaps irreconcilable, streams of thought: the formalism of Kant and the moral relativism of Nietzsche. By this I mean not that Kant and Nietzsche were Troeltsch's two lodestars (for in fact Nietzsche did not begin to make an impact on the thinking of Europeans until after his death, when Troeltsch's basic problematic had long been formulated). Rather, the central issue that occupied all of Troeltsch's extensive scholarly labors was the tension between asserting the Kantian primacy and underivative character of moral norms and coming to realize that, in the light of history, moral norms can be shown to change, and change radically.

The same applies to the history of dogma. By definition "dogma" pertains to what is taught as true, and in the Christian dispensation, dogma is taught as true by virtue of divine revelation, which implies that it must always have been true, at least *sub specie aeternitatis* (from the point of view of eternity). Indeed, one of the norms for establishing the truth of Catholic orthodoxy and the illegitimacy of the importation of heretical innovations was the standard of *quod ubique, quod semper, quod ab omnibus creditum est* (the standard for faith must be identified with what has been believed everywhere, always, and by all).[1]

But the history of dogma as a subdiscipline within the field of history (and not of theology, irrespective of whatever faculty in a university carried out this research) was beginning in the nineteenth century to make such a claim sound anachronistic. Of course, no one believed that first-century Christians, for example,

---

1. Vincent of Lérins, *Commonotorium,* ed. R. S. Moxon (Cambridge: Cambridge University Press, 1915), 2.3.

explicitly *held*, let alone were taught, such doctrines as the equality of the divine persons, Father, Son, and Spirit, in the Godhead (defined only in A.D. 325), or the unmixed presence of the divine and human natures in the one person of Christ (defined in 453), not to mention such later doctrines as Mary's bodily assumption into heaven. But by the historically formulated norms for orthodoxy these doctrines had to be at least genetically present, and it was this that the results of historical research were making harder and harder to accept.

Prior to Troeltsch, one could go one of two ways with this: either the way of Idealism, and see the historical manifestation of Christianity (or of morality) as but one expression of many of the universal natural religions (or morality) accessible to all human minds; or the way of Nietzsche, and fully embrace relativism and see man as the quintessentially self-creating animal, subject to no norms not of his making. The former traps humankind in a rigid ethical trellis of duty and its relentless demands (not even permitting, in Kant's notorious limit-example, a white lie) or a vision of alarming freedom from all moral norms such as in Nietzsche's unnerving manifesto:

> Let us look ahead a century and assume the case that my attempt to assassinate two millennia of anti-nature and human disfigurement has succeeded. That new party of life which would take the greatest of all tasks into its hands, the higher breeding (*Höherzuchtung*) of mankind, including the merciless extermination (*schonungslose Vernichtung*) of everything degenerate and parasitic, would make possible again that excess of life on earth from which the Dionysian state will grow again.[2]

Both these options are, for their differing reasons, impossible to subscribe to today, but before Troeltsch they also seemed to be mutually exclusive and mutually exhaustive. Troeltsch believed that either option meant abandoning essential aspects of the human. In fact, after World War I, he felt that Germany's disastrous estrangement from the democracies to its west was based on precisely the

---

2. Nietzsche, *Ecce Homo*, "The Birth of Tragedy," section 4; my translation. I agree that it is a vulgar ploy to read Nietzsche, as his sister did, as a direct forerunner of the Nazis, but I find it impossible to read this passage except in terms of later history.

inability of Germany to conceive of the state except as requiring absolute obedience in the manner of either Kant or Nietzsche. He thought that German political thinking had yet to learn how to compromise between absolutism and relativism. And the same challenge faced Christian theology as well, as we learn in his instructive essay "Christianity and the History of Religion."

"Christianity and the History of Religion"

For the historian of the life of the mind, it is axiomatic that the mind is an independent potency not to be derived from nature and, more importantly, that it does not actualize itself simply in a formal adjustment to nature. It also contains independent spiritual contents, dispositions, and drives that give rise, in interaction with the demands of empirical reality, to the rich world of history. The independence, autonomy, and creative power of the mind as they develop in religion, morality, and culture become so clearly apparent in these areas that the mind can be treated as at least relatively independent.

Now, as religion is a constitutive part of historical existence, its main questions arise in the area of history. The modern scientific study of history, which has extended its sway over previously unknown areas and eras, has confronted the Christian faith with entirely new problems. In fact, the rise of a comparative history of religion has shaken the Christian faith more deeply than anything else. The application of new pragmatic and critical methods, pioneered by the Deists and energetically deepened by the German theologians of the eighteenth century, showed the mutability of Christianity by reference to its own history. It destroyed the Catholic fiction that the church simply represented the continuation of original Christianity, as well as the Protestant fiction that the Reformation represented its restoration. All the questions raised by the previously prevailing confessional view of history were replaced by new ones that involved the history of the church and of revelation in an all-compassing historical pragmatism.

What the eighteenth century had begun — still hesitantly, always in search of an immutable truth of reason, and revering the "natural religion" in all religion but especially in Christianity —

the nineteenth century continued, with growing success and ever increasing scope. Above all, it developed concrete philological-historical methods both for particular areas and for history as a whole. The pragmatic approach was replaced by the genetic approach, which rests on the assumption that the development of the life of the mind is homogeneous and continuous; and which showed, by studying the laws governing the formation of traditions in the nations of antiquity, that the actual course of events can be clearly reconstructed out of these very traditions, even though they tend to obliterate every sign of development or natural conditioning. Myths and traditions, cultures and religious laws were now perceived in their natural relationship to the whole of life. Finally, there were the researches of ethnologists and anthropologists concerning the peoples-without-history, which were found to bear many features that showed a striking similarity to the oldest traces of the cultural and religious development of the civilized nations and thus threw a wholly new light on their beginnings. Out of the co-operation of the study of antiquity, oriental philology, and ethnology there accordingly emerged a grand new discipline, the history of religion. Its methods deeply affected the investigation of the Israelite and Christian religions.

As a result, Christianity lost its exclusive-supernatural foundation. It was now perceived as only one of the great world religions, along with Islam and Buddhism, and like these, as constituting the culmination of complicated historical developments. What would become now of Christianity's exclusive truth or even of its decisive superiority? Above all, what would become of the belief in an exclusive revelation? But the consequences go even further. Not only the truth and validity of Christianity but also those of religion itself, as a unique sphere of life, disappear in this maelstrom of historical diversity. What can be true in the religious belief in God when this belief manifests itself in a thousand different forms, clearly dependent on the situation and the conditions in which they arise; and goes back to revelations that purport to be infallible and universally valid, or at least a direct, supernatural work of the Deity, yet completely contradict one another? In view of the countless number and the deep differences of the *religions* how can there still be *religion* at all, if religion is truly to mean communion with the Deity? Must we not at least follow Schiller's well-known words:

Of the religions you name,
You ask me which one I profess.
Not one. And why not?
Religion prevents me.

But — like Odin's spear — the great historical crises often heal the very wounds they have caused. While the Enlightenment (due to the after-effects of supernaturalism) had sought the content of history in a rational truth that remains perpetually and rigidly the same, history has more recently been viewed as the manifestation of manifold basic tendencies of human nature and, in their inter-connection, as unfolding the totality of human reason in the course of the generations. This great modern conception of history has given rise to a new conception of religion and its historical development. Here, too, the aim is to understand and analyze the fundamental experience, and the resulting formation of religious groups and unfolding of the religious idea. Of course, a thorough knowledge of the empirical history of religion is requisite here, which up to now is only very partially available. On the whole, however, this is the way that corresponds to the general trend of scientific thought and has already led to many valuable insights. We simply must learn to view religion more sympathetically; to free ourselves from doctrinaire, rationalistic, and systematizing presuppositions; and to focus more intently on the characteristic, distinctively religious phenomena and personages rather than on average people. Then the deepest core of the religious history of humanity reveals itself as an experience that cannot be further analyzed, an ultimate and original phenomenon that constitutes, like moral judgment and aesthetic perception and yet with characteristic differences, a simple fact of psychic life. Everywhere the basic reality of religion is the same: an underivable, purely positive, again and again experienced contact with the Deity. This unity has its ground in a common dynamism of the human spirit which advances in different ways as a result of the mysterious movement of the divine Spirit in the unconscious depth of the human spirit, which is everywhere the same. Unable to attain its goal in the short span of individual life, this movement is effected through the cooperative efforts of countless generations as they are grasped and led by the divine activity, surrendering to it and experiencing its true import in ever greater fullness and profoundness.

Now, the more the great religions grasp their ultimate goal, the less likely is their self-seclusion. Instead, they strive for the truth in its totality and fullness, often with consuming passion. Only where the religions are filled with such passion do they unfold a truly progressive vitality of their own. What really counts, then, is to find the goal, or the direction of the goal, of the history of religion, which can only be found in a concrete religiosity of exceptional profundity, power, and lucidity, not in the related areas of art and science and not in an abstract religion derived from the multiplicity of the religions. This religiosity must comprehend, or be able to comprehend, the truth-moments of all the others. In any case, it must give living embodiment to the central idea taking shape in the evolutionary process.

The modern approach to history looks upon the history of religion as the history of God's relationship to humanity, a history of redemption which lifts both humanity as a whole and the individual person out of their bondage to mere sensual nature, with its needs and drives, into communion with God, into the freedom of the spirit transcending the mere positivity of a dull existence. Since the history of religion thus attains, or rather actualizes, the truth in varying degrees (depending on situation and conditions) and unites human beings with the deepest ground of their being and the quintessence of their spiritual goods, it is inseparable from the conviction that in it, and in it alone, there is genuine historical progress. It accordingly claims the right — a right not shared by the history of other spheres of life — to believe in the attainment of an ultimate, simple goal.

But the history of religion shows clearly that religion is not simply the direct work of God in the soul. That it is, is the theory of mysticism — that peculiar result of history of religion developments which obtains wherever particular concrete forms of the belief in God have been abandoned in favor of a completely ineffable working of God in the soul that is everywhere the same, or where the desire for a direct and inward communion with God leads to the rejection of all outward means. The self-centeredness of such piety, its lack of content and community, and its artificial concentration and withdrawal from the world, leading to overstimulation and exhaustion, show that such phenomena cannot be regarded as normal. The religious impression or, to use a term from empirical psychology, the religious stimulus always arises from inward and outward events and experiences in nature and history, in heart and conscience. For the vast majority of people the religious stimulus is mediated by the religious tradition, with non-traditional stimuli generally playing only a minor role. The peculiar mystery of individual religious development is how traditions that are at first strange, not understood at all, or childishly misinterpreted can gradually lead to an independent, inward, and personal piety that is conscious, at least at its high-points, of an inner communion and interaction with the divine life. Where it is possible to speak of the beginnings of a religion, we encounter predominantly original personages who are less closely bound to the mediation of tradition and whose great new visions are stimulated by great events in nature or history, by the outward course of their own life, or even by the processes of their inner life. Others are then attracted by the power of their piety and personality. The seers, ecstatics, and inspired people of the ancient religions, as well as prophets, reformers, and saints, are generally personages of this kind. Their chief characteristic is an enormous one-sidedness; only by pushing everything else aside are they able to make their religious impact.

If we go beyond the accidents of time and space, personality and tradition, we find everywhere a very similar truth. We note a great sense of awe before the mystery of a supersensible world that speaks its word within the course of everyday life: whether it comforts people or frightens them, it always disrupts the slumber of a purely inner-worldly existence. We also note the manifestation of divine forces in nature, and the authorization of moral and legal norms on the part of the Deity. Above all, we note the higher goods of eternal blessedness and the rise of the belief in redemption. All these phenomena are properly viewed as belonging together, as requiring a unified, comprehensive treatment.

There is also a "religious apperception," where the religious stimulus enters directly into the nexus of conceptions and feelings, is influenced by it, but also gives new directions to it. As the spiritual life reaches higher levels, the conditions of this apperception become correspondingly less transparent and more complicated, and religion now demands more insistently the concentration and quiet attention to the religious stimulus known as meditation and prayer. In this connection it must not be forgotten that individuals do not stand alone but that their close interaction gives certain inclinations and orientations a position of social dominance. This is why there are predominantly conservative and predominantly critical periods even in the history of religion. Periods of violent religious conflict, finally, can lead to periods where great masses of people turn against religion and prefer to concern themselves with secular, more easily ascertainable matters. Examples of this are the culture of the Roman empire, the Confucian morality of the higher classes of China, and the conditions of life in modern Europe.

Now comes the question whether this varied and partial apprehension of the truth [in the history of religion] has a point of convergence, an obviously visible high-point; or, more precisely, whether Christianity, which purports to be a such a high-point, can indeed be recognized as such. When we put the question in this way, it is because Christianity alone has made this claim with ever increasing urgency in the course of its development, and with ever more principled appeal to its own innermost essence. Sustained by the authority of its Master, it addresses itself exclusively to the essential inner core of the individual, to the most universal, profound, and simple needs for rest and peace of heart and for a positive, ultimate, absolutely valid meaning of existence. It addresses itself to every individual without exception, presupposing this essential core in everyone and with full assurance that it can educate all to recognize these needs. Peace of soul with God, overcoming the anguish of the world and all pains of conscience, living and doing the will of God, and the commandment to love the neighbor who is such because all have a common Father: this is its gospel. From it Christianity derives the firmest and most comprehensive community, by having the essential human nature originate in the divine Spirit and by pointing it to the goal of community with God and the neighbor, requiring every believer to co-operate in this universal community and the goal of a shared perfection. This is why it is the only religion to claim an absolute and unconditional universality; to have produced out of itself a philosophy of history linking the beginning, the center, and the end of human history; and to recognize in this history a coherent and unique reality promoting unconditionally worthwhile goals. Above all, Christianity does not simply assert its universal validity but derives it from an inner necessity in the being of God: creating the world out of love, the Creator *must* lead creatures out of the world, out of illusion, out of guilt and discouragement, back to the Divine Being.

Both God's grace and commandments flow from this essential nature and [creatures] find their inward fulfillment through love to the God who first loved them. Here the universal tendency of religion reaches its culmination: all particular, ethnic, and worldly conditionings are eliminated; and all dependence on a merely given (and ever changing) situation is overcome through the universality of a future goal that is grounded in nature (*Wesen*) and destiny (*Bestimmung*).

Also present, to be sure, is the one-sidedness of the predominantly religious type of life. But it is precisely in this one-sidedness that Christianity attains full inwardness and purely human universality. Only in tension with inner-worldly cultural values does it attain the character of a higher life of the mind, where unity must be attained again and again through conscious effort. Christianity has always shown this tendency toward the individual and personal, the universally human, and the totality with all its tensions. This is confirmed by comparison with the other great universal religions that represent its only competitors. Islam — Christianity's younger sibling since both descended from Judaism — has taken over from Judaism and Christianity in a purely external manner this universalism, revelation-by-the-Book, and a fragmentary philosophy of history. Only the unity of its God and the simplicity of its few paltry moral commandments reflect universalism; which does not, however, derive from an inner necessity of the essential nature of its God, who is hard, unpredictable, arbitrary. Islam thus represents a regression from Judaism and Christianity and has never been able to conceal its characteristic ties to the Arab nation and war.

Buddhism, which shows many parallels to Christianity, originates as merely the religion of a monastic order. All who have come to understand the nothingness of the will-to-be are admittedly allowed and encouraged to enter the order, which shows a considerable missionary vitality. But its universal validity derives only from the universal validity of this understanding, not from the essential nature of a single Deity that calls all to a common goal. The Deity has here been replaced by a merely impersonal order of redemption. The physical survival of the enlightened members of the order always depends on the great mass of the unenlightened laity. The vast majority of people remain caught up in the cycle of reincarnations, a mass from which the initiates separate themselves but on which they depend for sustenance until they disappear in Nirvana. This process repeats itself in successive world periods, without linkage or goal. Life and piety lack a uniform, positive goal, as does the world itself. The order recruits members and exalts the peace of redemption, but no inner necessity requires that all of humanity ever be gathered together in it. However much here, as in Islam, the universality of religion is asserted in one way or another, the claim is less intense than that of Christianity.

Only *one* religion has completely broken out of the spell of the religion of nature and stands unique in this respect: the religion of Israel and Christianity. In view of the impending catastrophe of the nation, the religion of Israel detached itself on principle from its particularistic and natural-religious foundations and linked faith in Yahweh to purity of heart and the assurance that at the end of days all the confusions of earthly life would be resolved. Christianity, in the person of Jesus, built on this core conviction, which (as its foundation) prevents it from relapse into the pantheism and mysticism of the perfected religion of nature. While Christianity experiences God more intimately in the individual heart and in more direct activity in the world, it waits for a higher world, in the conviction that the world of the senses passes away. A purely immanent absorption in God is thus excluded. Since Christianity redeems not only from the anguish of finitude and the oppression of nature but above all from the defiance and despondency of the human heart, from weakness and guilt-feelings, and since it bestows not only peace of heart and assurance concerning a supertemporal community with God but also the power to act and to love here on earth, it is a religion of redemption of a higher order, going equally far beyond the pessimism of Buddhism and the mysticism of Neo-Platonism, the two final developments of non-Christian piety. By breaking on principle with every kind of nature religion, Christianity alone among the religions completes the tendency toward redemption, just as it alone completes the related tendency toward a purely intrinsic universal validity. It is because of its empirical uniqueness and the inner coincidence of what it is with what it demands that we recognize in the Prophetic-Christian religion the high-point, or rather a new point of departure, in the history of religion; not a conclusion and end calling for rest but the beginning of a new day for the world, with new work and new struggles.

It is obvious that as the underlying view of history assumed in the present study derives from our classical literature and philosophy, so its view of the history of religion is close to the ideas of Lessing, Goethe, Herder, Kant, Hegel, Schleiermacher, and similar thinkers. It only seeks to free the understanding of religion from the all-too-great proximity to other areas of culture in which it was placed by these men. Lessing's "eternal gospel" was conceived in too close an analogy to the science of the Enlightenment. Herder brought religion too close to the ethical concept of humaneness; by finding instances of this humaneness everywhere, he largely obliterated the boundaries between religions. Schleiermacher practically dissolved religion in a romantic Spinozism that looked upon the religions as merely individually different ways of being conscious of one's immanence in God. Hegel likewise conformed religion too much to metaphysical monism; above all, he derived the evolution of religion in too doctrinaire and rigid a fashion from the logical necessity of the dialectic of the idea, thus failing to do justice to the mysterious power of religion and the contingency of its various movements.

More recently, of course, "modern" science has for the most part put a great distance between itself and these deepest foundations of our culture. This was not so much because of scientific considerations but because of changed external conditions resulting from the enormous practical transformations of the nineteenth century. The all-transforming achievements of the new technology, the burning social questions resulting from them, the reawakening of national egoism, and not least, the growth and improving living conditions of the population, have diverted all interest to practical cultural questions, focusing on the problems of inner-worldly happiness. The opinion of the day is dominated by the dogma of cultural progress, or culture-optimism, and all scientific achievements are viewed in this light. From the historicizing thought of the last century or more, every effort is being made to infer the consequence of relativism, but only to devalue the ideal powers of the past and especially Christianity; faith in progress and in an absolute cultural happiness of the future remains undisturbed. The natural sciences are cultivated assiduously in order to subject all life and reality to the "laws of nature," but only in order to undermine spiritual values that go beyond inner-worldly happiness; to the human will, on the other hand, an enormous power to manipulate these same laws of nature in the interests of cultural happiness is attributed.

Such general moods are not easily dissipated, least of all by the demonstration of their inconsistencies. Their practical consequences will have to become more clearly apparent. The desolation of the life of the mind, the continuing decline of moral strength and religious seriousness, and the deadening effects of self-gratification must show where this approach will lead us, in spite of all outward progress. It must demonstrate that a perfect inner-worldly cultural happiness is the most deceptive of all illusions. Only then will recourse be had to our best cultural heritage, which will readily permit the utilization of scientific advances. The serious dangers posed by the historicizing of all science, including the scientific study of religion, will also be more readily dealt with at that time than now.

This is not the place to discuss the extent to which the views expressed here can (and will be permitted to) affect the official theology of the churches and theological faculties. Theology is not a pure science, or at least not a free science, since it is bound to the legal enactments, the actual tradition, and the conditions and goals confronting it. It is more of a compromise with science than a genuine science. Its tasks are primarily practical, given with the actual state of the institutional church. Theologians, insofar as they are scholars, may indeed make significant contributions toward the solution of the great questions. But insofar as they also have to serve ecclesiastical interests, they are bound by practical tasks and circumstances. Actually, the great scientific questions have always been settled outside of theology, despite the contributions of individual theologians, who may well be entitled to distinguish between an exoteric and an esoteric theology so long as they are conscious of having the same aim in both. But the vicious circle, that theology's self-isolation intensifies the displeasure of science while the hostility of science increases the self-isolation of theology, will not be broken so long as the extraordinary significance of the church question for national life is not perceived by enlightened indifference.

The general interest attaches to something quite different from specifically theological disquisitions. It requires that precisely in the field of religion, the historical relativism that threatens in all fields to drown us in erudition and to paralyze all creative power be recognized and overcome as the most dangerous of all opponents. Indications are multiplying on all sides that people are getting tired of it. The attempt is made to overcome it through patriotic enthusiasm, through the ideal of social justice, through futurism, through non-religious altruism; there is a thirst for simple, absolute, universally valid ideals. All this will not do it. But the recognition will come that religion is the true home of all such ideals, and that, above all, an assured and joyous faith in an absolute goal must be found again in it. To be sure, this cannot be done by a sudden turning away from history and an abjuration of its methods. But it can be done if we recall the great basic ideas of our classical literature, philosophy, and historiography and see in history the unfolding of a uniform and essentially simple spiritual import; and if we seek in the greatest and most powerful of all religions no longer merely the interesting historical phenomenon but the connection with the eternal core of the life of the mind. Then it will also be seen that the history of religion has not only parts but also a spiritual bond, and that this bond is not as difficult to find as the careful people suppose who would reserve all historical study to the specialists. Even the possibility that the end of this bond has been placed in our own hand will no longer seem frightening. If history is indeed no more than the infinitely complicated struggle for the unfolding of a simple spiritual import, then should we be amazed if in Christianity we had attained to the core of this import and were now bound to fashion our present and future by reference to it and empowered by it?

Translated by James Luther Adams and Walter F. Bense

Max Scheler

It is often said of Max Scheler (1874–1928) that he was particularly volatile and intense as a personality, going from, for example, vigorous support for the German cause in World War I (even to the point of carrying out missions in Geneva for the German Foreign Office) to a thoroughgoing repudiation of war and its horrors after Armistice Day. In religion he was equally protean: he came from a long line of Protestant clergymen (though his mother was Jewish), yet converted to Catholicism after the war, publishing his epochal *On the Eternal in Man* in 1921; but by 1924 he was already moving away from orthodox Christianity and even theism to a kind of vitalistic pantheism. This fascinating display of serial metamorphoses is also reflected in the people who claim him as a guide to their thought: sociologists all recognize him as one of the founding fathers of the sociology of knowledge; theologians continue to wrestle with his change from orthodox theism to pantheism; and phenomenologists all hail him for his work in the description of such hidden emotions as resentment and envy. Clearly in Scheler we have a thinker who is teeming with ideas, a pioneer in an extraordinarily large number of fields of inquiry.

These wild swings of position make it difficult for an editor to select a reading from his work that captures the quintessential Scheler, presuming there is such a thing in this Proteus of a philosopher. After some reflection, however, I have chosen a section from his famous *On the Eternal in Man.* I have made this selection not simply because the book was hailed upon its publication as "just the book we have been looking for" or because it was said that with this work Scheler "became the great herald of a religious renewal."[1] Rather, I have made this choice in part because the text helps reveal that Scheler was not as self-contradictory as he has been portrayed. As James Collins has pointed out: "The most striking result of a close study of [Scheler's various books on religion from all periods of his life] is the uncovering of a large amount of common doctrine. Something of the arbitrary character of Scheler's evolution is thus removed."[2] A close reading of the following selection will help to demonstrate an underlying unity to his religious thought that pervaded all his thinking subsequent to the end of World War I.

From On the Eternal in Man

Repentance and Rebirth

Behind the stirrings of the conscience, its warnings, its counsel, its condemnations, the spiritual eye of Faith is ever aware of the outline of an invisible, everlasting Judge. These stirrings seem to form a wordless natural discourse from God to the soul, prompting the course of its salvation and the world's. It is here an open question whether it is at all possible to separate the peculiar unity and the sense of the so-called *stirrings* of conscience from this view of them as a secret "voice" and symbolic language of God, and yet preserve intact the unity of what we call conscience itself. I doubt it, and believe rather that if it were not for the participation of a divine Judge those very stirrings would disintegrate into a host of phenomena — feelings, images, opinions — and that there would no longer remain any basis for conceiving them as a unity.... We are not more led by a "causal inference" from these stirrings to God's existence than we are led to the existence of a red ball by a "causal inference" from its extended red appearance. But in both cases something *is presented* in the act of experience: some-

1. George Shuster, "Introduction to the Symposium on the Significance of Max Scheler of Philosophy and Social Science," *Philosophy and Phenomenological Research* 2 (1942): 270; and P. Wolff, *Christliche Philosophie in Deutschland: 1920–1945* (Regensburg: Habbel, 1949), 9.

2. James Collins, "Roots of Scheler's Evolutionary Pantheism," in *Crossroads in Philosophy* (Chicago: Henry Regnery, 1962), 109.

thing transcending the medium of presentation, yet nevertheless apprehended in it.

Problems of Religion

The Renewal of Religion

Whenever man is seized in his deepest being and overwhelmed — whether by rapture or grief — the hour does not pass before he has beheld, with the inner eye of the mind, the eternal and absolute, nor before that sight has wrung from him a loud, or muffled, or secret, or even inarticulate — cry of longing. For in the person whole and undivided, in the core of the human person — not, like the springs of social activity, in partial and peripheral functions, talents, needs of the person; not close by the surface of the psychic stream — in our deepest depth, then, there lies that wonderful mainspring which, mostly unnoticed and disregarded in wonted circumstances, is ever latent and active to lead us upward, over and beyond ourselves and all things finite, to the divine. When therefore such an event as awakens the core of the human soul and unpinions this mainspring for greater activity impinges not only on the individual soul, in the dumb secrecy of its suffering and struggle, but on the community of men; when it impinges on the world-wide community, divided in peoples, which has nothing over it but its God; when its impact is greater than that of any event in the whole of history; when the event is in addition so unimaginably saturated with tears, suffering, lifeblood as the late war — *then* one may expect the call to a renewal of religion to resound through the world with such power and strength as has not been for centuries.

Today this call takes on a singularly historic character in that what is stricken to the heart is nothing less than the *whole of humanity,* nothing less than this mysterious planetary species in its undivided state — that is, like one man, a man cast into the boundlessness of time and space, cast into a mute uncomprehending nature: he bends every member in a solidarity of effort to win the fight for existence, but it is also a fight for the meaning of his life and for his worth and dignity. Whatever exists in material reality apart from this species — flora and fauna, the sun and stars —

man knows that everything is *beneath* him, beneath him in status and value, even in strength. But what does this creature, that knows everything beneath itself and learns to master it, know to be above it save the pitiless stars — save God? Where could this creature find something stronger and worthier than itself? Countless sufferings in its struggles with nature and internecine conflicts has this species undergone, and countless themselves have been the struggles and conflicts throughout the course of its dark history, a history illumined with but one thread of light at its medial point. But wherever these vicissitudes appeared, whatever aspect they assumed, always, until the outbreak of the Great War, the subject that fought and suffered, the people and the nations, had at least one thing above it, above it in worth and strength: there was, then, something above man to which he imputed as it were a moral office of judge over himself, but something in which he could at the same time place a deep trust and hope and in whose bosom he could at least believe himself to lie in some way sheltered. This one thing was — *humanity.* The part had a right of appeal to the whole, the part had a right to hope through the whole. Every suffering and every despair could say: "The whole is not suffering, the whole does not despair." Today that appeal is no more. For the first time, no more, since as far as thought can reach. Gone is the right to say: "For mankind as a *whole,* the future remains, and the wealth of humanity, and undiminished strength." Gone, because this war, rightly called the World War, was the first experience to be undergone by humanity as *its collective* experience. It was not a thing taking place in only one section of humanity and reaching all other sections only as foreign rumor and report; nor was it an affair wherein one section fights and suffers, while the others look on merely to applaud or commiserate. And yet every contention known to us in history has hitherto been of that kind. The issue of world-war and world-peace is an issue common to all mankind, affecting directly every member of the race — to a greater or lesser degree — in life, in body, in soul.

Up to the time of the outbreak there existed in Europe a certain widespread fashion of thought. In philosophy it was called *positivism,* and it was also busily active in poetry and art. This way of thinking shifted all the love and veneration which man formerly brought in offering to his God, his invisible Lord and Creator, on to the "great being" — as A. Comte called humanity. "God was my first, reason my second, man my final thought" were the words of Ludwig Feuerbach even in the Germany of the 1860s. And so what Comte, Feuerbach, Zola called the great being of humanity was inflated to something distant and holy, to be approached in fear and trembling. A similar quasi-religious pathos over humanity is to be found in Friedrich Schiller, especially in the productions of his youth. It was to humanity that the cry of the injured and insulted went out, of all those, were they individuals or whole peoples, who felt themselves unjustly humbled and oppressed. Where is, where ever was, this humanity, which still seemed enthroned *above* us all as the *"grand être"*? The war, unlike all previous wars in history, was no longer within humanity, no longer in one of its sections. Humanity itself was in the war. Where now was that which used not to suffer, but reposed in remote sublimity while peoples suffered? Humanity itself was suffering violence committed by humanity. Where was the seat of the wicked, where the source of disturbance and peril, where the demonic element of turmoil and faction which attacked a people and made them to suffer, that humanity might arm to punish the transgressors? Let the politicians peer through their spectacles and seek it as best they may: it is nowhere. For it is in the whole of humanity itself and *is* humanity itself, suffering the violence upon violence which it inflicts upon itself. Where is the whole which, when a part strayed into evil ways, could yet lead the part back, teach it and educate it? Nowhere! For mankind has learned how to master everything *beneath* it — plants and animals, sunlight and all kinds of energy — but one thing alone it has not learned to master: *itself*. Where is the *grand être* to whom the people look up in reverence? It has been convulsed with pain and bloodletting, and is truly no more the "great being." It is only a small being, a quite small, suffering, being. For the first time humanity feels *alone* in the wide universe. It has seen that the god it made of itself was an idol — the basest of idols since time began — baser than graven images of wood, marble and gold.

This, then, is the new thing in the present call to religious renewal: *humanity* is rejecting its *idol-self*, and the *grand être* which so long hid God from sight, as a cloud veils the sun, has been blown away. In some unprecedented way humanity has become aware of its weakness, its lowliness, its crooked timber, as Kant put it. For this reason it is hard to understand why, precisely when the *grand être* has become so small and — like a caterpillar inquisitively swaying its head beyond the edge of the leaf — is powerlessly scanning its surroundings for some force that might help it to escape the clutches of the frightful mechanism in which it has trapped itself, — why at this moment Alfred Loisy is able to write a book which, on the basis of a wealth of religious scholarship, seeks to breathe new life into Comte's religion of humanity. Moral "obligation"? — that is supposed to be no more than the sense of what we owe to the work of past humanity. What *we* — owe to past humanity? Come now, whatever we owe to past humanity, "they" are indebted to us for the entire sum of human suffering endured by youth in the Great War: for that they are indebted to us, since to *them* we are indebted for the war. Without further investigating the extraordinary apparition of this somewhat belated book, we may affirm that *positivistic faith in humanity,* as a chosen makeshift for genuine religion, has collapsed in ruin.

It had necessarily to collapse at a time when mankind, divided into states and peoples, is at least showing the *first will* to embody itself in a league which represents *more* than a bare sum of compacts between states, in an independent, real, and collective moral corporation, armed with power and enthroned above peoples and states, a body which, like a state over its citizens, seeks to settle all disputes between states and peoples according to universally recognized norms and laws of right, and to enforce the idea of justice embodied in these laws even, if need be, between separate *sections* of humanity. For it is precisely this legislative moral *embodiment,* for the first time realizing the abstract natural concept of humanity in a "league of nations," which finally and emphatically precludes any deification of the object of that concept. Only while "humanity," as an ultimate unit of right and morality, still remained merely a distant *Utopia,* a shining figment of dreams and mystery, or at its highest a splendid vision of poet and seer, could it appear to certain intellectual groups as a substitute for the idea of God. The humanity *realizing* itself in humanity's world-war — the humanity now making the first attempt in its history to master itself and control its destiny in freedom according to supra-national law — can no longer be open to this delusion. Even as the age-old vision begins to be realized, in a realization hampered, like *every* realization, by obstacles, imperfections and disturbances, even the *apparent* gratification of religious cravings which the substance of the vision offers is eschewed. Likewise exactly, the *grand être* is left to fall into desuetude in accordance with that law of the soul whereby the realization of socialism has already begun to expose the redundance of the sham religious gratification offered by the quasi-messianic "ideal state." This is the law whereby, in general terms, every realization of the simplest dream of youth, let it be ever so perfect, destroys the power of the fantasy to shine and enchant. For it is only through the transforming psychic power of *longing*, which bathes everything in an ineffable medium of light and splendor, that essentially finite contents of our thoughts and aspirations can assume even an apparent power to satisfy the *religious* craving of our mind, to satisfy the demands of our reason for the final realization of our ideal of the world. Disenchantment ensues even when the substance of the ideal, as envisaged in the longing mind, is fully realized. For one element is bound to be absent from the *realization* — the shining splendor which *longing* itself casts over the ideal.

Nowadays humanity, as realized in one concrete, real and effective subject, will *finally* cease to mistake itself for God. The humanity which in the sphere of earthly justice has no longer any earthly thing above it, the humanity which has pledged itself to the task of eliminating, as far as possible, the blind hazards of chance and fatality from the relations between its parts, will doubly need some insight into an *eternal* order of good and right, by whose light it is taking the first great step toward the genuine mastery of itself.

In Germany, positivism and its religious pathos over humanity was never a considerable force. The more active, on the other hand, among our intellectuals, were the manifold forms of *pantheism*, bequeathed by classicism to our poetry and philosophy. For long it persisted in dilute form — though basically *counter* to the actual feeling of the times. But it is probably no exaggeration to say that of all philosophical attitudes and ways of life, idealistic pantheism is the one which has been struck the hardest blow by the deep revelation of the *nature of things* which the experiences of the Great War have brought in their wake. It has been stricken to the roots.

Pierre Bayle was perhaps the first to ask the ironic question (in his Dictionary's article, "Spinoza") whether God is at war with himself in time of war. But how more profoundly shattered is pantheism now than was indicated in that question! The seeds of its destruction were already sown in the development of pantheistic thought and feeling over the course of the nineteenth century and during the two decades of the twentieth.

Pantheism's system of thought and feeling rests more or less on the equation *God* = *World*. Its first error is the unproven hypothesis that the multiplicity of things, forces, relations surrounding us men form *one* world (not an unrestricted number of worlds, as was taught by every logically consequent materialism from Democritus on), and that it forms moreover, a *world* (not a *chaos*), hence one "sensibly" ordered whole. For this assumption is already founded on the unity and cosmic supremacy of a *single* creator-god. It is not only in a historical sense that one may demonstrate the truth of Christoph von Sigwart's dictum, which is that if man ceased to countenance the notion of regions of being without causal contact (the idea latent in all true polytheism) and instead envisaged a single, internally consistent cosmic whole, with its parts all in systematic relation, this change of attitude was a fruit of philosophical monotheism. It is also logically and objectively true that the assumption of cosmic unity and singularity *follows* from — before anything else — the assumption of a single creator-god. (For that reason, by the way, it is not quite so easy as is commonly believed to demonstrate the existence of God from the necessity of a first cause for the "world.") The world is world (not chaos), and the world is one world, only if and *because* it is God's world — if and because *one and the same* infinite will and spirit is latent and active in every entity. Just as the unity of human nature does not in the last resort lie in man's demonstrable natural characteristics but in his likeness to God, and just as humanity as a whole is only *one* humanity if all its component persons are, by virtue of their connection with God, also truly and morally bound one to another, so the world is *one* world only by virtue of *God's* oneness. Pantheism, which begins by postulating the world-character of subsistent being and the unity of the world, both independently of God, is only guilty — in a more blatant way — of the error committed by those who conclude the existence of God from a presupposed oneness and unity of a world-reality. From this we understand that wherever pantheism has made an appearance in history it has been always an end, never a beginning, never the dawning red of a sunrise of belief but always a sunset glow. It invariably rests on the fact that, in their outlook on the world, men cling to some of the consequences of a positive religious attitude, though its root and basis be forgotten. For the most part therefore, it is the way of thought typical of mature, synthetic, silver-age civilizations, and as such it may be endowed with a marvelous nobility, a greatness truly felicitous and harmonious. The god of pantheism is always a reflection of theistic belief, and is frequently of greater warmth and beauty than the theistic God. Few have so profoundly recognized this as Schopenhauer, who regarded all the pantheism of his age (represented by Fichte, Schelling and Hegel) as a residue of theistic attitudes — and for that very reason poured the more scorn on it. In ages of cataclysmic change and rebirth pantheism not only retreats in the face of reason (which has always put it to rout) but renounces the attempt to gratify religious cravings. It is even by reason of its endeavors to reconcile and harmonize, which leave no place for the moral either-or (the form of experience imposed by such ages), that pantheism is obliged to abdicate in crucial periods of history. . . .

It should occasion no astonishment that pantheism has developed in this direction. Pantheism was able — with certain allowances — to express as it were the religious formulation of the German temperament so long as the nation's intellectual life was lost in dreams of an ideal world of the spirit, representing the true homeland of man (for "man" read "German") — so long as the nation thought and felt itself to be first and foremost a *Kulturnation;* so long, finally, as there still existed an "art and science" of which one might still say with some claim to *sense* that whoever possessed them possessed religion, and that only those excluded from the cultural aristocracy need take to heart Goethe's famous *mot,* "If any possess not these two, let *him* possess religion!" For just as that art was an art of ideas with little tendency to specialization, that "science" was a synthetic, autodidactic pursuit of cultivated men in a strictly local *culture,* a science strongly colored by theology — most of the German speculative philosophers were former Protestant theologians. To say anything similar about the art of our time and its science, geared as it is to *work* and *research,* and specialized in the extreme, would be not only incorrect — as also is Goethe's dictum, by the way — but absurd and ridiculous. If then these German pantheistic traditions are to return in backwash to our present world, they must automatically take the shape of some highly colored and enticingly dangled *lie,* some illusionistic evasion of reality....

If these two worlds of thought, the positivist and the pantheistic, are unable to give *any* answer to the call for religious renewal, what is the significance of that call? It can signify a great deal, but it can also come and go like the call for help of a man who remains *unanswered* in the extremest danger of drowning. For however strong may be a pressure, a need, a deeply felt want, an emptiness in the heart that might be filled, the pressure itself, the need itself, have *not* the power nor the means to achieve their own satisfaction. Yet the attempt has been made to turn the need, the lack, the necessity into the creator of cultural and technical civilization. The great physiologist A. Pflüger even tried to prove that in the life of the bodily organism every need became ultimately the cause of its own satisfaction. Lamarck built the whole of his theory of evolution on a similar proposition. There is likewise the German proverb "Need teaches to pray," and it is true that we Germans are traditionally all too fond of believing in, and appealing to, the creative force of "holy" need. But in *no* field of human values is this proposition true in the sense in which it is meant. *Least of all* is it true in the field of religion.

With regard to higher culture, the free creations of the mind, philosophy and art, never and nowhere spring from necessity and dire need, but always from disengaged leisure. The ancients knew it well. Even technical skills and inventions, for which need and necessity mean considerably more, spring from them only in the sense that they control the choice of direction exercised by the mind's *inventive activity* — which, however, must always be present. But even in this case the very "needs" which are satisfied by the invented tool or machine are of *historical* origin; they have arisen through adaptation of instinctual life to types of good which as types were already present before they were, types which were thus already formed before the corresponding need, types which — finally — did *not* themselves proceed from needs, but from the free and positive creative force of the mind. Nearly everything which today is a need of the masses was once a luxury of the few.

The higher we climb from the utilitarian in the realm of values, the more *erroneous* the proposition becomes. For that reason it is at its most erroneous where types of the *highest,* the *religious,* the *truly holy good* are concerned. "Need teaches to pray" — certainly. But the fundamental act of the mind whereby we first open our inner eye to the eternal and are first enabled to pray to it, the act of *worship*, and thereafter the acts of reverence and devotion — these are *not* taught by need. And yet there is never any prayer without worship beforehand — neither thanksgiving, supplication, nor any kind of prayer. But at least pure need, necessity, emptiness, do tell us something about *what* we worship, what we pray to, what we pray, and how we should pray. There are Negroes in Africa dwelling in tribes by lakes with abundant fish, yet many die of starvation every year, since the dire need of hunger has not been able to provoke the invention of the angler's hook. How much easier it is to imagine that so great a need for religious renewal should remain without positive consequence. It is possible for the world's cry of need to hold great meaning only when it generates motion and activity in man's positive springs of religion, only when it brings our reason to act in renewed concentration on the idea of God and opens our mental eye to the positive benefits of revelation and grace which are already *present* in the world, though great multitudes are blind to them. Need, the empty heart, the heartfelt want, can and should have this effect: to that extent they are beacons, drawing souls on to explore new ground. But *more* they cannot do. For this world and human nature are everywhere so ordered that the lower, natural and instinctual forces can unleash higher forms of activity, but cannot create them; they bid them seek, but not *necessarily* bring them to find. The mental force which creates and finds is invariably a higher force, working according to its own inner law and owing nothing of its goal, substance and principle to that which merely set it in motion....

Christianity, some say, is bankrupt; No — simply the Churches, say others; Just this Church and that one, say others yet again. All these theses were prevalent long ago — long before the war. Among the older voices only *one* is almost wholly unheard today — the one which says, Religion itself is bankrupt: it is only an atavism in historical evolution. That this voice is missing shows that we should expect at all events an age of extreme *vitality* in matters of religion, an age characterized by quite new kinds of mighty spiritual conflicts. But for precisely that reason, in the coming age every existing positive religion and Church must cease to be a mere ice-box for old truths — as it was recently put by a

Swiss theologian. No doctrinal position — unless it wishes to surrender entirely — will be able to content itself with a mere wish to maintain its *status quo;* every such position will have to exert itself in addition to demonstrate positively to the world its overriding worth — and to be the warrant of its own truth. There we have certainly a new situation, to which none may remain blind. Consider the person who wishes merely to *preserve,* or at the most defend, his religious position: if he dare not see in it the positive means of salvation for suffering humanity, and will not extend to humanity this means in a gift of joy and love, then he will find even his more modest goal of self-preservation *no longer* attainable. As men reckon, his cause will vanish from the face of the earth. For this is how things stand: neither mass-indifference, however widespread, nor even heresy and unbelief, nor sham piety nor superstition were ever a real, an ultimate danger to the existence of a positive religion and Church. Rather the opposite — the outworn, the decadent, custom and inertia were never so mightily propped and preserved in Church-religion as by — *inter alia* — indifference and unbelief. Especially among the educated. Only one true possible danger threatens the existence of a positive religion — the greater enthusiasm and the deeper faith of those who practice *another religion.* It was skeptic indifference and unbelief which enabled the Churches to live such an easy life before the war and to be so content with "maintaining" their position. But the time will come when unbelief's sterile negation and the apparent tolerance of religion by lazy indifference will have come to an end. Then religion will once again be recognized and attacked from all sides for what it is — the highest concern of man. Then will be an end of the easy life. And with it there will cease the perfunctory frontier-patrol of one's values and ideas, or the airtight, quasi-paralyzed self-mummification in the coffin of exclusive organizations and places apart. Only one alternative will then be valid — either one must gird up one's loins and with open, succoring arms *give,* present or lavish something on humanity, heal its heart's open wound, or one must be prepared to find that the world, though thirsting feverishly for religion, believes one has nothing to give; to find, even, that one no longer feels oneself wholly in the right or in possession of the true and the good — of, in short, the divine verities. But in the latter case one must also be prepared to find that this catalytic conviction also penetrates one's own ranks, and that the mere policy of "holding fast" — that gesture of pride and avarice — brings on the destruction of the very things which one wished to preserve. Any positive religion which today fails in the above sense to carry out its spiritual mission, to bear new and living witness to its cause in every way, is most certainly doomed to defeat and decline in the spiritual struggles which we have before us. Not in the sense of outward power and might, but in the sense of the proofs of heart and soul, every positive religion must win victory *or* suffer defeat. He who has nothing to give in *this* crisis of the world will lose what he possesses.

Translated by Bernard Noble

Albert Schweitzer

Because of his renown as a medical missionary in Africa, as an interpreter of Bach's organ music, and as the recipient of the Nobel Peace Prize in 1952, Albert Schweitzer (1875–1965) is perhaps not as well known to the general public for his religious writings, although every New Testament scholar is familiar with his works on the search for the historical Jesus, *Von Reimarus zu Wrede* (1906), and on the theology of St. Paul, *Die Mystik des Apostels Paulus* (1930). Schweitzer's writings are very much a reflection of his life and display all of the virtues that gave him such wide recognition outside the narrow field of biblical scholarship: technical mastery of the material, a deep respect for the religious striving of all humankind, and an openness to every possible point of view.

His impact was revolutionary, but perhaps nowhere more so than in his technical scholarship, for it is to Schweitzer — and almost Schweitzer alone — that one must credit the total turnaround in the study of Jesus: nineteenth-century German scholarship had operated under the presupposition that the Gospels were written under the influence of faith and that it should be possible to strip away this dogmatic "overlay" and reach the historical Jesus. Schweitzer's book on the search for this historical Jesus was a survey of these efforts, and he deftly showed that nearly every one of them reached the same conclusion: that Jesus was a benign liberal Protestant in the Adolf von Harnack mode, who ultimately preached merely "the Fatherhood of God and brotherhood of man." Schweitzer, however, showed that on the contrary Jesus was very much an eschatological prophet in the Jeremiah mode, who preached the wrath of God as fully as any Old Testament prophet. He further showed, at least to his satisfaction, that Jesus grew increasingly anxious at the delay in the arrival of the Kingdom whose imminent coming he preached; and so he resolutely faced Jerusalem to provoke that Kingdom and died in despair when it did not arrive as he had expected.

The selection we have chosen does not come from this work or from his book on Paul, not only because the work of later scholars has to a great extent superseded these two insightful books but also because it seemed best to draw on a work dealing with religion more generally. Schweitzer had a truly open mind and could synthesize positions that to a more ordinary mortal would seem to be irreconcilable;[1] and one of his more important works is a book on Indian philosophy, *Die Weltanschauung der indischen Denker* (1935). This selection accordingly comes from a lecture entitled "Christianity and the Religions of the World," which admirably brings together both his acute biblical erudition and his passionate humanistic vision.

From "Christianity and the Religions of the World"

Let us together try to find out whether Christianity, simple though it is, can really maintain its claim to be the deepest expression of the religious mind.

Do not expect me to furnish an apologetic of the type that is, unfortunately, so frequently met with — an apologetic which con-

---

1. This is ably brought out in the observations of Don Cupitt: "Even at this early age Schweitzer's attitude to religion was uncommon by today's standards. He was enquiring, undogmatic and remarkably independent-minded. Although he could describe the supernaturalist beliefs of the past with great insight, he seems never to have held them himself. He stood at the end of the great tradition of Protestant rationalism, and all of his life he took it for granted that the unreserved pursuit of truth was compatible, was indeed identical, with a Protestant's loyalty to Christ. Following Kant, he was a metaphysical agnostic who saw religion primarily in terms of ethics and the will. Great though his abilities were, he accordingly regarded himself as destined to be a man of action rather than a pure scholar.... During the 1890's the thinkers who were to mean most to him made their mark on his mind: Goethe, Kant, probably Schopenhauer and certainly Nietzsche. All were highly unorthodox figures, and two were militant atheists, yet Schweitzer's heroic Protestant temper of mind was able to accommodate them readily without the inner conflict and 'doubts' that would be expected of him today. Indeed he never wavered in his loyalty to his village Lutheran background and his singularly tough old father, who continued to work in the parish ministry until the age of ninety-seven" (Don Cupitt, *The Sea of Faith: Christianity in Change* [New York: Cambridge University Press, 1988], 102–3).

sists in the assertion that Christianity contains truths which are above all reasoning, and which, therefore, do not have to enter into contest with philosophy. This appears to me like a retiring into a mountain fortress, which is excellent indeed for defense, but useless as far as exercise of power over the surrounding country is concerned.

From my youth I have held the conviction that all religious truth must in the end be capable of being grasped as something that stands to reason. I, therefore, believe that Christianity, in the contest with philosophy and with other religions, should not ask for exceptional treatment, but should be in the thick of the battle of ideas, relying solely on the power of its own inherent truth.

In the first place I have to touch upon the results obtained by those who have carried on research work in the sphere of history of religions as to the past of Christianity. You know that some have gone so far as to cast doubt upon its originality. The first to do this was Bruno Bauer (1809–82). He maintains that the ideas of Christianity originated in the piety of the Graeco-Roman world at the beginning of our era: first, some pious people, who longed for "redemption," formed a congregation; then a tradition arose that made a Jewish rabbi, called Jesus, the preacher of this "religion of redemption."

Arthur Drews, at present professor of philosophy at the School of Technology in Karlsruhe, a deeply religious thinker, influenced by the philosopher Eduard von Hartmann, considers Christianity to be the offspring of a myth about a dying and rising Savior-god. Out of this myth (so Drews declares) grew the history of Jesus as we now read it in the Gospels.

Others, again, assume that there really was a Jewish teacher called Jesus, who was crucified on account of his teaching, but that Paul was the real author of Christianity. Paul's mind, they say, was filled with the Hellenistic ideas of "redemption"; in Tarsus he had become familiar with the mystery-cults which were at that time practiced in Asia Minor, and he was equally acquainted with mystical ideas of redemption which had grown in the soil of Zarathushtra's religion. Later on he connected these Graeco-Oriental redemption-ideas with reflections concerning the person and the work of the crucified Jesus of Nazareth, whom he represented to be the Savior dying for the redemption of men. Also, it was Paul who gave Christianity its sacramental character. The chief representative of this view is the German philologist Richard Reitzenstein.

How can men who think seriously come to the conclusion that the ideas of Christianity do not go back to Jesus, but merely represent a transformation of ideas which stirred religious circles in the then heathen world?

As a matter of fact, there is a certain analogy between Christianity and Hellenistic piety. In both, the assurance of redemption plays a part; in both, the attainment of redemption is thought of as being connected with sacramental rites.

In the beginning of our era the longing for redemption sought satisfaction in cults which had originated in Greece or in the Orient or in Egypt, and which claimed the power to mediate redemption to men through mysterious initiations. These cults have only recently become the object of historical research, and their significance for the spiritual life of the period when the ancient world was passing away has been recognized. (Pioneers in this sphere were the German philologists, Herman Usener, Erwin Rohde, and Albrecht Dieterich, and the Belgian scholar, Franz Cumont). Greece contributed the Eleusinian Mysteries, Asia Minor the worship of Attis and of Cybele, Egypt the cult of Isis and Serapis, Persia the cult of Mithras.

The attempt to prove that Christianity is derived from these mystery-religions of redemption does not lead to positive results. Christianity is much richer than they, for it comprises elements of a very different type. However much one may idealize the Graeco-Oriental mystery-religions — and some of the investigators have idealized them beyond measure — they are still poverty-stricken, compared with Christianity. If one forms an unbiased judgment, on the basis of the extant records concerning them, a great deal of the charm with which they are being surrounded today vanishes. They are concerned solely with the bestowal of immortality upon men through magic. The ethical element, which plays such a predominant part in Christianity, they contain in words, at best, but not in reality. The Mithras-cult alone is really ethical. It derives its ethical energies from the religion of Zarathushtra, of which it is a fragment that for some time whirled, like a flaming comet, in the Graeco-Oriental and Graeco-Roman world. But not even the wildest fanatic disputing the originality of Christianity can think of maintaining that it sprang from the cult of Mithras, for that cult appeared in the Graeco-Oriental world only after Christianity had attained to full development. It was, however, the very vitality of its ethical ideas that made the Mithras-religion, which Roman soldiers brought into Western Europe and Africa, the most powerful rival of Christianity.

A fundamental difference between the redemption-idea found in the cults of the Hellenistic period and that of Christianity lies in this: the one knows nothing of the conception of the Kingdom of God, whereas the other is dominated by that conception.

Hellenistic religion is exclusively concerned with the destiny of spirit in the world of matter. It seeks to understand how the life from above came down into the lower life, and how it can be released from this captivity. Its interest centers in this restoration of the spiritual element to its original sphere, and not in the fate of mankind or of the world. Christianity, on the other hand, lives by the glowing hope of a better world. Redemption, according to the Christian conception, is the action of God, who brings this better world, the Kingdom of God, into existence and receives into it those men who have proved themselves to be of an honest and good heart.

The teaching of Jesus and of Paul concerning the Kingdom of God is, briefly, as follows: The end of this world and the dawn of the supernatural world are regarded as near at hand. The "Saints," not being conformed to this world, have thereby proved their election to God's Kingdom, and they will live in that Kingdom together with the Messiah, in transfigured bodies, until the end comes and all things return unto God, so that God may be all in all, as in the beginning (1 Cor. 15:28).

Of such an eschatological hope — that is, an expectation of the end of the world, and of its transfiguration — nothing is to be found in the Graeco-Oriental mystery-religions. Where there is any kind of expectation of the end of the world, and of the Kingdom of God, we certainly have to do with a type of religious thinking which cannot be traced back to those mystery-religions, but which is derived from that Jewish outlook we find in the prophets. Amos and Isaiah have created the conception of the Kingdom of God. Late Judaism developed it in fantastic ways, no doubt partly under the influence of ideas from Zarathushtra's religion, with which the exile made the Jews acquainted. Jesus brings the

Kingdom-idea to its ethical perfection, without inveighing against its late-Jewish form.

From every point of view, therefore, the contention that Christianity can be explained by being traced back to Graeco-Oriental religious thought, has to be regarded as fantasy introduced into the sphere of the comparative study of religions. Christianity is the creation of Jesus, whose spiritual background was late-Jewish piety.

Later, when Christianity had to relinquish the hope for the speedy coming of the end of the world and for the immediate realization of the Kingdom of God, and when, through Greek converts, Greek thought came to influence it, it entered, to a certain degree, the world of the Graeco-Oriental mystery-religions and was thereby impoverished.

As yet we know few details concerning the process by which Christianity, in an irrepressible development, casts off Jewish thought and is hellenized. This much, however, is certain: as the Jewish outlook is abandoned, the ideas which constitute the uniqueness and greatness of the teaching of Jesus — the ideas of the Kingdom of God and of an ethic directed toward that Kingdom — lose their vitality in the Christian religion. The first representative of that hellenized Christianity was Ignatius, who lived in the latter part of the first and the beginning of the second centuries. In his letters there is not much of the vital teaching of Jesus to be found. He is chiefly interested in the sacraments and in the manner in which they become efficacious. He refers to the Lord's Supper as the "medicine of immortality."

Let us not be satisfied with having ascertained that Christianity cannot be traced to the religious mind of the Graeco-Oriental type, but is something original and goes back to the personality of Jesus, who worked in Galilee and died at Jerusalem. In determining what is the difference between Christianity and the Graeco-Oriental religion, let us try to discover what Christianity essentially is.

What again and again misleads people into the belief that the religious mind of the Graeco-Oriental type and that of the Christian type are identical is the fact that both are pessimistic. They despair of the natural world. Just here, however, a most important difference is revealed. Graeco-Oriental piety is merely pessimistic. The only question with which it concerns itself is how the spiritual element is set free from the world of matter. The Gnostics of the second century — Basilides, Valentinus, Marcion and the rest — have reinterpreted Christianity on the lines of that pessimism and have tried to fit it into their impressive systems of doctrines concerning the descent of the spiritual into matter and its return to its origin. Manichaeism, which arose in the third century, is dominated by the same thought.

Christianity, however, is not so consistent. In the bedrock of its pessimism there are optimistic veins, for it is not only the religion of redemption but of the Kingdom of God. Therefore, it wishes and hopes for a transformation of the world.

Connected with this is the fact that its ethic is quite different from that of the Graeco-Oriental religion. The latter is concerned with liberation from the world only; it is not a dynamic ethic. Jesus, on the contrary, like the prophets and like Zarathushtra, who has much in common with the prophets, demands that we should become free from the world, and at the same time that we should be active in the world. The only experience the religious mind of the Graeco-Oriental type knows is the longing after the spiritual; but according to the teaching of Jesus men are to be gripped by God's will of love, and must help to carry out that will in this world, in small things as in great things, in saving as in pardoning. In this imperfect world already to be glad instruments of God's love is the service to which men are called, and it forms a preparatory stage to the bliss that awaits them in the perfected world, the Kingdom of God.

In doing God's will of love they experience communion with the Messiah, without being conscious of it. On that basis they will, on the Day of Judgment, enter into the Kingdom of God by the Messiah's decree. That is the meaning of that weighty word of Jesus (Matt. 25:40): "Inasmuch as ye have done it unto one of the least of these my brethren, ye have done it unto me."

Graeco-Oriental piety, Plato, the mystery-religions and the Gnostics, all alike say to man: "Free thyself from the world!" Jesus says: "Get free from the world, in order to work in this world in the spirit and in the love of God, till God transplants you into another, more perfect world."

Wherein does the difference lie? In the Graeco-Oriental religion there is no living conception of God. To it God is nothing but pure spirituality. The God of Jesus is an active God, who works in man. Therefore, the religion of Jesus is not consistent pessimism, completely systematized, but it is a chaotic mixture of pessimism and optimism.

Thus, the religious philosophy of Jesus is not unified. His judgment of the natural world, it is true, is pessimistic; but to him God is other than the sum-total of the forces at work in the world, other than a pure spirituality, of which part was lost into the world and has to be restored. He is a dynamic Power for good, a mysterious Will, distinct from the world and superior to the world. To Him we yield our will; to Him we leave the future of the world. In the contrast between the world and God, who is an ethical Personality, and in the peculiar tension between pessimism and optimism lies the uniqueness of the religion of Jesus. The fact that it is not a unified system constitutes its greatness, its truth, its depth, its strength.

At this point I must observe that we modern men are inclined to interpret the thoughts of Jesus in a modern way. We are familiar with the idea that by the active ethical conduct of individuals the Kingdom of God may be realized on earth. Finding that Jesus speaks of ethical activity and also of the Kingdom of God, we think that he, too, connected the two in the way which seems so natural to us. In reality, however, Jesus does not speak of the Kingdom of God as of something that comes into existence in this world and through a development of human society, but as of something which is brought about by God when He transforms this imperfect world into a perfect one. In the thought of Jesus, the ethical activity of man is only like a powerful prayer to God, that He may cause the Kingdom to appear without delay. In this sense we have to take the word of Jesus (Matt. 11:12) that from the days of John the Baptist the Kingdom of God has been suffering violence, and the violent have been seizing it by force.

For about a century and a half the modernizing interpretation of the ideas of Jesus has ruled in Protestant theology as a matter of course. Only quite recently have we ventured to admit that he, living in the late-Jewish expectation of the end of the world, holds views of the Kingdom which differ from ours.

There is a deep significance in the fact that Jesus does not establish the organic connection, which to us seems so natural, between the ethical acts of men and the realization of the Kingdom of God. It signifies that we are to be ethical, not in the expectation of thereby fulfilling some purpose but from inward necessity, so as to be children of God's spirit and in this world already to enter into His will.

Jesus does not build up his ethic with a view to solving the problem of how to organize a perfectly ethical society, but he preaches the ethic of men who together strive to attain to a perfect yielding of themselves to the will of God. Because he thus turns away from the utilitarian, he attains to the absolute ethic. An ethic which is formulated on a principle of utility is always relative.

An illustration: Jesus tells us that we must always forgive, that we must never fight for our rights nor resist evil; he does not consider whether observance of these commandments makes legally ordered conditions possible in human society, but he leads us beyond all considerations of utility into the inward constraint to do the will of God.

As modern men we imagine the state of the perfect human society to be one of harmony between legal organization and the practice of love. Jesus does not attempt to harmonize justice and love but says to man: If you want to be in the spirit of God, you may not think or act otherwise than in love.

It is because Jesus does not think in a utilitarian way, but only according to the absolute ethic of "not being conformed to the world," that there is such a remarkable contrast between his thoughts and our modern views. Only when we experience this contrast, have we entered into relationship to the true Jesus. Therefore, we must not allow ourselves to be tempted into modernizing his views and inadvertently putting thoughts as we think them into his words. His significance for us is that he fights against the spirit of the modern world, forcing it to abandon the low level on which it moves even in its best thoughts and to rise to the height whence we judge things according to the superior will of God, which is active in us, and think no more in terms of human utilitarianism but solely in terms of having to do God's will — becoming forces of God's ethical personality.

Translated by Johanna Powers

Martin Buber

The influence of Martin Buber (1878–1965) in the world of thought has been immense, but it stems, perhaps paradoxically, from a complete fidelity to his own religious tradition of Judaism. Yet he understood that fidelity so dialogically that his influence has perhaps been greater on Christians than on Jews, and on philosophers more than on theologians. Born in Vienna, he spent most of his childhood in Lvov, Galicia, at the home of his grandfather, a businessman and scholar of rabbinic literature. An early advocate of the Zionist movement, he also had the unusual distinction of being appointed (from 1924 to 1933) to the chair of the philosophy of Jewish religion and ethics at the University of Frankfurt am Main, the only chair in Jewish religion at any German university. He left for Palestine in 1938, where he was appointed professor of sociology of religion at Hebrew University. He was also heavily involved in the Yihud movement, which was devoted to Arab-Jewish understanding and in fact envisioned Zionism as entailing the creation of a binational state.

After the war he traveled and lectured widely and accepted various German awards for his humanitarian efforts and his contributions to German literature. When this led to criticism from some Jewish quarters, Buber remained steadfast: he insisted that Germans should be encouraged to face the past, and to those who realized the magnitude of the Nazi crimes and repented on behalf of their nation he offered nothing but encouragement.

This was clearly a man of extraordinary openness, but he never tried to prove the ecumenicity of that openness by moving away from his tradition; rather, his openness came from a fidelity to that tradition, marking a real sea change in the response of Jewish thinkers to the Enlightenment: rejecting both ghettoization and assimilation. Perhaps the best example of the appreciation that this stance generated among Christian thinkers comes from an author who will conclude this book, Hans Urs von Balthasar:

> Martin Buber is one of the creative minds of our age. Most of those who know something of the riches of his work and have felt the appeal of his personality, are alive to one or more of the aspects of this many-sided man: the sage, the philosopher of religion, the anthropologist, the originator of the "dialogical principle," and the brilliant translator of the Scriptures who achieved what Herder and Hamann and the Romantics had always longed for, a translation of the Hebrew in which the genius of the Semitic language sounds through the German without distorting it. Furthermore, there is the man who saved the Hasidic tradition, and worked tirelessly to restore and interpret it. And finally there is the theoretician and "theologian" of present-day Judaism. Those who know him at all realize that he is not simply another writer of the Jewish race who has been admitted into the German pantheon, but the man — and, what is more, the only one — who remained in the forefront of German literature throughout the last half century, representing the Jewish race in the face of a blind hatred of everything Jewish.
>
> From the days of Moses Mendelssohn and his grandchildren in the Biedermeier salons of Berlin, down to the period of Hermann Cohen and the philosophers of the turn of the century, the tendency among the Jewish intelligentsia has all along been one of assimilation; their aim has been to present the spirit of Jewry as broadly humanistic. Martin Buber's work flies in the face of that long literary tradition, and his whole endeavor has been to recapture the essential spirit of Judaism, and to recollect its nature. He has expounded his reflections in a classical German untainted by those fatal lapses of taste which mar the work of some Jewish writers, and its form no less than its content disarmed the equally fatal prejudices against the Jews. That wholesale reversal of a centuries-old tradition deserves to be pondered.[1]

---

1. Hans Urs von Balthasar, *Martin Buber and Christianity: A Dialogue between Israel and the Church*, trans. Alexander Dru (London: Hatrill Press, 1961/1958), 9–10.

Our selection is drawn from a relatively little-known piece by Buber, which nicely exemplifies these qualities so appreciatively set forth by Balthasar.

From Eclipse of God

Prelude: Report on Two Talks

I shall tell about two talks. One apparently came to a conclusion, as only occasionally a talk can come, and yet in reality remained unconcluded; the other was apparently broken off and yet found a completion such as rarely falls to the lot of discussions.

Both times it was a dispute about God, about the concept and the name of God, but each time of a very different nature.

On three successive evenings I spoke at the adult folk-school of a German industrial city on the subject "Religion as Reality." What I meant by that was the simple thesis that "faith" is not a feeling in the soul of man but an entrance into reality, an entrance into the *whole* reality without reduction and curtailment. This thesis is simple but it contradicts the usual way of thinking. And so three evenings were necessary to make it clear, and not merely three lectures but also three discussions which followed the lectures. At these discussions I was struck by something which bothered me. A large part of the audience was evidently made up of workers but none of them spoke up. Those who spoke and raised questions, doubts, and reflections were for the most part students (for the city had a famous old university). But all kinds of other circles were also represented; the workers alone remained silent. Only at the conclusion of the third evening was this silence, which had by now become painful for me, explained. A young worker came up to me and said: "Do you know we can't speak in there, but if you would meet with us tomorrow, we could talk together the whole time." Of course I agreed.

The next day was a Sunday. After dinner I came to the agreed place and now we talked together well into the evening. Among the workers was one, a man no longer young, whom I was drawn to look at again and again because he listened as one who really wished to hear. Real listening has become rare in our time. It is found most often among workers, who are not indeed concerned about the person speaking, as is so often the case with the bourgeois public, but about what he has to say. This man had a curious face. In an old Flemish altar picture representing the adoration of the shepherds one of them, who stretches out his arms toward the manger, has such a face. The man in front of me did not look as if he might have any desire to do the same; moreover, his face was not open like that in the picture. What was notable about him was that he heard and pondered, in a manner as slow as it was impressive. Finally, he opened his lips as well. "I have had the experience," he explained slowly and impressively, repeating a saying which the astronomer Laplace is supposed to have used in conversation with Napoleon, "that I do not need this hypothesis 'God' in order to be quite at home in the world." He pronounced the word "hypothesis" as if he had attended the lectures of the distinguished natural scientist who had taught in that industrial and university city and had died shortly before. Although he did not reject the designation "God" for his idea of nature, that naturalist spoke in a similar manner whether he pursued zoology or *Weltanschauung*.

The brief speech of the man struck me; I felt myself more deeply challenged than by the others. Up till then we had certainly debated very seriously, but in a somewhat relaxed way; now everything had suddenly become severe and hard. How should I reply to the man? I pondered awhile in the now severe atmosphere. It came to me that I must shatter the security of his *Weltanschauung*, through which he thought of a "world" in which one "felt at home." What sort of a world was it? What we were accustomed to call world was the "world of the senses," the world in which there exists vermilion and grass green, C major and B minor, the taste of apple and of wormwood. Was this world anything other than the meeting of our own senses with those unapproachable events about whose essential definition physics always troubles itself in vain? The red that we saw was neither there in the "things," nor here in the "soul." It at times flamed up and glowed just so long as a red-perceiving eye and a red-engendering "oscillation" found themselves over against each other. Where then was the world and its security? The unknown "objects" there, the apparently so well-known and yet not graspable "subjects" here, and the actual and still so evanescent meeting of both, the "phenomena" — was that not already three worlds which could no longer be comprehended from one alone? How could we in our thinking place together these worlds so divorced from one another? What was the being that gave this "world," which had become so questionable, its foundation?

When I was through a stern silence ruled in the now twilit room. Then the man with the shepherd's face raised his heavy lids, which had been lowered the whole time, and said slowly and impressively, "You are right."

I sat in front of him dismayed. What had I done? I had led the man to the threshold beyond which there sat enthroned the majestic image which the great physicist, the great man of faith, Pascal, called the God of the Philosophers. Had I wished for that? Had I not rather wished to lead him to the other, Him whom Pascal called the God of Abraham, Isaac, and Jacob, Him to whom one can say Thou?

It grew dusk, it was late. On the next day I had to depart. I could not remain, as I now ought to do; I could not enter into the factory where the man worked, become his comrade, live with him, win his trust through real life-relationship, help him to walk with me the way of the creature who *accepts* the creation. I could only return his gaze.

Some time later I was the guest of a noble old thinker. I had once made his acquaintance at a conference where he gave a lecture on elementary folk-schools and I gave one on adult folk-schools. That brought us together, for we were united by the fact that the word "folk" has to be understood in both cases in the same all-embracing sense. At that time I was happily surprised at how the man with the steel-grey locks asked us at the beginning of his talk to forget all that we believed we knew about his philosophy from his books. In the last years, which had been war years, reality had been brought so close to him that he saw everything with new eyes and had to think in a new way. To be old is a glorious thing when one has not unlearned what it means *to begin,* this old man had even perhaps first learned it thoroughly in old age. He was not at all young, but he was old in a young way, knowing how to begin.

He lived in another university city situated in the west. When the theology students of that university invited me to speak about prophecy, I stayed with the old man. There was a good spirit in his house, the spirit that wills to enter life and does not prescribe to life where it shall let it in.

One morning I got up early in order to read proofs. The evening before I had received galley proofs of the preface of a book of mine, and since this preface was a statement of faith, I wished to read it once again quite carefully before it was printed. Now I took it into the study below that had been offered to me in case I should need it. But here the old man already sat at his writing-desk. Directly after greeting me he asked me what I had in my hand, and when I told him, he asked whether I would not read it aloud to him. I did so gladly. He listened in a friendly manner but clearly astonished, indeed with growing amazement. When I was through, he spoke hesitatingly, then, carried away by the importance of his subject, ever more passionately. "How can you bring yourself to say 'God' time after time? How can you expect that your readers will take the word in the sense in which you wish it to be taken? What you mean by the name of God is something above all human grasp and comprehension, but in speaking about it you have lowered it to human conceptualization. What word of human speech is so misused, so defiled, so desecrated as this! All the innocent blood that has been shed for it has robbed it of its radiance. All the injustice that it has been used to cover has effaced its features. When I hear the highest called 'God,' it sometimes seems almost blasphemous."

The kindly clear eyes flamed. The voice itself flamed. Then we sat silent for awhile facing each other. The room lay in the flowing brightness of early morning. It seemed to me as if a power from the light entered into me. What I now answered, I cannot today reproduce but only indicate.

"Yes," I said, "it is the most heavy-laden of all human words. None has become so soiled, so mutilated. Just for this reason I may not abandon it. Generations of men have laid the burden of their anxious lives upon this word and weighed it to the ground; it lies in the dust and bears their whole burden. The races of man with their religious factions have torn the word to pieces; they have killed for it and died for it, and it bears their finger-marks and their blood. Where might I find a word like it to describe the highest! If I took the purest, most sparkling concept from the inner treasure-chamber of the philosophers, I could only capture thereby an unbinding product of thought. I could not capture the presence

of Him whom the generations of men have honored and degraded
with their awesome living and dying. I do indeed mean Him whom
the hell-tormented and heaven-storming generations of men mean.
Certainly, they draw caricatures and write 'God' underneath; they
murder one another and say 'in God's name.' But when all madness and delusion fall to dust, when they stand over against Him in
the loneliest darkness and no longer say 'He, He' but rather sigh
'Thou,' shout 'Thou,' all of them the one word, and when they
then add 'God,' is it not the real God whom they all implore, the
One Living God, the God of the children of man? Is it not He who
hears them? And just for this reason is not the word 'God,' the
word of appeal, the word which has become a *name*, consecrated
in all human tongues for all times? We must esteem those who in-
terdict it because they rebel against the injustice and wrong which
are so readily referred to 'God' for authorization. But we may not
give it up. How understandable it is that some suggest we should
remain silent about the 'last things' for a time in order that the
misused words may be redeemed! But they are not to be redeemed
thus. We cannot cleanse the word 'God' and we cannot make it
whole; but, defiled and mutilated as it is, we can raise it from the
ground and set it over an hour of great care."

It had become very light in the room. It was no longer dawning,
it was light. The old man stood up, came over to me, laid his hand
on my shoulder and spoke: "Let us be friends." The conversation
was completed. For where two or three are truly together, they are
together in the name of God.

Religion and Reality

1

The relationship between religion and reality prevailing in a given
epoch is the most accurate index of its true character. In some
periods, that which men "believe in" as something absolutely independent of themselves is a reality with which they are in a
living relation, although they well know that they can form only
a most inadequate representation of it. In other periods, on the
contrary, this reality is replaced by a varying representation that
men "have" and therefore can handle, or by only a residue of

the representation, a concept which bears only faint traces of the original image.

Men who are still "religious" in such times usually fail to realize that the relation conceived of as religious no longer exists between them and a reality independent of them, but has existence only within the mind — a mind which at the same time contains hypostatized images, hypostatized "ideas."

Concomitantly there appears, more or less clearly, a certain type of person, who thinks that this is as it should be: in the opinion of this person, religion has never been anything but an intra-psychic process whose products are "projected" on a plane in itself fictitious but vested with reality by the soul. Cultural epochs, such men say, can be classified according to the imaginative strength of this projection; but in the end, man, having attained to clear knowledge, must recognize that every alleged colloquy with the divine was only a soliloquy, or rather a conversation between various strata of the self. Thereupon, as a representative of this school in our time has done, it becomes necessary to proclaim that God is "dead." Actually, this proclamation means only that man has become incapable of apprehending a reality absolutely independent of himself and of having a relation with it — incapable, moreover, of imaginatively perceiving this reality and representing it in images, since it eludes direct contemplation. For the great images of God fashioned by mankind are born not of imagination but of real encounters with real divine power and glory. Man's capacity to apprehend the divine in images is lamed in the same measure as is his capacity to experience a reality absolutely independent of himself....

4

Understandably, the thinking of the era, in its effort to make God unreal, has not contented itself with reducing Him to a moral principle. The philosophers who followed Kant have tried essentially to reinstate the absolute, conceived of as existing not "within us," or at least not only within us. The traditional term "God" is to be preserved for the sake of its profound overtones, but in such a way that any connection it may have with our concrete life, as a life exposed to the manifestations of God, must become meaningless. The reality of a vision or a contact that directly determines our existence, which was a fundamental certainty to thinkers such as Plato and Plotinus, Descartes and Leibniz, is no longer found in the world of Hegel (if we disregard his youthful works, which have a completely different orientation). "The spiritual principle that which we call God," and which "alone is real," is, by its nature, accessible only to reason, not to the whole of man as he lives his concrete life. The radical abstraction, with which philosophizing begins for Hegel, ignores the existential reality of the I and of the Thou, together with that of everything else. According to Hegel, the absolute — universal reason, the Idea, i.e., "God" — uses everything that exists and develops in nature and in history, including everything that relates to man, as an instrument of its, i.e., God's, self-realization and perfect self-awareness; but God never enters into a living, direct relation to us, nor does He vouchsafe us such a relation to Him.

At the same time, however, Hegel takes a peculiarly ambivalent attitude toward Spinoza's *amor Dei.* "The life of God and of the divine element," he says, "might be described as love in love with itself" (*ein Spielen der Liebe mit sich selbst*). But he adds at once, "This idea degenerates to mere edification and even insipidity if it does not include the seriousness, the pain, the patience, and the labor of the negative." For Hegel, it follows from this quite correct insight (which, it is true, does not at all apply to Spinoza's thought) that God Himself must be drawn into the dialectical process, in which negations emerge in order to be transcended. But thereby the concrete *encounter* between God and the contradiction, as it is documented with human existence, personal and historical, is relegated to the domain of fiction. The substance which, from among the infinity of its attributes, reveals to us only two, nature and spirit, and yet lets its infinite love shine in our finite love, here becomes the subject of an absolute process encompassing nature and spirit, which in this very process "achieves its truth, its consciousness of itself" in "an irresistible urge." In this process, in which the use of universal reason "mobilizes the passions for its own purposes," as Hegel puts it, "individuals are sacrificed and surrendered." The basic theme of all religions, which even so-called atheistic philosophies could only vary, the dramatic conflict between limited and unlimited being, is extinguished, because it is replaced by the exclusive rule of a universal spirit wrestling with and for itself, using everything as a means and consuming everything. Hegel, who wanted to preserve religion by renewing its form, by amending "revealed" (*offenbarte*) religion and transforming it into "manifest" (*offenbare*) religion, has denuded it of reality for the era now closing. "There is no longer anything mysterious about God," he says of this stage of development which he regards as the highest. Nothing mysterious indeed, except that what is here and now called God can no longer be for man that God which he encounters, both deeply mysterious and manifest, in his despairs and in his raptures.

5

Nietzsche's saying that God is dead, that we have slain Him, dramatically sums up the end situation of the era. But even more eloquent than this proclamation, which recapitulates a proposition of Hegel* with a change of accent and meaning, are the attempts to fill the horizon that has been declared empty. I shall mention here only two of the most important of these attempts.

Bergson's point of departure is the fact of the *effort créateur que manifeste la vie*. This *effort,* he says, "is of God (*est de Dieu*), if it is not God Himself." The second part of the sentence nullifies the first. An effort, i.e., a process, or the preliminary forms of a process, cannot be named God, without making the concept of God utterly meaningless. Further, and most especially, the crucial religious experiences of man do not take place in a sphere in which creative energy operates without contradiction; but in a sphere in which evil and good, despair and hope, the power of destruction and the power of rebirth, dwell side by side. The divine force which man actually encounters in life does not hover above the demonic, but penetrates it. To confine God to a producing function is to remove Him from the world in which we live — a world filled with burning contradictions and with yearning for salvation.

The conception represented by Heidegger is of an essentially different kind. Unlike Bergson, he does not aim at a new concept of God. He accepts Nietzsche's statement about the death

*The connection has recently been pointed out by Heidegger. Hegel, in his essay "Faith and Knowledge," written in 1802, sought to express the essence of the feeling "on which the religion of the modern era rests" in the words, "God himself is dead." He refers in explanation to Pascal's phrase, "the lost God." But these three expressions actually mark three very different stages on one road. [Buber's note]

of God and interprets it. This interpretation is doubtless correct to some extent. He holds the sentence "God is slain" to mean that contemporary man has shifted the concept of God from the realm of objective being to the "immanence of subjectivity." Indeed, specifically modern thought can no longer endure a God who is not confined to man's subjectivity, who is not merely a "supreme value," and, as we have seen, this thought leads us down a path which although by no means straight, is ultimately unmistakable. But then Heidegger goes on to say: "The slaying means the elimination of the self-subsisting suprasensual world by man." This sentence likewise, taken by itself, is correct, but it leads to crucial problems that neither Nietzsche — if Heidegger interprets him correctly — nor Heidegger has perceived or acknowledged. By the "self-subsisting suprasensual world" Heidegger means "the highest ends, the foundations and principles of the existent, the ideals, as well as the suprasensual, God and the gods." But the living God who approaches and addresses an individual in the situations of real life is not a component part of such a suprasensual world; His place is no more there than it is in the sensible world, and whenever man nonetheless has to interpret encounters with Him as self-encounters, man's very structure is destroyed. This is the portent of the present hour.

Heidegger rightfully looks upon this hour of night. Thus he refers to a verse of Hölderlin, the great poet to whose work he has devoted some of his most important interpretative writings. Hölderlin says:

Aber weh! es wandelt in Nacht, es wohnt, wie im Orkus,
Ohne Göttliches unser Geschlecht.

(But alas! our generation walks in night, dwells as in Hades, without the divine.)

It is true that Heidegger holds out the promise, even though only as a possibility, of an intellectual transformation from which day may dawn again, and then "the appearing of God and the gods may begin again." But this coupling of an absolute singular with an iridescent plural has a ring different from that of the verses in which Hölderlin a century and a half ago praised God and His manifestations in the active forces of nature, i.e., the gods. Today, when we are faced by the question of our destiny, the question as to the essential difference between all subjectivity and that which transcends it, the juxtaposition of such a singular and such a plural seems to indicate that after the imageless era a new procession of images may begin — images of God and images of gods, images of God and gods together — without man's again experiencing and accepting his real encounters with the divine as such. But, without the truth of the encounter, all images are illusion and self-deception. And who would dare, in this hour when all speech must have a deadly seriousness, to juxtapose God and the gods on the plane of the real encounter? Indeed, there was once a time when a man invoking a god in true dedication to him, really meant God Himself, the divinity of God, manifesting itself to him as a force or a form, at that moment and in that place. But this time is no longer. And even Hölderlin, when, associating singular and plural, said, *der Götter Gott*, "the God of the gods," meaning not merely the most high of the gods, but Him whom the "gods" themselves worship as their god.

6

Eclipse of the light of heaven, eclipse of God — such indeed is the character of the historic hour through which the world is passing. But it is not a process which can be adequately accounted for by instancing the changes that have taken place in man's spirit. An eclipse of the sun is something that occurs between the sun and our eyes, not in the sun itself. Nor does philosophy consider us blind to God. Philosophy holds what we lack today is only the spiritual orientation which can make possible a reappearance "of God and the gods," a new procession of sublime images. But when, as in this instance, something is taking place between heaven and earth, one misses everything when one insists on discovering within earthly thought the power that unveils the mystery. He who refuses to submit himself to the effective reality of the transcendence as such — our vis-à-vis — contributes to the human responsibility for the eclipse.

Assume that man has now fully brought about "the elimination of the self-subsisting suprasensual world," and that the principles and the ideals which have characterized man in any way, to any extent, no longer exist. His true vis-à-vis, which, unlike principles and ideals, cannot be described as It, but can be addressed and reached as Thou, may be eclipsed for man during the process of elimination; yet this vis-à-vis lives intact behind the wall of darkness. Man may even do away with the name "god," which after all implies a possessive, and which, if the possessor rejects it, i.e., if there is no longer a "God of man," has lost its *raison d'être:* yet He who is denoted by the name lives in the light of His eternity. But we, "the slayers," remain dwellers in darkness consigned to death.

According to a Jewish legend, Adam and Eve, when they rejected God on the day of their creation and were driven out of the Garden, saw the sun set for the first time. They were terrified, for they could interpret this phenomenon only as a sign that the world was to sink back into chaos because of their guilt. Both of them wept, sitting face to face, the whole night through, and they underwent a change of heart. Then morning dawned. Adam rose, caught a unicorn, and offered it as a sacrifice in place of himself.

Translator unknown

Karl Jaspers

Along with Jean Paul Sartre, Karl Jaspers (1883–1969) is perhaps the only existentialist who was content with the term (all the other thinkers who were lumped under this term, such as Heidegger and Marcel, resisted the label). This alone makes his views on religion significant in the history of thought, but perhaps even more significant is the range of skills and backgrounds Jaspers was able to bring to his religious reflections: he first studied law at the universities of Heidelberg and Munich (his father was a jurist and constable), but then transferred to medicine, earning his M.D. in 1909 with a dissertation entitled "Nostalgia and Crime." This interest in psychopathology led him to specialize in psychiatry, and his textbook *General Psychopathology* (1913) is still regarded as a benchmark in the history of psychiatric writing (much the way William James's *Principles of Psychology* still contains matters of interest to psychologists as well as philosophers). In 1916 he became professor of psychology at Heidelberg, and in 1919 he published *Psychology of World Views,* a psychological analysis of why thinkers are emotionally drawn to certain philosophies. This rather neglected but important work marks Jaspers's transition from psychology to philosophy, on the basis of which he was named in 1921 to be professor of philosophy at Heidelberg. In 1932 he published the first volume of his most important work, the three-volume *Philosophie,* wherein he fully outlines his existentialist philosophy. In 1937 he was suspended from his position by the Nazi government, but was reinstated in 1945 (in 1948, however, he accepted a chair of philosophy at the University of Basel, where he remained until his death in 1969).

His connection with religion had always been deep but also deeply ambivalent. This comes through most especially in a lecture that Jaspers gave on the views of the famous Protestant theologian Rudolf Bultmann (whose own essay immediately follows this chapter), where he insists that

> no philosophy can comprehend religion as a historical phenomenon or as a living faith. Philosophic thinking confronts religion as an ever-perplexing ultimate, a weight it cannot lift, or a resistance it cannot surmount. When, occasionally, it seems to us that the resistance has been surmounted, we do not experience the gratification produced by the discovery of a truth; rather, we feel something like terror, as before a sudden void.[1]

In his important work published in 1962, *Philosophical Faith and Revelation*, Jaspers managed to develop this diffidence into a fully developed philosophy of religion: whereas so many previous thinkers in Germany saw the tension between a historical (and therefore particular) revelation and the generic concept of natural religion and therefore resolved that tension by absorbing the particular into the general (Kant, Lessing, Hegel, Schleiermacher, etc.), Jaspers insisted that revelation cannot by definition be absorbed by philosophy. But he also insisted that revelation cannot satisfactorily establish the grounds of its validity before the bar of philosophy, so that in this sense Lessing's parable of the three rings is still true: philosophy is like the Court Assayer called in to judge the authenticity of the rings given to the three sons, and yet he cannot do so.

But philosophy can, as Jaspers says of himself, "notice things as an outsider which the native misses. I am like a traveler in a foreign country, looking at things from the outside."[2] What makes Jaspers's views so rich is the paradox that, over against the views of Bultmann (who was an explicit believer and always wrote as a theologian), Jaspers more often than not defended the mystical content of revelation in the face of Bultmann's challenge that the theologian must strip the Bible of its mythological clothing, a paradox that comes through most strongly in the two passages chosen for this chapter.

---

1. Karl Jaspers, "Myth and Religion," in Karl Jaspers and Rudolf Bultmann, *Myth and Christianity: An Inquiry into the Possibility of Religion without Myth,* trans. Norbert Guterman (New York: Noonday Press, 1958), 3.

2. Ibid.

From Philosophical Faith and Revelation

a: A medieval verse reads as follows:

> I come I know not whence,
> I am I know not who,
> I die I know not when,
> I go I know not where,
> I wonder why I am of good cheer.

This is not a "Christian" verse. For the faith in revelation provides answers to everything. It lives by marvelous pledges and would perhaps conclude its answer by saying, "I wonder why I am sad."

It was this question that prepared the Nordic race to follow Christian promises. The Venerable Bede tells of an Anglo-Saxon king who in A.D. 627 had to decide whether to accept Christianity or to reject it: "My liege," said one of his counselors, "compared with the time unknown to us, men's present life on earth reminds me of your sitting at mead with your lords in winter. A blazing fire warms the hall, but outside a storm is raging. Then a sparrow flies in and swiftly flits through the hall, in one door and out the other. For the moment of being indoors it is safe from the wintry blasts; but after the quick passage through the short, pleasant span it disappears from sight and returns from winter to winter. So, too, this human life is but like one single instant. We do not know what has gone before, nor what will follow. Hence, if this new religion reassures us on that point, I deem it right to accept it."

The deliberation of these men, why they should try the Christian religion, is without an impulse of faith, utterly rational, derived from concern about what might come after death. But the parable of the sparrow shows how serious our eerie existential situation seemed to them on reflection.

b: What the world in which we find ourselves is as a whole, whence it comes, where it goes — this we do not know, and never will know. But the mere question changes man's inner condition. Answers have been given and, from the earliest times on, have only intensified the question. In the Rig Veda, the oldest Hindu text, we find these lines:

> There was not non-being, nor Being, . . . there was neither death nor immortality. . . . Moved by no breeze, the One

breathes.... Nothing was but this.... Yet who has been able to bring it to light, who has learned whence Creation comes? The gods do not reach that far.... Whence and when this Creation has come, whether it is created or uncreated, he alone knows, the All-seeing One in the highest heaven — or does he not know either?

The pure, unsurpassable basic thoughts may have occurred to men at all times. How secondary is the meaning of ages and history! Essentially we know no more than that Hindu sage of three thousand years ago knew about what concerned him, and what concerns us.

c: What we are is as mysterious as the world. If our knowledge of worldly realities has increased immeasurably over scores of centuries, notably in the past few, we still know as little as then what we ourselves really are. The basic question — which may arise even in early childhood, astounding and changing the individual — has at all times been put in various deeply moving forms, as in the Hindu Mahabharata: "Man is ignorant, helpless before his own joy and grief, sent by God...." Or by St. Augustine: "I am cast into the world.... I have become a question unto myself...."

We are more than all our knowledge. What we know confronts an infinitely encompassing unknown. The world is a mystery, and each of us is a mystery to himself.

d: We might add to the historic instances; yet the issue is peculiar to the human being as such. Its particular forms differ vastly in the ways of their concern, their questing and answering. But what is immutable in all this historic diversity?

First: with such questioning views man has really awakened. Before, he was living in the world as behind a veil that served to conceal the essence. He has no inkling of the inscrutable as long as the shrouds remain unquestioned matters of course.

Second: with this questioning man takes a leap. Not until then does human life proper begin, with man aware of his humanity. Before the leap he is only potentially human; now he is really human. Once this ascertainment has begun, nothing remains a matter of course. Existence, previously unquestioned, has become an immediately boundless sum of questions, answered each time by an act, a creation, a love, a community, in an unceasing process.

Not until then does man set out on the conscious venture of his history. He wants to be shown what is. He wants it manifested. It cannot be nothing. I have not come into this existence in vain, for nothing. But what it signifies goes beyond all definite significance.

Third: the question is linked to a powerful impulse. Appearing together with awe is the will to move from boundless blights to endless blessings.

The urge to learn from the source of things what is, what can be, and what may come to be, has one sole goal that can be phrased in many ways. We long to be sure of the source, to return to it, to be sheltered in it, to find contentment in its being. We want the source to reveal the goal we seek in it, to find our way in its light. We want the attraction of Being to uplift us, to give us, amid the currents of change, a part in eternity.

There is an interrelation: the urge to know what really is means a will to selfhood; the consciousness of not really being oneself urges to Being. To come into being, selfhood seeks to exceed itself. This is the cause of man's infinite restlessness. He wants to think, to act, to live so that salvation will come to him. Its most remotely perceptible trace grants him a matchless tranquility.

Translated by E. B. Ashton

From Myth and Religion

2. Myth and Science

Bultmann, in keeping with a tradition that goes back to Aristotle, distinguishes between myth and science. He regards mythological thinking as obsolete, as something that scientific thinking has left behind. However, insofar as the myth conceals a content that was expressed in a language suitable only to the age in which it was created, it must be translated. The myth, says Bultmann, is to be interpreted, divested of its mythological garb, and transposed into a truth valid today.

I deny this. Mythical thinking is not a thing of the past, but characterizes man in any epoch. It is true that the term "myth" is by no means unequivocal. It contains the following elements:

(1) The myth tells a story and expresses intuitive insights, rather than universal concepts. The myth is historical, both in the form of its thinking and in its content. It is not a cloak or disguise put over a general idea, which can be better and more directly grasped intellectually. It explains in terms of historical origin rather than in terms of a necessity conceived as universal law.

(2) The myth deals with sacred stories and visions, with stories about gods rather than with empirical realities.

(3) The myth is a carrier of meanings which can be expressed only in the language of myth. The mythical figures are symbols which, by their very nature, are untranslatable into other language. They are accessible only in the mythical element, they are irreplaceable, unique. They cannot be interpreted rationally; they are interpreted only by new myths, by being transformed. Myths interpret each other.

How wretched, how lacking in expressiveness our life would be, if the language of myth were no longer valid! To fill mythical forms with banal content is to commit an unpardonable error. The splendor and wonder of the mythical vision is to be purified, but must not be abolished. To speak of "demythologization" is almost blasphemous. Such a depreciation of myth is not enlightenment, but sham enlightenment. Does the splendor of the sunrise cease to be a tangible, ever new and inspiring reality, a mythical presence, just because we know that the earth is revolving around the sun, so that properly speaking there is no sunrise? Does the appearance of the godhead on Mount Sinai or in the burning bush cease to be a poignant reality even when we know that in terms of space and time the phenomena in question were human experiences? To demythologize would be to do away with an essential faculty of our reason. Nevertheless, the impulse to demythologize contains a half-truth derived from genuine enlightenment:

A. *The Degradation of the Myth.* The truth of mythical thinking has been perverted in all periods, including our own: the myth is interpreted not as a code, but literally, and material reality is ascribed to its symbols. Contact with true reality by way of its unique language slips into the materialism of tangibility and usability. Therefore, thinkers of all ages, and Bultmann too, are right in denying assertions which give myth the tangible reality of things in the world, a reality that is accessible to our quite different real knowledge, a knowledge that modern science has developed and clearly delimited. A corpse cannot come to life and rise from the grave. Stories based on the reports of contradictory witnesses and containing scanty data cannot be regarded as historical facts. Because materialism is a common way of thinking, the cipher language of myth will always be degraded into a language of the tangible, which is guaranteed and provides guarantees; this took place among the earliest Christians, and has taken place everywhere in the world. Every epoch has the critical task of correcting such perversions. Bultmann hits on something true insofar as he means by "demythologization" the fulfillment of this task — that of denouncing reification, or conceiving the myth as an alleged reality, opaque and tangible.

B. *Recovery of the Myth.* But the demand for demythologization is justified only if at the same time it insists on restoring the reality of the mythical language. We should seek not to destroy, but to restore the language of myth. For it is the language of a reality that is not empirical, but existential, whereas our mere empirical existence tends continually to be lost in the empirical, as though the latter were all of reality. Only he has the right to demythologize, who resolutely retains the reality contained in the cipher language of the myth.

The real task, therefore, is not to demythologize, but to recover mythical thought in its original purity, and to appropriate, in this form of thinking, the marvelous mythical contents that deepen us morally, enlarge us as human beings, and indirectly bring us closer to the lofty, imageless transcendence, the idea of God which no myth can fully express for it surpasses them all.

Mythical thinking can achieve a unique and legitimate effectiveness in our lives provided that two critical ideas are not lost sight of.

First: Whereas mythical language is historical, and hence its truth can lay no claim to the universal validity of knowledge, it is precisely by virtue of this quality that it can lend the historical *Existenz* something of the unconditional. The unconditional thus brought to light remains conditioned in expression, historically relative, and objectively uncertain. It is one of the basic insights of philosophical reflection that universally valid truth is valid only relatively, from the standpoint of abstract consciousness, while it is existentially neutral; and that existential truth, on the contrary, which becomes identified with the thinker so that he lives and dies in it, precisely for that reason must be historical, and cannot achieve universally valid expression. Only he has a right to live in the mythical who does not confuse the unconditionality of historical *Existenz,* which becomes clear to itself in myth, with the universal validity of an assertion, which, being an assertion concerning an empirical reality, is valid for all. Indeed, the reality that has come down to us in the myth would be lost if it were dissolved into general philosophical ideas.

However, it is impossible to foresee where mythical language achieves validity in the moment of unconditional decision. To learn this language, to appropriate the vision it expresses, makes decision possible and prepares us for it. But even that takes place historically. By entrusting ourselves to our own historical origins we are brought closer to the Bible and to antiquity, despite the partly Oriental contents of the former.

Second: All mythical images are ambiguous. This idea is inherent in the Biblical commandment: Thou shalt not make unto thee any graven image. Everything mythical is a language that grows faint before the transcendence of the one godhead. While we see, hear, and think in the language of myth conceived as code, while we cannot become concretely aware of transcendence without a code language, we must at the same time keep in mind that there are no demons, that there is no magic causality, no such thing as sorcery. There nevertheless remains a deeply moving series of images — the three angels visiting Abraham, Moses receiving the tablets of the law, Isaiah seeing in his vision not God himself but only his manifestation, God addressing one man in thunder and another in a gentle breeze, Balaam's she-ass possessed of better vision than her rider, the Resurrected saying, Touch me not, His Ascension, the Descent of the Holy Ghost, and so on to infinity.

Now, the three distinctions — between the tangible presence and the language of cipher, between mythical contents and the transcendent God, and finally between unconditional historicity and relative universal validity — are proper only to the philosophical consciousness. What we thus distinguish may have been one originally, and it becomes one again where it is alive. For the philosophically naïve, tangible presence and cipher language are not distinct. Some pious people conceive of this tangible presence as an empirical reality. True piety, as a matter of course, eliminates the materialistic, magical, and utilitarian misuse of literal interpretation. There is also an impious, materialistic conception of the myth as tangible reality, which no longer regards the myth as a cipher, and which leads to superstition.

C. *Struggle for Existential Possibilities of Faith.* However, the great and most essential task for anyone who enters the field of mythical thinking is to struggle for the true faith within that thinking. One myth confronts another, not in rational discussion, and not necessarily with the aim of destroying it, but in spiritual struggle. This struggle is fought dishonestly if the outward form of the myth is attacked, if its opponent denounces it as a mode of thinking, denying that such a mode of thinking is necessary to his own faith. Such a struggle is fought fairly and illuminates, when it goes back to the original meanings, to the deeper sources. Depending on the consequences a given myth has for a given individual, he will accept or reject it, realizing how it affects his actions and conduct. But no man can deny in the name of all, what he rejects for himself. He must concede that a myth which he cannot accept may be valid for others. What is in question is existential truth, which is spiritually efficacious only in mythical thinking, but which without the myth would remain beyond our horizon.

We acquire strength when we read the Bible not in a spirit of slavish literalness, but participating in the inner meanings, rejecting or appropriating them. The mythical contents put the reader in certain states, which he experiences as possibilities; he sees their meanings in the various and variously important images that appear to him, and that all point beyond themselves to something no image can express. It is not rational knowledge, but existential clarification in the sphere of the contradictory, mutually exclusive or complementary possibilities of the Bible that gives us the daily strength to go forward or to resist. For us, the Bible is the favorite arena of spiritual contest; another one is provided by the Greek epic poems and tragedies, and still another by the sacred books of Asia.

Translation, explication, and interpretation in terms of universal concepts — methods which have been practiced since antiquity — may help us to appropriate the contents of the Bible in a limited sense; but the clarifying struggle in which the rejected elements are not destroyed, but retained as discarded possibilities, requires that we come to grips with the living contents of the myth.

Now, it seems to me that in this struggle for the truth of certain Biblical contents against other Biblical contents, Bultmann reaches conclusions which I cannot accept. Here lies the crucial point of the debate. Bultmann, who has made important contributions to our historical knowledge of the New Testament, is interested in all of the Bible as a historian; but as a theologian, he appears in an entirely different light, namely, as a man whose interest in the Bible is singularly restricted. He is almost indifferent to the Old Testament. Study of the Synoptic Gospels proves to him that we have little historical knowledge of Jesus, and that many views contained in those books were a common possession of the non-Christian world at the time. But he attaches the highest value to St. Paul and to the Gospel according to St. John. For him the revelation is found not in a historically knowable Jesus, but in a redemptive history which can be discovered in these later texts. The redemptive history conceived by Christ's disciples and apostles is the very meaning of these texts. Here the emphasis lies on the mythical idea of justification by faith alone — an idea which is most alien to our philosophizing. As a believing reader of the New Testament, Bultmann is attracted by the theology expressed in it, but less so, if at all, by the actual teachings of Jesus. The spiritualized Christ of the Gospel according to St. John, though noble and captivating as a fairytale hero, seems to us far less significant than the living figure of Jesus in the Synoptics. But Bultmann is not concerned with this. He is scarcely troubled by the absurdity of the Gnostic myth in the Gospel of St. John — although he was the first to recognize it clearly as a myth — and he interprets this Gospel as a surmounting of the myth. His interpretation goes into detail, yet he is scarcely troubled by the fact that this Gospel mythically justifies the earliest Christian anti-Semitism, absent from both St. Paul and the Synoptics and indicative of the sort of faith animating the author of this gospel of love. Selection, emphasis, evaluation, and acceptance or rejection of given contents of the Bible can be clarified only if these are discussed in terms of mythical thinking itself, and we can do this (and do it) today as always.

Translator unknown

Rudolf Bultmann

Although Rudolf Bultmann (1884–1976) is known primarily as a New Testament scholar, he had a profound influence on German religious thought in general. This is because he was not content with merely analyzing the data of the New Testament and then leaving it at that; rather, his whole work was motivated by his sharp sense of the remoteness and unacceptability of the thought forms of the New Testament to the citizens of the twentieth century. According to Bultmann, the very fact that we can walk into a room and throw on an electric light means that we do not, and cannot, see our world as a theater of conflict between supernatural powers, with the demonic seeking to possess and destroy us, and God intervening to secure our salvation through a manipulation of the natural course of history (via miracles, the incarnation, etc.).

But Bultmann's is not the voice of Feuerbach or Freud, even less of Nietzsche, for he does not argue from this starting point to the rejection of Christianity. Rather, he boldly asserts the opposite: that the mythical material of the New Testament is not an embarrassment and need not be rejected out of hand. On the contrary, it can be "reinterpreted" as images that refer not to the cosmos itself, as it would first seem, but to the conditions and possibilities of human existence. Myth for Bultmann opens up new options for human existence, and in that openness lies the possibility for reinterpreting New Testament mythology. Thus New Testament accounts of Christ's death and resurrection are mediated to modern humankind via the early church's *kerygma* (proclamation), which is couched in the form of an announcement proclaiming the good news of salvation that must be taken on faith. And that faith is an act of decision, which opens up the possibility for a more authentic existence.

The following essay is drawn from the Shaffer Lectures at Yale University, delivered in October 1951, in which Bultmann has summarized all these views with admirable brevity and concision.

From "Jesus Christ and Mythology"

The hope of Jesus and of the early Christian community was not fulfilled. The same world still exists and history continues. The course of history has refuted mythology. For the conception "Kingdom of God" is mythological, as is the conception of the eschatological drama. Just as mythological are the presuppositions of the expectation of the Kingdom of God, namely, the theory that the world, although created by God, is ruled by the devil, Satan, and that his army, the demons, is the cause of all evil, sin and disease. The whole conception of the world which is presupposed in the preaching of Jesus as in the New Testament generally is mythological; i.e., the conception of the world as being structured in three stories, heaven, earth and hell; the conception of the intervention of supernatural powers in the course of events; and the conception of miracles, especially the conception of the intervention of supernatural powers in the inner life of the soul, the conception that men can be tempted and corrupted by the devil and possessed by evil spirits. This conception of the world we call mythological because it is different from the conception of the world which has been formed and developed by science since its inception in ancient Greece and which has been accepted by all modern men. In this modern conception of the world the cause-and-effect nexus is fundamental. Although modern physical theories take account of chance in the chain of cause and effect in subatomic phenomena, our daily living, purposes and actions are not affected. In any case, modern science does not believe that the course of nature can be interrupted or, so to speak, perforated, by supernatural powers.

The same is true of the modern study of history, which does not take into account any intervention of God or of the devil or of demons in the course of history. Instead, the course of history is considered to be an unbroken whole, complete in itself, though differing from the course of nature because there are in history spiritual powers which influence the will of persons. Granted that not all historical events are determined by physical necessity and that persons are responsible for their actions, nevertheless nothing happens without rational motivation. Otherwise, responsibility would be dissolved. Of course, there are still many superstitions among modern men, but they are exceptions or even anomalies. Modern men take it for granted that the course of nature and of history, like their own inner life and their practical life, is nowhere interrupted by the intervention of supernatural powers.

Then the question inevitably arises: is it possible that Jesus' preaching of the Kingdom of God still has any importance for modern men and the preaching of the New Testament as a whole is still important for modern men? The preaching of the New Testament proclaims Jesus Christ, not only his preaching of the Kingdom of God but first of all his person, which was mythologized from the very beginnings of earliest Christianity. New Testament scholars are at variance as to whether Jesus himself claimed to be the Messiah, the King of the time of blessedness, whether he believed himself to be the Son of Man who would come on the clouds of heaven. If so, Jesus understood himself in the light of mythology. We need not, at this point, decide one way or the other. At any rate, the early Christian community thus regarded him as a mythological figure. It expected him to return as the Son of Man on the clouds of heaven to bring salvation and damnation as judge of the world. His person is viewed in the light of mythology when he is said to have been begotten of the Holy Spirit and born of a virgin, and this becomes clearer still in Hellenistic Christian communities where he is understood to be the Son of God in a metaphysical sense, a great, pre-existent heavenly being who became man for the sake of our redemption and took on himself suffering, even the suffering of the cross. It is evident that such conceptions are mythological, for they were widespread in the mythologies of Jews and Gentiles and then were transferred to the historical person of Jesus. Particularly the conception of the pre-existent Son of God who descended in human guise into the world to redeem mankind is part of the Gnostic doctrine of redemption, and nobody hesitates to call this doctrine mythological. This raises in an acute form the question: *what is the importance of the preaching of Jesus and of the preaching of the New Testament as a whole for modern man?*

For modern man the mythological conception of the world, the conceptions of eschatology, of redeemer and redemption, are over and done with. Is it possible to expect that we shall make a sacrifice of understanding, *sacrificium intellectus,* in order to accept what we cannot sincerely consider true — merely because such conceptions are suggested by the Bible? Or ought we to pass over those sayings of the New Testament which contain such mythological conceptions and to select other sayings which are not such stumbling-blocks to modern man? In fact, the preaching of Jesus is not confined to eschatological sayings. He proclaimed also the will of God, which is God's demand, the demand for the good. Jesus demands truthfulness and purity, readiness to sacrifice and to love. He demands that the whole man be obedient to God, and he protests against the delusion that one's duty to God can be fulfilled by obeying certain external commandments. If the ethical demands of Jesus are stumbling-blocks to modern man, then it is to his selfish will, not to his understanding, that they are stumbling-blocks.

What follows from all this? Shall we retain the ethical preaching of Jesus and abandon his eschatological preaching? Shall we reduce his preaching of the Kingdom of God to the so-called social gospel? Or is there a third possibility? We must ask whether the eschatological preaching and the mythological sayings as a whole contain a still deeper meaning which is concealed under the cover of mythology. If that is so, let us abandon the mythological conceptions precisely because we want to retain their deeper meaning. This method of interpretation of the New Testament which tries to recover the deeper meaning behind the mythological conceptions I call *de-mythologizing* — an unsatisfactory word, to be sure. Its aim is not to eliminate the mythological statements but to interpret them. It is a method of hermeneutics. The meaning of this method will be best understood when we make clear the meaning of mythology in general.

It is often said that mythology is a primitive science, the intention of which is to explain phenomena and incidents which are strange, curious, surprising, or frightening, by attributing them to supernatural causes, to gods or to demons. So it is in part, for example, when it attributes phenomena like eclipses of the sun or of the moon to such causes; but there is more than this in mythology. Myths speak about gods and demons as powers on which man knows himself to be dependent, powers whose favor he needs, powers whose wrath he fears. Myths express the knowledge that man is not master of the world and of his life, that the world within which he lives is full of riddles and mysteries and that human life also is full of riddles and mysteries.

Mythology expresses a certain understanding of human existence. It believes that the world and human life have their ground and their limits in a power which is beyond all that we can calculate or control. Mythology speaks about this power inadequately and insufficiently because it speaks about it as if it were a worldly power. It speaks of gods who represent the power beyond the visible, comprehensible world. It speaks of gods as if they were men and of their actions as human actions, although it conceives of the gods as endowed with superhuman power and of their actions as incalculable, as capable of breaking the normal, ordinary order of events. It may be said that myths give to the transcendent reality an immanent, this-worldly objectivity. Myths give worldly objectivity to that which is unworldly.

All this holds true also of the mythological conceptions found in the Bible. According to mythological thinking, God has his domicile in heaven. What is the meaning of this statement? The meaning is quite clear. In a crude manner it expresses the idea that God is beyond the world, that He is transcendent. The thinking which is not yet capable of forming the abstract idea of transcendence expresses its intention in the category of space; the transcendent God is imagined as being at an immense spatial distance, far above the world: for above this world is the world of the stars, of the light which enlightens and makes glad the life of men. When mythological thinking forms the conception of hell, it expresses the idea of the transcendence of evil as the tremendous power which again and again afflicts mankind. The location of hell and of men whom hell has seized is below the earth in darkness, because darkness is tremendous and terrible to men.

These mythological conceptions of heaven and hell are no longer acceptable for modern men since for scientific thinking to speak of "above" and "below" in the universe has lost all meaning, but the idea of the transcendence of God and of evil is still significant....

*　　*　　*

An objection often heard against the attempt to demythologize is that it takes the modern worldview as the criterion of the interpretation of the Scripture and the Christian message and that Scripture and Christian message are not allowed to say anything that is in contradiction with the modern worldview.

It is, of course, true that de-mythologizing takes the modern worldview as a criterion. To de-mythologize is to reject not Scripture or the Christian message as a whole, but the worldview of Scripture, which is the worldview of a past epoch, which all too often is retained in Christian dogmatics and in the preaching of the Church. To de-mythologize is to deny that the message of Scripture and of the Church is bound to an ancient worldview which is obsolete.

The attempt to de-mythologize begins with this important insight: Christian preaching, insofar as it is preaching of the Word of God by God's command and in His name, does not offer a doctrine which can be accepted either by reason or by a *sacrificium intellectus.* Christian preaching is *kerygma,* that is, a proclamation addressed not to the theoretical reason, but to the hearer as a self. In this manner Paul commends himself to every man's conscience in the sight of God (2 Cor. 4:2). De-mythologizing will make clear this function of preaching as a personal message, and in doing so it will eliminate a false stumbling-block and bring into sharp focus the real stumbling-block, the word of the cross.

For the worldview of the Scripture is mythological and is therefore unacceptable to modern man whose thinking has been shaped by science and is therefore no longer mythological. Modern man always makes use of technical means which are the result of science. In case of illness modern man has recourse to physicians, to medical science. In case of economic and political affairs, he makes use of the results of psychological, social, economic and political sciences, and so on. Nobody reckons with direct intervention by transcendent powers.

Of course, there are today some survivals and revivals of primitive thinking and superstition. But the preaching of the Church would make a disastrous mistake if it looked to such revivals and conformed to them. The nature of man is to be seen in modern literature, as, for instance, in the novels of Thomas Mann, Ernst Jünger, Thornton Wilder, Ernest Hemingway, William Faulkner, Graham Greene and Albert Camus, or in the plays of Jean-Paul Sartre, Jean Anouilh, Jean Giraudoux, etc. Or let us think simply of the newspapers. Have you read anywhere in them that political or social or economic events are performed by supernatural powers such as God, angels or demons? Such events are always ascribed to natural powers, or to good or bad will on the part of men, or to human wisdom or stupidity.

The science of today is no longer the same as it was in the nineteenth century, and to be sure, all the results of science are relative, and no worldview of yesterday or today or tomorrow is definitive. The main point, however, is not the concrete results of scientific research and the contents of a worldview, but the method of thinking from which worldviews follow. For example, it makes no difference in principle whether the earth rotates round the sun or the sun rotates round the earth, but it does make a decisive difference that modern man understands the motion of the universe as a motion which obeys a cosmic law, a law of nature which human reason can discover. Therefore, modern man acknowledges as reality only such phenomena or events as are comprehensible within the framework of the rational order of the universe. He does not acknowledge miracles because they do not fit into this lawful order. When a strange or marvelous accident occurs, he does not rest until he has found a rational cause.

The contrast between the ancient worldview of the Bible and the modern worldview is the contrast between two ways of thinking, the mythological and the scientific. The method of scientific thinking and inquiry is in principle the same today as it was at the beginning of methodical and critical science in ancient Greece. It begins with the question about the origin from which the world is conceivable as unity, as *Kosmos*, as systematic order and harmony. It begins therefore also with the attempt to give reasonable proofs for every statement. These principles are the same in modern science, and it does not matter that the results of scientific research are changing over and over again, since the change itself results from the permanent principles.

Certainly it is a philosophical problem whether the scientific worldview can perceive the whole reality of the world and of human life. There are reasons for doubting whether it can do so, and we shall have to say more about this problem in the following chapters. But for present purposes it is enough to say that the thinking of modern men is really shaped by the scientific worldview, and that modern men need it for their daily lives.

Therefore, it is mere wishful thinking to suppose that the ancient worldview of the Bible can be renewed.

Translator unknown

Franz Rosenzweig

Franz Rosenzweig (1886–1929) is one of the towering figures of religious existentialism, a man whose main work, *The Star of Redemption* (1921), continues to have a steady influence in both theology and philosophy. What makes this work especially epochal is that it moved the terms of Jewish-Christian dialogue forward in a way that could also do justice to the self-understanding of both Judaism and Christianity.

Born the only son of a prosperous and completely assimilated Jewish family in Cassel, Germany, Rosenzweig studied medicine, natural science, history, and philosophy at the universities of Göttingen, Munich, Freiburg, and finally Berlin, where he earned a doctorate in philosophy in 1912 with a dissertation on Hegel's political thought. His precocity as a scholar was demonstrated when, in the course of this work, he discovered a one-page manuscript in Hegel's handwriting, marked "Essay on Ethics." Rosenzweig's close analysis of the text proved the page to be Hegel's transcribed copy of a text composed by Schelling.

Clearly he was a man destined for an appointment to an important academic post, and indeed in 1922 he was named to the lectureship for Jewish philosophy and ethics at the University of Frankfurt, but had to decline for reasons of health (he had been diagnosed with amyotrophic lateral sclerosis [Lou Gehrig's disease] just prior to the nomination). But Rosenzweig's diffidence toward an academic position had deeper roots than that, and in fact went all the way back to 1913, when he suffered what he called a "collapse" but which in fact was a religious crisis set on by his disenchantment with Hegel. This disenchantment had its roots in the following line of thought: according to Idealism, God and the world can be, and are, deduced from the positing activity of human consciousness — consciousness, of course, understood as consciousness in general (the so-called World-Spirit, which eclipses the importance of the individual consciousness). But thought, Rosenzweig came to believe, is only one of the components of human existence and in fact does not precede it. Man is important not because he thinks but because he is alive.

This insight forced him to see that the triad God–man–world could not be collapsed into Hegel's dialectical monism, and this is what provoked his religious crisis. Based on his friendship and conversations with the sociologist Eugen Rosenstock-Huessy, a Protestant Christian, he decided to prepare for baptism, during which preparation period he would live as a Jew so that he might explicitly convert *from* Judaism and not merely from the rather casually adopted secular Hegelianism of his past. In the course of this preparation period he attended a Yom Kippur service in a traditional synagogue in Berlin (October 11, 1913). It is not known exactly what happened to him during this service, as he left behind no explicit account of the day, only allusions in his later writings. But clearly this was a moment of intense revelation for him, confirming him in his rejection of Hegelianism but also diverting him from his prior choice of Protestant baptism. From this experience he came to see, as he said in a letter that forms part of the Rosenzweig selection below, that although it is true that for the Christian no one can come to the Father except through Christ, the situation is different for those who do not have to go to the Father because they are already with him.

This, however, interestingly enough, did not lead to a polemic against Christian missions to the Jews, for he recognized that in the Christian dispensation what is granted to Israel in general (to be spared to the end of time) is not granted to the individual Jews. But then again, the position of the believing Jew is also valid: "Shall I become converted, I who was born 'chosen'? Does the alternative of conversion even exist for me?" The selection that follows comes from some of the letters he wrote to his cousin Rudolf Ehrenberg (who had himself become a Christian and who was to serve as Rosenzweig's godfather at the baptism), as well as to Eugen Rosenstock, explaining his position about the different ways of looking at Judaism and Christianity from their respective points of view.

From Letters to Rudolf Ehrenberg and Eugen Rosenstock-Huessy

To Rudolf Ehrenberg

November 1, 1913

Christianity recognizes the God of Judaism, not as God, but as the "Father of Jesus Christ." It embraces the "Lord," but only because it knows that he alone is the way to the Father. He will remain with his church as the Lord forever, until the end of the world. Then, however, he will cease to be the Lord and he too will come under the domain of the Father, and the Father will be "all in all" (1 Cor. 15:28). What Christ and his church mean in the world — on that we agree: no one comes to the Father save through him (John 14:6).

No one *comes* to the Father — but it is different when one no longer needs to come to the Father, because he is already with him. And this is the case with the people of Israel (not with the individual Jew). The people of Israel, chosen by its Father, fixes its glance on that ultimate, most distant point, beyond world and history, of where its Father, the Father himself, will be the One and the Only — will be "All in All"! At that point, when Christ will cease to be the Lord, Israel will cease to be chosen; on that day God will lose the name by which only Israel calls on him; God will then no longer be "their" God. Until that day, however, Israel will live to anticipate it in belief and deed, to stand tall as a living harbinger of that day, a nation of priests, following the law which requires that one make the name of God holy by being holy oneself. We are in agreement, however, on the status of this people of God in the world, and on the suffering which it has borne on account of its seclusion, both from without (persecution) and from within (rigidity).

And yet, both the synagogue and the church have borne their sufferings in the same ultimate hope, the synagogue the sufferings of world-negation, and the church the sufferings of world-affirmation. This hope is not merely a hope for some unconscious and coincidental rendezvous in *eternity* (as would be the case, for instance, between the believer and the "universal-humanistic" pacifist). For both of them this hope — the God of all *time* — is rooted in a common origin. This common origin is the revelation of the Old Testament. For all these reasons, synagogue and church are mutually dependent on one another.

The synagogue, immortal, but with broken staff and a blindfold over her eyes, has to renounce all work in the world and concentrate all its energy on sustaining its own life, while maintaining its purity in the face of life. Thus, it relegates work in the world to the church and acknowledges that the church brings salvation for all heathens, for all time. It knows that what is accomplished within Judaism by works of ritual is accomplished for the world outside of Israel by works of love. But it refuses to concede to the church that the power which enables the church to do works of love is more than divine in *quality*, to concede that it is itself a power of God. Here its glance is fixed on that future yet to *come*.

And the church, with its unbreakable staff, and its eyes open to the world, a warrior confident of victory, always runs the risk that the vanquished might impose its own law on the victor. Although the church reaches out to all, it still must not lose itself in universality. For all time, its teaching is to remain a folly and a stumbling block (1 Cor. 1:23). That it remain a folly is assured by the Greeks, then and now and in the future. Again and again they will be asking: why is *this* supposed to be a divine power, and not just as well some other teaching or yet another — why Jesus and not (or not also) Goethe? And the voice of the Greeks will resound until the last day, only it will grow ever softer, softer with every external or internal victory by the church. For when wisdom is aware that it is wise, it is dumbstruck whenever confronted with the obvious; and when the last Greek has been dumbstruck by the workings of the church in time, the word of the cross at the *end* of time, but still *in* time — will no longer be a folly to anyone. Yet it will remain, all the same, as a stumbling block, even then. It was not a stumbling block for any Greek to acknowledge a divine power in the world: after all, he saw the world full of gods; what was incomprehensible to him was that he was to worship only this one savior on the cross; so it is today and so it will be in the future. The synagogue, however, was blind-folded; it saw no world at all — how was it to see gods in it? It saw only out of its inner prophetic eye, and saw, therefore, only that which is last and most distant. The demand that the synagogue view that which is closest, something in the present, in the same way that it viewed the most distant thus became a stumbling block; that is how it is now and so it shall be in the future. For this reason, whenever the church forgets that it is a stumbling block, when it tries to reconcile itself with what is "universally human" — a reconciliation which would be welcomed by the Greeks, who would, like the Roman emperor, erect a statue of the Christ in their temple of gods — then the church finds in the synagogue a silent admonisher who is not tempted by the "universally human" and knows only of the stumbling block; and then the church feels positive about itself once again, and recites its word of the cross. And thus the church knows that Israel will be preserved until the day when the last Greek vanishes, the work of love is finished, and until that later day when the harvest day of hope arrives. However, what the church concedes to Israel as a whole, it refuses to the individual Jew; it is on the individual Jew that it will and ought to test its power and see whether it can win him over. For to the church, to look to the future is not the same as it is to the synagogue. The future is not the power source of its faith, but only an image of the goal of its hopes. The power of its faith requires it to be aware of its own surroundings and to do the work of its love in the *present.*

With that I have said the essentials, at least with regard to dialogue and confrontation with Christianity....

As I said before, I have been trying of late to clarify for myself the whole system of Jewish doctrine, developing it on its own Jewish foundation. I am no longer the heretic of your eighteenth sermon, who takes from faith and not from love; I now deal with other names and teach other doctrines. And nevertheless, I know that I am a thing of the past only before the will of your *Lord*, but have not been forgotten by *God* — by that God to whom someday even your Lord will be subject. That is the connection between community and non-community (community which is necessary, because it is nourished by the same root, a community based on the eternal goal, involving mutual interdependence and, therefore, differentiation for all time) — which I present to you, so that you might see and recognize it objectively. What is at issue is not that the church recognize that each individual Jew belongs to the people of Israel (for the church, this status of belonging has always been a problem, and, when in doubt, considered to be non-existent); what is at issue is that it recognize the people of Israel itself, from the standpoint of Christian *theology.*

To Rudolf Ehrenberg

Berlin, November 4, 1913

...*Our* recognition of Christianity actually is based on Christianity itself, that is, on its recognition of *us*. It is, after all, the Torah which the Bible Societies distribute even to the remotest "isles." Any Jew will grant me that. However, Jewish consciousness is not *grounded* in the relationship of the Christian church to the world; it only recognizes its own reflection in it. In and of itself, Jewish consciousness takes no note of it: Isaiah 55:5. For this reason, it has no need, in time, of a new mandate; its mission did not change as a result of the events of the first century, only its destiny. Since then conditions have changed, and, I believe, they have taken on their final temporal form; but only the conditions changed. The Mishnah, the work through which Judaism laid a new foundation, after the destruction of the Temple, claims to be *only* a "repetition" of the Torah (that is the meaning of *mishnah*). The purpose of the entire Talmud is to demonstrate that this is, in fact, the case. From a purely theoretical standpoint, in the [previous] letter I showed you what the significance of the existence of Israel is for the church; that is also the standpoint of the church, only with a certain practical emphasis. The synagogue can only see itself; it has no consciousness of the *world*. Thus, to the church it can only say: we have already arrived at the destination, you are still enroute. The church answers: certainly, at the destination you are the last ones, because you are the most stubborn, *absolutely* stubborn. It does not see that there is a purpose in the existence of this point of stubbornness which gets in its way (to the church, the "purpose" is a *mystērion* [mystery]); it only knows *that* it is so. And yet, from the church's standpoint, then, the position of Judaism is not a position *within* the church; on the contrary, it is absolutely outside it, a position which in the course of time will never be overcome. That is the reason why the church interprets what seems "stubbornness" as rejection, by God. From our standpoint things look quite different. To us, our "stubbornness" is fidelity, and our "infidelity toward God" is remedied—just because it is infidelity, and not an original, primeval estrangement ("Adam's" fall into sin!)—only by repentance and return, not by a transformation or conversion. The concept of repentance, the Hebrew word for which, *teshuvah*, means "return," was rendered as *metanoia* [change of mind] in the New Testament. This is one of those cases where world history is chronicled in the pages of a dictionary.... We interpret the "wrath" of God in an entirely different way. For us, it did not begin with the Exile. Divine wrath has been with us since the election of Israel, and followed as a result of it (Amos 3:2). We see perfect piety realized not in the history of our people, but in the age of the patriarchs; that is the age to which we "appeal" before God. To be sure, the year 70 marks a line of demarcation, but a line like one which separates the time of church history from the end-time. Since then, after each particular instance of infidelity, we have no longer been compelled to hope, to hope for particular reconciliation. Now we hope only for the great reconciliation on the very last day. Before the year 70, certain prophets appeared at certain times, since then we have expected no more prophets, but only the one prophet on that last day.

To Eugen Rosenstock-Huessy

[October 1916]

... Yes, the stubbornness of the Jews is a Christian dogma. So much so that the Church, after she had built up the substantial part of her particular dogma — the part having to do with God and Man — in the first century, during the whole of the second century turned aside to lay down the "second dogma" (the formal part of her dogma, i.e., her historical consciousness of herself). And in its after-effects this process continued through the third and fourth centuries and beyond; and Augustine applied himself to it personally, though the Church had already for some time been moving away from it. That is, it had been becoming a Church of writings or rather of tradition, instead of spirit; in other words, it was becoming exactly the Church that history knows. Paul's theory concerning the relation of the Gospels to the Law could have remained a "personal opinion"; the Hellenizing "spiritual" Church (of John's Gospel) of the first century, in the marvelous naïveté of her "spiritual believers," had scarcely worried about it. Then came gnosticism, which laid its finger on Paul and sought to weed out the personal element from his theory and to develop its objective aspects in distinction from the personal in it. (Paul said: "The Jews are spurned, but Christ came from them." Marcion said: "Therefore the Jews belong to the devil, Christ to God.") Then the Church, which hitherto had been quite naïve in its own gnosticism (in St. John we read that salvation comes from the Jews), suddenly seeing this, pushed the spirit [pneuma] to one side in favor of tradition, and through a great *ritornar al segno* fixed this tradition by returning to its cardinal point, to its founder Paul; that is, she deliberately established as dogma what previously had been considered Paul's personal opinion. The Church established the identity of the Creator (and the God revealed at Sinai) with the Father of Jesus Christ on the one hand, and the perfect manhood of Christ on the other hand, as a definite, correlated Shibboleth against all heresy — and thereby the Church established herself as a power in human history. You know the rest better than I do. (N.B. I have just read all this in Tertullian, of whom I bought a complete edition.... I prefer his rhetoric, as that of a real lawyer, to the professorial rhetoric of Augustine, just because it is more genuine — at least according to our modern ideas.)

Thus, in the firm establishment of the Old Testament in the Canon, and in the building of the Church on this double scripture (Old Testament and New Testament) the stubbornness of the Jews is in fact brought out as the other half of the Christian dogma (its formal consciousness itself — the dogma of the Church — if we may point to the creed as the dogma of Christianity).

But could this same idea (that of the stubbornness of the Jews) also be a Jewish dogma? Yes, it could be, and in fact it is. But this Jewish consciousness of being rejected has quite a different place in our dogmatic system, and would correspond to a Christian consciousness of being chosen to rule, a consciousness that is in fact present beyond any doubt. The whole religious interpretation of the significance of the year 70 is tuned to this note. But the parallel that you are looking for is something entirely different. A dogma of Judaism about its relation to the Church must correspond to the dogma of the Church about its relation to Judaism. And this you know only in the form of the modern liberal-Jewish theory of the "daughter religion" that gradually educates the world for Judaism. But this theory actually springs from the classical period in the formation of Jewish dogma — from the Jewish high scholasticism which, in point of time and in content, forms a mean between Arab and Christian scholasticism (al-Ghazali–Maimonides–Thomas Aquinas). For it was only then that we had a fixing of dogma, and that corresponds with the different position that intellectual conceptions of faith hold with us and with you. In the period when you were developing dogma, we were creating our canon law, and vice versa. There is a subtle connection running all through. For instance, when you were systematizing dogma, we were systematizing law; with you the mystical view of dogma followed its definition, while with us the mystical view preceded definition, etc. This relation is rooted throughout in the final distinction between the two faiths. Indeed with us, too, this theory is not part of the substance of our dogma; with us, too, it was not formed from the content of the religious consciousness but belongs only to a second stratum, a stratum of learning concerning dogma. The theory of the daughter religion is found in the clearest form in both of the great scholastics. Beyond this, it is found, not as dogma but as a mystical idea (see above), in the literature of the old Synagogue, and likewise in the Talmudic period. To find it is no easy task, however. For whereas the substantial dogma in our scholasticism was based on trials, the connection between the old mysticism and medieval philosophy is brought about by the free religious spirit of the people, not by a lettered relationship to the past. But I should like to quote you one such legend. The Messiah was born exactly at the moment when the Temple was destroyed, but when he was born, the winds blew him forth from the bosom of his mother. And now he wanders unknown among the peoples, and when he has wandered through them all, then the time of our redemption will have come.

So that Christianity is like a power that fills the world (according to the saying of one of the two scholastics, Yehudah ha-Levi: it is the tree that grows from the seed of Judaism and casts its shadows over the earth; but its fruit must contain the seed again, the seed that nobody who saw the tree noticed). This is a Jewish dogma, just as Judaism as both the stubborn origin and last convert is a Christian dogma.

But what does all that mean for me, apart from the fact that I know it? What does this Jewish dogma mean for the Jew? Granted that it may not belong to the dogmas of the substantial group, which like the corresponding Christian dogmas can be won from an analysis of the religious consciousness. It is rather like the corresponding Christian one, a theological idea. But theological ideas must also mean something for religion. What, then, does it mean?

What does the Christian theological idea of Judaism mean for the Christian? If I am to believe E. R.'s letter before last (or before the one before the last?): Nothing! ...

And so the corresponding Jewish outcome of the theological idea of Christianity as a preparer-of-the-way is the *pride of the Jews*. This is hard to describe to a stranger. What you see of it appears to you silly and petty, just as it is almost impossible for the Jew to see and judge anti-Semitism by anything but its vulgar and stupid expressions. But (I must say again, *believe me*) its metaphysical basis is, as I have said, the three articles: (1) that we have the truth, (2) that we are at the goal, and (3) that any and every Jew feels in the depths of his soul that the Christian relation to God, and so in a sense their religion, is particularly and extremely pitiful, poverty-stricken, and ceremonious; namely, that as a Christian one has to learn from someone else, whoever he may be, to call God "our Father." To the Jew, that God is our Father is the first and most self-evident fact — and what need is there for a third person between me and my father in Heaven? That is no discovery of modern apologetics but the simplest Jewish instinct, a mixture of failure to understand and pitying contempt.

These are the two points of view, both narrow and limited just as points of view, and so in theory both can be surpassed; one can understand why the Jew can afford his unmediated closeness to God and why the Christian may not; and one can also understand how the Jew must pay for this blessing....

You recollect the passage in the Gospel of John where Christ explains to his disciples that they should not leave the world, but should remain within it. Even so, the people of Israel — who indeed could use all the sayings of the Gospel — could speak to its members in such a way, and as a matter of fact it does so: "to hallow the name of God in the world," is a phrase that is often used. From this follows all the ambiguity of Jewish life (just as all the dynamic character of the Christian life follows from it). The Jew, insofar as he is "in the world," stands under these laws and no one can tell him that he is permitted to go just so far and no farther, or that there is a line that he may not cross. Such a simple "as little as possible" would be a bad standard, because if I wished to govern all of my actions by the standard "as little as possible from outside

Judaism" it would mean, in the circumstances, a diminution of my inner Jewish achievement. So I say to myself as a rule: "as much as possible of the inner Jewish life" — though I well know that in the particular case I cannot anxiously avoid a degree of life outside Judaism. I also know that thereby, in your eyes, I open the way to a charge of soullessness. I can only answer fully at the center and source of my activity; at the periphery it escapes me. But should I then let the citadel fall in order to strengthen these precarious outworks? Should I "be converted," when I have been "chosen" from birth? Is that a real alternative for me? Have I only been thrown into the galley? Is it not *my* ship? You became acquainted with me on land, but you have scarcely noticed that my ship lies in harbor and that I spend more time than is necessary in sailors' taverns, and therefore you could well ask what business I have on the ship. And for you really to believe that it is my ship, and that I therefore belong to it — for you really to believe me will only be possible if the voyage is once more free and I launch out.

Or only when we meet out on the open sea? You might! . . .

Translated by Fritz A. Rothschild

Karl Barth

Karl Barth (1886–1968) is by common consent the only Protestant theologian of modern times whose greatness matches that of Luther and Calvin. What makes him perhaps the most towering figure of all the thinkers who appear in this book is the way he has managed to absorb the critique of religion and revelation that forms so crucial an aspect of German religious philosophy and turn it to his own purposes as a Christian theologian. Moreover, he has done this not by conceding the modern worldview from the outset, in the manner of Bultmann, or by insisting on the inerrancy of the Scriptures against modern science, in the manner of fundamentalism, but by insisting that *because* Feuerbach is right — that all religion is a projection of human needs — all religions, including empirical Christianity, stand under God's judgment "against the nations," that is, against idolatry.

Barth's central concern was how to prevent theology from becoming this "idolatry." That is, his whole effort was dedicated to ensuring that theology not become an artifact of human culture. And this is what he resisted so strenuously in the liberal theology into which he had been trained.

What jolted him out of this worldview was the support given to the German kaiser and his war-making policies in 1914 *by* several of his liberal teachers:

> One day in early August 1914 stands out in my personal memory as a black day. 93 German intellectuals impressed public opinion by their proclamation in support of the war policy of Wilhelm II and his counsellors. Among those intellectuals I discovered to my horror almost all of my theological teachers whom I had greatly venerated. In despair over

what this indicated about the signs of the times, I suddenly realized that I could not any longer follow either their ethics and dogmatics or their understanding of the Bible and history. For me, at least, 19th century theology no longer held any future.[1]

Active at the time in a parish in an industrial village in Safenwil, Switzerland, Barth lived through the slaughter of World War I more convinced than ever of the doctrine that had always been the undoing of liberal theology and the philosophical defense of natural religion: the doctrine of original sin, or man's innate iniquity. Groping his way along a difficult and untrod path, he came to feel that Paul's Letter to the Romans contained the key to the enigma, for here more clearly than anywhere else in the New Testament was the assertion that if theology moved from man, it could not reach God — that is, that God can only be known through God. And out of these painful reflections came his epochal commentary, *The Epistle to the Romans,* a book whose revolutionary outlook can best be shown in the stunned reaction it received from the theological world: the first edition (1919) sold out immediately, and a substantially revised edition that came out in 1922 not only sold out (there were six editions during Barth's lifetime) but led to Barth being called to a chair of Reformed theology at the University of Göttingen (and later Münster). In a stroke the direction of Protestant theology had been changed:

As I look back upon my course, I seem to myself as one who, ascending the dark staircase of a church tower and trying to steady himself, reached out for the banister, but got hold of the bell-rope instead. To his horror, he had then to listen to

---

1. Karl Barth, "Evangelical Theology in the 19th Century," in *The Humanity of God,* trans. Thomas Wieser (Richmond: John Knox Press, 1960), 14. Balthasar expresses a similar worry in his short essay "A Note on Lay Theologians" (in *New Elucidations* [San Francisco: Ignatius Press, 1986], 198–203), an opinion piece that was much attacked at the time for its alleged attempt to reclericalize theology. But perhaps his admonitions will carry more weight when we consider the Barthian parallel. In any event, Balthasar was not attacking either the professionalization of theology per se or the entry of large numbers of laypeople into the profession, but it would be foolhardy to overlook the dangers amid the benefits.

what the great bell had resounded over him, and not over him alone.[2]

As a dogmatic theologian, Barth eventually came to recognize, from his reading of St. Anselm, that theology is also a rational quest. But for Barth the real meaning of Anselm's ontological argument is that theology contains within itself its own rationale. The admission led, in any case, to an optimism about human religiosity not otherwise evident in his earlier work: for now religion can become the object of God's grace as well as his judgment. This, however, represents no real contradiction to his earlier thought, for as Paul himself says in Romans, "God has imprisoned all men in their own disobedience only to show mercy on them all" (Rom. 11:32).

From The Epistle to the Romans

The First Chapter
Introduction
The Author to His Readers

Paul, a servant of Jesus Christ, called to be an apostle. Here is no "genius rejoicing in his own creative ability" (Zündel). The man who is now speaking is an emissary, bound to perform his duty; the minister of his King; a servant, not a master. However great and important a man Paul may have been, the essential theme of his mission is not within him but above him — unapproachably distant and unutterably strange. His call to apostleship is not a familiar episode in his own personal history: "The call to be an apostle is a paradoxical occurrence, lying always beyond his personal self-identity" (Kierkegaard). Paul, it is true, is always himself, and moves essentially on the same plane as all other men. But, in contradiction to himself and in distinction from all others, he is — called by God and sent forth. Are we then to name him a Pharisee? Yes, a Pharisee — "separated," isolated, and distinct. But he is a Pharisee of a higher order. Fashioned of the same stuff as

---

2. Karl Barth, *Die christliche Dogmatik im Entwurf* (Munich: Kaiser Verlag, 1927), ix.

all other men, a stone differing in no way from other stones, yet in his relation to God—and in this only—he is unique. As an apostle—and only as an apostle—he stands in no organic relationship with human society as it exists in history: seen from the point of view of human society, he can be regarded only as an exception, nay, rather, as an impossibility. Paul's position can be justified only as resting in God, and so only can his words be regarded as at all credible, for they are as incapable of direct apprehension as is God Himself. For this reason he dares to approach others and to demand a hearing without fear either of exalting himself or of approximating too closely to his audience. He appeals only to the authority of God. This is the ground of his authority. There is no other.

Paul is authorized to deliver — **the Gospel of God.** He is commissioned to hand over to men something quite new and unprecedented, joyful and good,—the truth of God. Yes, precisely—*of God!* The Gospel is not a religious message to inform mankind of their divinity or to tell them how they may become divine. The Gospel proclaims a God utterly distinct from men. Salvation comes to them from Him, because they are, as men, incapable of knowing Him, and because they have no right to claim anything from Him. The Gospel is not one thing in the midst of other things, to be directly apprehended and comprehended. The Gospel is the Word of the Primal Origin of all things, the Word which, since it is ever new, must ever be received with renewed fear and trembling. The Gospel is therefore not an event, nor an experience, nor an emotion — however delicate! Rather, it is the clear and objective perception of what eye hath not seen nor ear heard. Moreover, what it demands of men is more than notice, or understanding, or sympathy. It demands participation, comprehension, cooperation; for it is a communication which presumes faith in the living God, and which creates that which it presumes.

Being the Gospel of God it was—**promised afore.** The Gospel is no intrusion of today. As the seed of eternity it is the fruit of time, the meaning and maturity of history—the fulfillment of prophecy. The Gospel is the word spoken by the prophets from time immemorial, the word which can now be received and has now been accepted. Such is the Gospel with which the apostle has been entrusted. By it his speech is authorized, but by it also that which he says is judged. The words of the prophets, long fastened under lock and key, are now set free. Now it is possible to hear what Jeremiah and Job and the preacher Solomon had proclaimed long ago. Now we can see and understand what is written, for we have an "entrance into the Old Testament" (Luther). Therefore the man who now speaks, stands firmly upon a history which has been expounded and veritably understood: "From the outset he disclaims the honor due to an innovator" (Schlatter).

Jesus Christ our Lord. This is the Gospel and the meaning of history. In this name two worlds meet and go apart, two planes intersect, the one known and the other unknown. The known plane is God's creation, fallen out of its union with Him, and therefore the world of the "flesh" needing redemption, the world of men, and of time, and of things — our world. This known plane is intersected by another plane that is unknown — the world of the Father, of the Primal Creation, and of the final Redemption. The relation between us and God, between this world and His world, presses for recognition, but the line of intersection is not self-evident. The point on the line of intersection at which the relation becomes observable and observed is Jesus, Jesus of Nazareth, the historical Jesus, — **born of the seed of David according to the flesh.** The name Jesus defines an historical occurrence and marks the point where the unknown world cuts the known world. This does not mean that, at this point, time and things and men are in themselves exalted above other times and other things and other men, but that they are exalted inasmuch as they serve to define the neighborhood of the point at which the hidden line, intersecting time and eternity, concrete occurrence and primal origin, men and God, becomes visible. The years A.D. 1–30 are the era of revelation and disclosure; the era which, as is shown by the reference to David, sets forth the new and strange and divine definition of all time. The particularity of the years A.D. 1–30 is dissolved by this divine definition, because it makes every epoch a potential field of revelation and disclosure. The point on the line of intersection is no more extended onto the known plane than is the unknown plane of which it proclaims the existence. The effulgence, or, rather, the crater made at the percussion point of an exploding shell, the void by which the point on the line of intersection makes itself known in the concrete world of history, is not — even though it be named the Life of Jesus — that other world which touches our world in Him. Insofar as our world is touched in Jesus by the other world, it ceases to be capable of direct observation as history, time, or thing. Jesus has been — declared to be the Son of God with power, according to the Holy Spirit, through his resurrection from the dead. In this declaration and appointment — which are beyond historical definition — lies the true significance of Jesus. Jesus as the Christ, as the Messiah, is the End of History; and He can be comprehended only as Paradox (Kierkegaard), as Victor (Blumhardt), as Primal History (Overbeck). As Christ, Jesus is the plane which lies beyond our comprehension. The plane which is known to us, He intersects vertically, from above. Within history, Jesus as the Christ can be understood only as Problem or Myth. As the Christ, He brings the world of the Father. But we who stand in this concrete world know nothing, and are incapable of knowing anything, of that other world. The Resurrection from the dead is, however, the transformation: the establishing or *declaration* of that point from above, and the corresponding discerning of it from below. The Resurrection is the revelation: the disclosing of Jesus as the Christ, the appearing of God, and the apprehending of God in Jesus. The Resurrection is the emergence of the necessity of giving glory to God: the reckoning with what is unknown and unobservable in Jesus, the recognition of Him as Paradox, Victor, and Primal History. In the Resurrection the new world of the Holy Spirit touches the old world of the flesh, but touches it as a tangent touches a circle, that is, without touching it. And, precisely because it does not touch it, it touches it as its frontier — as the new world. The Resurrection is therefore an occurrence in history, which took place outside the gates of Jerusalem in the year A.D. 30, inasmuch as it there "came to pass," was discovered and recognized. But inasmuch as the occurrence was conditioned by the Resurrection, insofar, that is, as it was not the "coming to pass," or the discovery, or the recognition, which conditioned its necessity and appearance and revelation, the Resurrection is not an event in history at all. Jesus is *declared to be the Son of God* wherever He reveals Himself and is recognized as the Messiah, before the first Easter Day and, most assuredly, after it. This declaration of the Son of man to be the Son of God is the significance of Jesus, and, apart from this, Jesus has no more significance or insignificance than may be attached to any man or thing or period of history in itself. — *Even though we have known Christ after the flesh, yet now we know him so no longer.* What He was, He is. But what He is underlies what He was. There is here no merging or fusion of God and man, no exaltation of humanity to divinity, no overflowing of God into human nature. What touches us — and yet does not touch us — in Jesus the Christ, is the Kingdom of God who is both Creator and Redeemer. The Kingdom of God has become actual, is nigh at hand (iii. 21, 22). And this Jesus Christ is — our **Lord**. Through His presence in the world and in our life we have been dissolved as men and established in God. By directing our eyes to Him our advance is stopped — and we are set in motion. We tarry and — hurry. Because Jesus is Lord over Paul and over the Roman Christians, the word "God" is no empty word in the Epistle to the Romans.

From Jesus Christ Paul has received — **grace and apostleship.** Grace is the incomprehensible fact that God is well pleased with a man, and that a man can rejoice in God. Only when grace is recognized to be incomprehensible is it grace. Grace exists, therefore, only where the Resurrection is reflected. Grace is the gift of Christ, who exposes the gulf which separates God and man, and, by exposing it, bridges it. But inasmuch as God knows men from afar and is known by them in His undiscoverable majesty, the man of God must inevitably approach his fellow men as an "emissary": *Necessity is laid upon me; yea, woe is unto me, if I preach not the gospel* (1 Cor. ix. 16). And yet the distinction between Paul and other Christians can be a matter of degree only. For, where the grace of God is, men participate in proclaiming the transformation of time and of things, the Resurrection — however reservedly and with whatever skepticism they proclaim it. Where the grace of God is, the very existence of the world and the very existence of God become a question and a hope with which and for which men must wrestle. For we are not now concerned with the propaganda of a conviction or with its imposition on others; grace means bearing witness to the faithfulness of God which a man has encountered in Christ, and which, when it is encountered and recognized, requires a corresponding fidelity toward God. The fidelity of a man to the faithfulness of God — the faith, that is, which accepts grace — is itself the demand for obedience and itself demands obedience from others. Hence the demand is a call which enlightens and rouses to action; it carries with it mission, beside which no other mission is possible. For the name of Him in whom the two worlds meet and are separated must be honored, and for this mission grace provides full authority, since men are shattered by it (v. 2).

The same God who had made Paul the apostle of the Gentiles (i. 1) had also pressed the Roman Christians into the service of His imminent and coming Kingdom. As men called unto holiness, they belong no longer to themselves or to the old world which is passing to corruption. They belong to Him who has called them. Not for Paul only, but for them also, has the Son of man been appointed Son of God through the power of the Resurrection. They too are here and now imprisoned in the knowledge of great tribulation and of great hope. They too after their fashion are separated and isolated for God. They too are constituted anew by the — **grace and peace from God our Father and the Lord Jesus Christ.** May this presupposition occur ever afresh! May their peace be their disquiet, and their disquiet be their peace! This is beginning, theme, and end, of the Epistle to the Romans.

The Theme of the Epistle
1. 16, 17

"I am not ashamed of the Gospel," says Paul. The Gospel neither requires men to engage in the conflict of religions or the conflict of philosophies, nor does it compel them to hold themselves aloof from these controversies. In announcing the limitation of the known world by another that is unknown, the Gospel does not enter into competition with the many attempts to disclose within the known world some more or less unknown and higher form of existence and to make it accessible to men. The Gospel is not a truth among other truths. Rather, it sets a question mark against all truths. The Gospel is not the door but the hinge. The man who apprehends its meaning is removed from all strife, because he is engaged in a strife with the whole, even with existence itself. Anxiety concerning the victory of the Gospel — that is, Christian Apologetics — is meaningless, because the Gospel is the victory by which the world is overcome. By the Gospel the whole concrete world is dissolved and established. It does not require representatives with a sense of responsibility, for it is as responsible for those who proclaim it as it is for those to whom it is proclaimed. It is the advocate of both. Nor is it necessary for the Gospel that Paul should take his stand in the midst of the spiritual cosmopolitanism of Rome; though he can, of course, enter the city without shame, and will enter it as a man who has been consoled by the Gospel. God does not need us. Indeed, if He were not God, He would be ashamed of us. We, at any rate, cannot be ashamed of Him.

The Night
Its Cause
1. 18–21

v. 18. For the wrath of God is revealed from heaven against all ungodliness and unrighteousness of men, who hold the truth imprisoned in the chains of their unrighteousness.

In the name of God! We know not what we should say to this. The believer knows our ignorance. With Job, he loves the God who in His unsearchable eminence is only to be feared: with Luther, he loves the *deus absconditus*. To him is manifested the righteousness of God. He shall be saved, and he alone. "Only the prisoner shall be free, only the poor shall be rich, only the weak strong, only the humble exalted, only the empty filled, only nothing shall be something" (Luther). But against the ungodliness and unrighteousness of men there is revealed the wrath of God.

The wrath of God is the judgment under which we stand insofar as we do not love the Judge; it is the "No" which meets us when we do not affirm it; it is the protest pronounced always and everywhere against the course of the world insofar as we do not accept the protest as our own; it is the questionableness of life insofar as we do not apprehend it; it is our boundedness and corruptibility insofar as we do not acknowledge their necessity. The judgment under which we stand is a fact, quite apart from our attitude to it. Indeed, it is the fact most characteristic of our life. Whether it enters within the light of salvation and of the coming world depends upon the answer we give to the problem of faith. But it is a fact, even should we choose the scandal rather than faith (i. 16). That time is nothing when measured by the standard of eternity, that all things are semblance when measured by their origin and by their end, that we are sinners, and that we must die — all these things ARE, even though the barrier be not for us the place of exit. Life moves on its course in its vast uncertainty and we move with it, even though we do not see the great question mark that is set against us. Men are lost, even though they know nothing of salvation. Then the barrier remains a barrier and does not become a place of exit. The prisoner remains a prisoner and does not become the watchman. Then is waiting not joyful but a bitter-sweet surrender to what is inevitable. Then is the contradiction not hope, but a sorrowful opposition. The fruitful paradox of our existence is then that which consumes it like a worm. And Negation is then — what is normally meant by the word. In the place of the Holy God there then appear Fate, Matter, the Universe, Chance, ANANKE. Indeed, a certain perception is betrayed when we begin to avoid giving the name "God" to the "No-God" of unbelief (i. 17). That which we, apart from faith in the Resurrection, name "God," is also a final consequence of the divine wrath. But the God who, contradicting His own name, affirms the course of this world, is God — God in His wrath, God who sorrows on our behalf, God who can only turn Himself from us and say only "No." And yet, for this very reason, no upright man can unreservedly name Him "God." For the wrath of God cannot be His last word, the true revelation of Him! "Not-God" cannot seriously be named "God." Nevertheless, it is, in fact, always God against whom we are thrust. Even the unbeliever encounters God, but he does not penetrate through to the truth of God that is hidden from him, and so he is broken to pieces on God, as Pharaoh was (ix. 18). "Everything that thwarts and damages the life that has been made by God, all the frailty and bondage of the creaturely life, including the sentence of death under which it lies, is a reaction of the power of God" (Zündel). Yes, but we must add that, if we do not make the apprehension of this divine reaction our own, we must perish at its hands. The whole world is the footprint of God; yes, but, insofar as we choose scandal rather than faith, the footprint in the vast riddle of the world is the footprint of His wrath. The wrath of God is to unbelief the discovery of His righteousness, for God is not mocked. The wrath of God is the righteousness of God — apart from and without Christ.

But what does "apart from and without Christ" mean? **The wrath of God is revealed against all ungodliness and unrighteousness of men.** These are the characteristic features of our relation to God, as it takes shape on this side resurrection. Our relation to God is *ungodly.* We suppose that we know what we are saying when we say "God." We assign to Him the highest place in our world: and in so doing we place Him fundamentally on one line with ourselves and with things. We assume that He *needs something:* and so we assume that we are able to arrange our relation to Him as we arrange our other relationships. We press ourselves into proximity with Him: and so, all unthinking, we make Him nigh unto ourselves. We allow ourselves an ordinary communication with Him, we permit ourselves to reckon with Him as though this were not extraordinary behavior on our part. We dare to deck ourselves out as His companions, patrons, advisers, and commissioners. We confound time with eternity. This is the *ungodliness* of our relation to God. And our relation to God is *unrighteous.* Secretly we are ourselves the masters in this relationship. We are not concerned with God, but with our own requirements, to which God must adjust Himself. Our arrogance demands that, in addition to everything else, some super-world should also be known and accessible to us. Our conduct calls for some deeper sanction, some approbation and remuneration from another world. Our well-regulated, pleasurable life longs for some hours of devotion, some prolongation into infinity. And so, when we set God upon the throne of the world, we mean by God ourselves. In "believing" on Him, we justify, enjoy, and adore ourselves. Our devotion consists in a solemn affirmation of ourselves and of the world and in a pious setting aside of the contradiction. Under the banners of humility and emotion we rise in rebellion against God. We confound time with eternity. That is our *unrighteousness.* — Such is our relation to God apart from and without Christ, on this side resurrection, and before we are called to order. God Himself is not acknowledged as God and what is called "God" is in fact Man. By living to ourselves, we serve the "No-God."

Who hold the truth imprisoned in unrighteousness. This second characteristic is in point of time the first. Men fall a prey first to themselves and then to the "No-God." First is heard the promise — *shall be as God!* — and then men lose the sense for eternity. First mankind is exalted, and then men obscure the distance between God and man. The nodal point in the relation between God and man apart from and without Christ is the unrighteousness of slaves. Thinking of ourselves what can be thought only of God, we are unable to think of Him more highly than we think of ourselves. Being to ourselves what God ought to be to us, He is no more to us than we are to ourselves. This secret identification of ourselves with God carries with it our isolation from Him. The little god must, quite appropriately, dispossess the great God. Men have *imprisoned* and encased the *truth* — the righteousness of God; they have trimmed it to their own measure, and thereby robbed it both of its earnestness and of its significance. They have made it ordinary, harmless, and useless; and thereby transformed it into untruth. This has all been brought to light by their ungodliness, and this ungodliness will not fail to thrust them into ever new forms of unrighteousness. If mankind be itself God, the appearance of the idol is then inevitable. And whenever the idol is honored, it is inevitable that men, feeling themselves to be the true God, should also feel that they have themselves fashioned the idol. This is the rebellion which makes it impossible for us to see the new dimensional plane which is the boundary of our world and the meaning of our salvation. Against such rebellion there can be revealed only the wrath of God.

Translated by Edwyn C. Hoskyns

Ludwig Wittgenstein

Ludwig Wittgenstein (1889–1951) is not normally understood to be a religious philosopher, in either sense of that term: neither was he taken to be particularly religious himself in sensibility, nor did his published works seem to devote much attention to the issue of religion. In fact, as an early associate of the Vienna Circle of logical positivists and in light of the deeply antimetaphysical thrust of his first book, the *Tractatus Logico-philosophicus,* he would seem to be one of the twentieth-century thinkers least likely to be included in this volume.

After his death, however, Wittgenstein's literary executors decoded his rather simply enciphered journals, portions of which were published as *Culture and Value,* and it has turned out not only that Wittgenstein's interest in religion was much more intense than had been previously suspected but also that his remarks were unusually insightful and provocative. Moreover, a recent biography — written by a man who was given complete access to the unpublished journals as well as having been granted the reminiscences of various friends and relations — reveals that Wittgenstein adopted the vocation of philosopher because of a "mystical" or quasi-mystical experience in 1911.[1]

The selections that follow are all drawn from his journals. Admittedly, this can lead to distortions, as Wittgenstein himself seems to note in this one entry:

---

1. Ray Monk, *Ludwig Wittgenstein: The Duty of Genius* (New York: Free Press, 1991). On all of these recent developments, see Edward T. Oakes, S.J., "Ludwig Wittgenstein Confesses," *First Things* 24 (June/July 1992): 37–41; and Russell Nieli, *Wittgenstein: From Mysticism to Ordinary Language: A Study of Viennese Positivism and the Thought of Ludwig Wittgenstein* (Albany: State University of New York Press, 1987).

Engelmann told me that when he rummages around at home in a drawer full of his own manuscripts, they strike him as so splendid that he thinks it would be worth making them available to other people. (He says it's the same when he is reading through letters from his dead relations.) But when he imagines publishing a section of them, the whole business loses its charm and value and becomes impossible.[2]

But it was this same Engelmann who reported that "the notion of a Last Judgment was of profound concern to him. 'When we meet again at the Last Judgment' was a recurrent phrase with him, which he used in many a conversation at a particularly momentous point. He would pronounce the words with an indescribably inward-gazing look in his eyes, his head bowed, the picture of a man stiffed to his depths."[3] This is clearly a man whose views on religion merit more attention than they have been given.

From Culture and Value

1929

What is good is also divine. Queer as it sounds, that sums up my ethics. Only something supernatural can express the Supernatural.

You cannot lead people to what is good; you can only lead them to some place or other. The good is outside the space of facts.

1930

l once said, perhaps rightly: The earlier culture will become a heap of rubble and finally a heap of ashes, but spirits will hover over the ashes.

---

2. Ludwig Wittgenstein, *Culture and Value*, ed. G. H. von Wright, trans. Peter Winch (Chicago: University of Chicago Press, 1980), 4e.
3. Paul Engelmann, *Letters from Ludwig Wittgenstein: With a Memoir*, trans. L. Furtmüller (Oxford: Basil Blackwell, 1967), 77–78.

In Renan's *History of the People of Israel* I read: "Birth, sickness, death, madness, catalepsy, sleep, dreams, all made an immense impression and, even nowadays, only a few have the gift of seeing clearly that these phenomena have causes within our constitution."

On the contrary there is absolutely no reason to wonder at these things, because they are such everyday occurrences. If primitive men can't help but wonder at them, how much more so dogs and monkeys. Or is it being assumed that men, as it were, suddenly woke up and, noticing for the first time these things that had always been there, were understandably amazed? — Well, as a matter of fact we might assume something like this; though not that they become aware of these things for the first time but that they do suddenly start to wonder at them. But this again has nothing to do with their being primitive. Unless it is called primitive not to wonder at things, in which case the people of today are really the primitive ones, and Renan himself too if he supposes that scientific explanation could intensify wonderment.

As though lightning were more commonplace or less astounding today than two thousand years ago.

Man has to awaken to wonder — and so perhaps do peoples. Science is a way of sending him to sleep again.

In other words it's just false to say: Of course, these primitive peoples couldn't help wondering at everything. Though perhaps it is true that these peoples *did* wonder at all the things around them. — To suppose they couldn't help wondering at them is a primitive superstition. (It is like supposing that they *had* to be afraid of all the forces of nature, whereas we of course have no need to be afraid. On the other hand we may learn from experience that certain primitive tribes are very strongly inclined to fear natural phenomena. — But we cannot exclude the possibility that *highly* civilized peoples will become liable to this very same fear once again; neither their civilization nor scientific knowledge can protect them against this. All the same it's true enough that the *spirit* in which science is carried on nowadays is not compatible with fear of this kind.)

1931

We are struggling with language.
We are engaged in a struggle with language.

The Jew is a desert region, but underneath its thin layer of rock lies the molten lava of spirit and intellect.

What would it feel like not to have heard of Christ?
Should we feel left alone in the dark?
Do we escape such a feeling simply in the way a child escapes it when he knows there is someone in the room with him?

Religion as madness is a madness springing from irreligiousness.

I look at the photograph of Corsican brigands and reflect: these faces are too hard and mine too soft for Christianity to be able to make a mark on them. The brigands' faces are terrible to look at and yet they are certainly no farther than I am from a good life; it is just that they and I find our salvation on different sides of such a life.

Within Christianity it's as though God says to men: Don't act a tragedy, that's to say, don't enact heaven and hell on earth. Heaven and hell are *my* affair.

People say again and again that philosophy doesn't really progress, that we are still occupied with the same philosophical problems as were the Greeks. But the people who say this don't understand why it has to be so. It is because our language has remained the same and keeps seducing us into asking the same questions. As long as there continues to be a verb "to be" that looks as if it functions in the same way as "to eat" and "to drink," as long as we still have the adjectives "identical," "true," "false," "possible," as long as we continue to talk of a river of time, of an expanse of space, etc. etc., people will keep stumbling over the same puzzling difficulties and find themselves staring at something which no explanation seems capable of clearing up.
    And what's more, this satisfies a longing for the transcendent, because insofar as people think they can see the "limits of

human understanding," they believe of course that they can see beyond these.

It is often said that a new religion brands the gods of the old one as devils. But in reality they have probably already become devils by that time.

A curious analogy could be based on the fact that even the hugest telescope has to have an eye-piece no larger than the human eye.

A confession has to be a part of your new life.

I never more than half succeed in expressing what I want to express. Actually not as much as that, but by no more than a tenth. That is still worth something. Often my writing is nothing but "stuttering."

Among Jews "genius" is found only in the holy man. Even the greatest of Jewish thinkers is no more than talented. (Myself for instance.)

I think there is some truth in my idea that I really only think reproductively. I don't believe I have ever *invented* a line of thinking, I have always taken one over from someone else. I have simply straightaway seized on it with enthusiasm for my work of clarification. That is how Boltzmann, Hertz, Schopenhauer, Frege, Russell, Kraus, Loos, Weininger, Spengler, Sraffa have influenced me. Can one take the case of Breuer and Freud as an example of Jewish reproductiveness? — What I invent are new *similes*.

At the time I modeled the head for Drobil, too, the stimulus was essentially a work of Drobil's and my contribution once again was really clarification. What I do think essential is carrying out the work of clarification with COURAGE: otherwise it becomes just a clever game.

The Jew must see to it that, in a literal sense, "all things are as nothing to him." But this is particularly hard for him, since in a sense he has nothing that is peculiarly his. It is much harder to accept poverty willingly when you *have* to be poor than when you might also be rich.

It might be said (rightly or wrongly) that the Jewish mind does not have the power to produce even the tiniest flower or blade of grass; its way is rather to make a drawing of the flower or blade of grass that has grown in the soil of another's mind and to put it into a comprehensive picture. We aren't pointing to a fault when we say this and everything is all right as long as what is being done is quite clear. It is only when the nature of a Jewish work is confused with that of a non-Jewish work that there is any danger, especially when the author of the Jewish work falls into the confusion himself, as he so easily may. (Doesn't he look as proud as though he had produced the milk himself?)

It is typical for a Jewish mind to understand someone else's work better than he understands it himself.

Rousseau's character has something Jewish about it.

"Look on this tumor as a perfectly normal part of your body!" Can one do that, to order? Do I have the power to decide at will to have, or not to have, an ideal conception of my body?

Within the history of the peoples of Europe the history of the Jews is not treated as circumstantially as their intervention in European affairs would actually merit, because within this history they are experienced as a sort of disease, and anomaly, and no one wants to put a disease on the same level as normal life (and no one wants to speak of a disease as if it had the same rights as healthy bodily processes [even painful ones]).

We may say: people can only regard this tumor as a natural part of the body if their whole feeling for the body changes (if the whole national feeling for the body changes). Otherwise the best they can do is *put up with* it.

You can expect an individual man to display this sort of tolerance, or else to disregard such things; but you cannot expect this of a nation, because it is precisely not disregarding such things that makes it a nation. I.e., there is a contradiction in expecting someone *both* to retain his former aesthetic feeling for the body and *also* to make the tumor welcome.

Power and possession aren't the *same* thing. Even though possessions also bring us power. If Jews are said not to have any sense of property, that may be compatible with their liking to be rich since for them money is a particular sort of power, not property. (For instance I should not like my people to become poor, since

I wish them to have a certain amount of power. Naturally I wish them to use this power properly too.)

1937

If you offer a sacrifice and are pleased with yourself about it, both you and your sacrifice will be cursed.

The *edifice of your pride* has to be dismantled. And that is terribly hard work.

The horrors of hell can be experienced within a single day; that's plenty of time.

The way to solve the problem you see in life is to live in a way that will make what is problematic disappear.

The fact that life is problematic shows that the shape of your life does not fit into life's mould. So you must change the way you live and, once your life does fit into the mould, what is problematic will disappear.

But don't we have the feeling that someone who sees no problem in life is blind to something important, even to the most important thing of all? Don't I feel like saying that a man like that is just living aimlessly — blindly, like a mole, and that if only he could see, he would see the problem?

Or shouldn't I say rather: a man who lives rightly won't experience the problem as *sorrow*, so for him it will not be a problem, but a joy rather; in other words for him it will be a bright halo round his life, not a dubious background.

Christianity is not a doctrine, not, I mean, a theory about what has happened and will happen to the human soul, but a description of something that actually takes place in human life. For "consciousness of sin" is a real event and so are despair and salvation through faith. Those who speak of such things (Bunyan for instance) are simply describing what has happened to them, whatever gloss anyone may want to put on it.

Thinking too has a time for ploughing and a time for gathering the harvest.

The effect of making men think in accordance with dogmas, perhaps in the form of certain graphic propositions, will be very peculiar: I am not thinking of these dogmas as determining men's opinions but rather as completely controlling the *expression* of all opinions. People will live under an absolute, palpable tyranny, though without being able to say they are not free. I think the Catholic Church does something rather like this. For dogma is expressed in the form of an assertion, and is unshakable, but at the same time any practical opinion *can* be made to harmonize with it; admittedly more easily in some cases than in others. It is not a *wall* setting limits to what can be believed, but more like a *brake* which, however, practically serves the same purpose; it's almost as though someone were to attach a weight to your foot to restrict your freedom of movement. This is how dogma becomes irrefutable and beyond the reach of attack.

Religious similes can be said to move on the edge of an abyss. B[unyan]'s for example. For what if we simply add: "and all these traps, quicksands, wrong turnings, were planned by the Lord of the Road and the monsters, thieves, and robbers were created by him"? Certainly, that is not the sense of the simile! But such a continuation is all too obvious! For many people, including me, this robs the simile of its power.

But more especially if this is — as it were — suppressed. It would be different if at every turn it were said quite honestly: "I am using this as a simile, but look: it doesn't fit here." Then you wouldn't feel you were being cheated, that someone was trying to convince you by trickery. Someone can be told for instance: "Thank God for the good you receive but don't complain about the evil: as you would of course do if a human being were to do you good and evil by turns." Rules of life are dressed up in pictures. And these pictures can only serve to *describe* what we are to do, not *justify* it. Because they could provide a justification only if they held good in other respects as well. I can say: "Thank these bees for their honey as though they were kind people who have prepared it for you"; that is *intelligible* and describes how I should like you to conduct yourself. But I cannot say: "Thank them because, look, how kind they are!" — since the next moment they may sting you.

Religion says: *Do this!* — *Think like that!* — but it cannot justify this and once it even tries to, it becomes repellent; because for every reason it offers there is a valid counter-reason. It is more convincing to say: "Think like this! however strangely it may strike you." Or: "Won't you do this? — however repugnant you find it."

Predestination: It is only permissible to write like this out of the most dreadful suffering — and then it means something quite different. But for the same reason it is not permissible for someone to assert it as a truth, unless he himself says it in torment. — It simply isn't a theory. — Or, to put it another way: If this is truth, it is not the truth that seems at first sight to be expressed by these words. It's less a theory than a sigh, or a cry.

The spring which flows gently and limpidly in the Gospels seems to have *froth* on it in Paul's Epistles. Or that is how it seems *to me.* Perhaps it is just my own impurity which reads turbidness into it; for why shouldn't this impurity be able to pollute what is limpid? But to me it's as though I saw human passion here, something like pride or anger, which is not in tune with the humility of the *Gospels.* It's as though he *is* insisting here on his own person, *and doing so moreover as a religious gesture,* something which is foreign to the Gospel. I want to ask — and may this be no blasphemy — : "What might Christ have said to Paul?" But a fair rejoinder to that would be: What business is that of yours? Attend to making *yourself* more honorable! In your present state you are quite incapable of understanding what may be the truth here.

In the Gospels — as it seems to me — everything is *less pretentious,* humbler, simpler. There you find huts; in Paul a church. There all men are equal and God himself is a man; in Paul there is already something like a hierarchy; honors and official positions. — That, as it were, is what my NOSE tells me.

Kierkegaard writes: If Christianity were so easy and cozy, why should God in his Scriptures have set Heaven and Earth in motion and threatened *eternal* punishments? — Question: But in that case why is this Scripture so unclear? If we want to warn someone of a terrible danger, do we go about it by telling him a riddle whose solution will be the warning? — But who is to say that the Scripture really is unclear? Isn't it possible that it was essential in this case to "tell a riddle"? And that, on the other hand, giving a more direct warning would necessarily have had the *wrong* effect? God has *four* people recount the life of his incarnate Son, in each case differently and with inconsistencies — but might we not say: It is important that this narrative should not be more than quite averagely historically plausible *just so that* this should not be taken as the essential, decisive thing? So that the *letter* should not be believed more strongly than is proper and the *spirit* may receive its due. I.e., what you are supposed to see cannot be communicated even by the best and most accurate historian; and *therefore* a mediocre account suffices, is even to be preferred. For that too can tell you what you are supposed to be told. (Roughly in the way a mediocre stage set can be better than a sophisticated one, painted trees better than real ones, — because these might distract attention from what matters.)

The Spirit puts what is essential, essential for your life, into these words. The point is precisely that your are only SUPPOSED to see clearly what appears clearly even in *this* representation. (I am not sure how far all this is exactly in the spirit of Kierkegaard.)

In religion every level of devoutness must have its appropriate form of expression which has no sense at a lower level. This doctrine, which means something at a higher level, is null and void for someone who is still at the lower level; he *can* only understand it *wrongly* and so these words are *not* valid for such a person.

For instance, at my level the Pauline doctrine of predestination is ugly nonsense, irreligiousness. Hence it is not suitable for me, since the only use I could make of the picture I am offered would be a wrong one. If it is a good and godly picture, then it is so for someone at a quite different level, who must use it in his life in a way completely different from anything that would be possible for me.

Christianity is not based on a historical truth; rather, it offers us a (historical) narrative and says: now believe! But not, believe this narrative with the belief appropriate to a historical narrative, rather: believe, through thick and thin, which you can do only as the result of a life. *Here you have a narrative, don't take the same attitude to it as you take to other historical narratives!*

Make a *quite different* place in your life for it. — There is nothing *paradoxical* about that!

Queer as it sounds: The historical accounts in the Gospels might, historically speaking, be demonstrably false and yet belief would lose nothing by this: *not*, however, because it concerns "universal truths of reason"! Rather, because historical proof (the historical proof-game) is irrelevant to belief. This message (the Gospels) is seized on by men believingly (i.e., lovingly). *That* is the certainty characterizing this particular acceptance-as-true, not something *else*.

A believer's relation to these narratives is *neither* the relation to historical truth (probability), *nor yet* that to a theory consisting of "truths of reason." There is such a thing. — (We have quite different attitudes even to different species of what we call fiction!)

I read: "No man can say that Jesus is the Lord, but by the Holy Ghost." And it is true: I cannot call him *Lord;* because that says nothing to me. I could call him "the paragon," "God" even — or rather, I can understand it when he is called thus; but I cannot utter the word "Lord" with meaning. *Because I do not believe* that he will come to judge me; because *that* says nothing to me. And it could say something to me, only if I lived *completely* differently.

What inclines even me to believe in Christ's Resurrection? It is as though I play with the thought. — If he did not rise from the dead, then he decomposed in the grave like any other man. *He is dead and decomposed.* In that case he is a teacher like any other and can no longer *help;* and once more we are orphaned and alone. So we have to content ourselves with wisdom and speculation. We are in a sort of hell where we can do nothing but dream, roofed in, as it were, and cut off from heaven. But if I am to be REALLY saved, — what I need is *certainty* — not wisdom, dreams, or speculation — and this certainty is faith. And faith is faith in what is needed by my *heart,* my *soul,* not my speculative intelligence. For it is my soul with its passions, as it were with its flesh and blood, that has to be saved, not my abstract mind. Perhaps we can say: Only *love* can believe the Resurrection. Or: It is *love* that believes the Resurrection. We might say: Redeeming love believes even in the Resurrection; holds fast even to the Resurrection. What combats doubt is, as it were, *redemption.* Holding fast to *this* must be holding fast to that belief. So what that means is: first you must be redeemed and hold on to your redemption (keep hold of your redemption) — then you will see that you are holding fast to this belief. So this can come about only if you no longer rest your weight on the earth but suspend yourself from heaven. Then *everything* will be different and it will be "no wonder" if you can do things that you cannot do now. (A man who is suspended looks the same as one who is standing, but the interplay of forces within him is nevertheless quite different, so that he can act quite differently than can a standing man.)

You cannot write anything about yourself that is more truthful than you yourself are. That is the difference between writing about yourself and writing about external objects. You write about yourself from your own height. You don't stand on stilts or on a ladder but on your bare feet.

1940

Sometimes an expression has to be withdrawn from language and sent for cleaning: — then it can be put back into circulation.

How hard I find it to see what is *right in front of my eyes!*

You can't be reluctant to give up your lie, and still tell the truth.

1941

Our greatest stupidities may be very wise.

1942

A man will be *imprisoned* in a room with a door that's unlocked and opens inward as long as it does not occur to him to *pull* rather than push it.

Put a man in the wrong atmosphere and nothing will function as it should. He will seem unhealthy in every part. Put him back into his proper element and everything will blossom and look healthy. But if he is not in his right element, what then? Well, then he just has to make the best of appearing before the world as a cripple.

Circa 1944

A miracle is, as it were, a *gesture* which God makes. As a man sits quietly and then makes an impressive gesture, God lets the world run on smoothly and then accompanies the words of a saint by a symbolic occurrence, a gesture of nature. It would be an instance if, when a saint has spoken, the trees around him bowed, as if in reverence. — Now, do I believe that this happens? I don't.

The only way for me to believe in a miracle in this sense would be to be *impressed* by an occurrence in this particular way. So that I should say, e.g.: "It was *impossible* to see these trees and not to feel that they were responding to the words." Just as I might say "It is impossible to see the face of this dog and not to see that he is alert and full of attention to what his master is doing." And I can imagine that the mere report of the *words* and life of a saint can make someone believe the reports that the trees bowed. But I am not so impressed.

People are religious to the extent that they believe themselves to be not so much *imperfect,* as *ill.*

Any man who is half-way decent will think himself extremely imperfect, but a religious man thinks *himself wretched.*

Go on, believe! It does no harm.

Believing means submitting to an authority. Having once submitted, you can't then, without rebelling against it, first call it in question and then once again find it acceptable.

No cry of torment can be greater than the cry of one man.

Or again, *no* torment can be greater than what a single human being may suffer.

A man is capable of infinite torment therefore, and so too he can stand in need of infinite help.

The Christian religion is only for the man who needs infinite help, solely, that is, for the man who experiences infinite torment.

The whole planet can suffer no greater torment than a *single* soul.

The Christian faith — as I see it — is a man's refuge in this *ultimate* torment. Anyone in such torment who has the gift of opening his heart, rather than contracting it, accepts the means of salvation in his heart.

Someone who in this way penitently opens his heart to God in confession lays it open for other men too. In doing this he loses the dignity that goes with his personal prestige and becomes like a child. That means without official position, dignity, or disparity from others. A man can bare himself before others only out of a particular kind of love. A love which acknowledges, as it were, that we are all wicked children.

We could also say: Hate between men comes from our cutting ourselves off from each other. Because we don't want anyone else to look inside us, since it's not a pretty sight in there.

Of course, you must continue to feel ashamed of what's inside you, but not ashamed of yourself before your fellow men.

No greater torment can be experienced than One human being can experience. For if a man feels lost, that is the ultimate torment.

Circa 1945

It isn't sensible to be furious even at Hitler; how much less so at God!

After someone has died we see his life in a conciliatory light. His life appears to us with outlines softened by a haze. There was no softening for *him* though, his life was jagged and incomplete. For him there was no reconciliation; his life is naked and wretched.

It is as though I had lost my way and asked someone the way home. He says he will show me and walks with me along a nice smooth path. This suddenly stops. And now my friend tells me: "All you have to do now is find your way home from here."

1946

In former times people went into monasteries. Were they stupid or insensitive people? — Well, if people like that found they needed to take such measures in order to be able to go on living, the problem cannot be an easy one!

The way you use the word "God" does not show *whom* you mean — but, rather, what you mean.

If life becomes hard to bear we think of a change in our circumstances. But the most important and effective change, a change in our own attitude, hardly even occurs to us, and the resolution to take such a step is very difficult for us.

I believe that one of the things Christianity says is that sound doctrines are all useless. That you have to change your *life*. (Or the *direction* of your life.)

It says that wisdom is all cold; and that you can no more use it for setting your life to rights than you can forge iron when it is *cold*.

The point is that a sound doctrine need not *take hold* of you; you can follow as you would a doctor's prescription. — But here you need something to move you and turn you in a new direction. — (I.e., this is how I understand it.) Once you have been turned round, you must *stay* turned round.

Wisdom is passionless. But faith by contrast is what Kierkegaard calls a *passion*.

Religion is, as it were, the calm bottom of the sea at its deepest point, which remains calm however high the waves on the surface may be. —

I cannot kneel to pray because it's as though my knees were stiff. I am afraid of dissolution (of my own dissolution), should I become soft.

1947

A man's dreams are virtually never realized.

Wisdom is cold and to that extent stupid. (Faith on the other hand is a passion.) It might also be said: Wisdom merely *conceals* life from you. (Wisdom is like cold grey ash, covering up the glowing embers.)

Don't *for heaven's sake,* be afraid of talking nonsense! But you must pay attention to your nonsense.

The miracles of nature.
   One might say: art *shows* us the miracles of nature. It is based on the *concept* of the miracles of nature. (The blossom, just opening out. What is *marvelous* about it?) We say: "Just look at it opening out!"

"Wisdom is grey." Life on the other hand and religion are full of color.

It strikes me that a religious belief could only be something like a passionate commitment to a system of reference. Hence, although it's *belief,* it's really a way of living, or a way of assessing life. It's passionately seizing hold of *this* interpretation. Instruction in a religious faith, therefore, would have to take the form of a portrayal, a description, of that system of reference, while at the same time being an appeal to conscience. And this combination would have to result in the pupil himself, of his own accord, passionately taking hold of the system of reference. It would be as though someone were first to let me see the hopelessness of my situation and then show me the means of rescue until, of my own accord, or not at any rate led to it by my *instructor,* I ran to it and grasped it.

1948

Religious faith and superstition are quite different. One of them results from *fear* and is a sort of false science. The other is a trusting.

If God really does choose those who are to be saved, there is no reason why he should not choose them according to nationality, race or temperament. Or why the choice should not find expression in the laws of nature. (Certainly he was *able* so to choose that his choice should follow a law.)

I have read excerpts from the writings of St. John of the Cross where he says that people have fallen into the pit because they did not have the good fortune to find a wise spiritual director at the right moment.

And if that is so, how can anyone say that God does not try men beyond their strength?

What I really feel like saying here is that distorted concepts have done a lot of mischief, but the truth is that I just *do not know* what does good and what does mischief.

If someone can believe in God with complete certainty, why not in Other Minds?

An honest religious thinker is like a tightrope walker. He almost looks though he were walking on nothing but air. His support is the slenderest imaginable. And yet it really is possible to walk on it.

Humor is not a mood but a way of looking at the world. So if it is correct to say that humor was stamped out in Nazi Germany, that does not mean that people were not in good spirits, or anything of that sort, but something much deeper and more important.

1949

There are remarks that sow and remarks that reap.

Could you explain the concept of the punishments of hell without using the concept of punishment? Or that of God's goodness without using the concept of goodness?

If you want to get the right *effect* with your words, certainly not.

Suppose someone were taught: there is a being who, if you do such and such or live thus and thus, will take you to a place of everlasting torment after you die; most people end up there, a few get to a place of everlasting happiness. — This being has selected in advance those who are to go to the good place and, since only those who have lived a certain sort of life go to the place of torment, he has also arranged in advance for the rest to live like that.

What might be the effect of such a doctrine?

Well, it does not mention punishment, but rather a sort of natural necessity. And if you were to present things to anyone in this light, he could only react with despair or incredulity to such a doctrine.

Teaching it could not constitute an ethical upbringing. If you wanted to bring someone up ethically while yet teaching him such a doctrine, you would have to teach it to him *after* having educated him ethically, representing it as a sort of incomprehensible mystery.

"Out of his goodness he has chosen them and he will punish you" makes no sense. The two halves of the proposition belong to different ways of looking at things. The second half is ethical, the first not. And taken together with the first, the second is absurd.

If Christianity is the truth then all the philosophy that is written about it is false.

1950

If someone who believes in God looks round and asks, "Where does everything I see come from?," "Where does all this come from?," he is *not* craving for a (causal) explanation; and his question gets its point from being the expression of a certain craving. He is, namely, expressing an attitude to all explanations. — But how is this manifested in his life?

The attitude that's in question is that of taking a certain matter seriously and then, beyond a certain point, no longer regarding it as serious, but maintaining that something else is even more important.

Someone may for instance say it's a very grave matter that such and such a man should have died before he could complete a certain piece of work; and yet, in another sense, this is not what matters. At this point one uses the words "in a deeper sense."

Actually I should like to say that in this case too the *words* you utter or what you think as you utter them are not what matters, so much as the difference they make at various points in your life. How do I know that two people mean the same when each says he believes in God? And just the same goes for belief in the Trinity. A theology which insists on the use of *certain particular* words and phrases, and outlaws others, does not make anything clearer (Karl Barth). It gesticulates with words, as one might say, because it wants to say something and does not know how to express it. *Practice* gives the words their sense.

A proof of God's existence ought really to be something by means of which one could convince oneself that God exists. But I think that what *believers* who have furnished such proofs have wanted to do is give their "belief" an intellectual analysis and foundation, although they themselves would never have come to believe as a result of such proofs. Perhaps one could "convince someone that God exists" by means of a certain kind of upbringing, by shaping his life in such and such a way.

How God judges a man is something we cannot imagine at all. If he really takes strength of temptation and the frailty of nature into account, whom can he condemn? But otherwise the resultant of these two forces is simply the end for which the man was predestined. In that case he was created so that the interplay of forces would make him either conquer or succumb. And that is not a religious idea at all, but more like a scientific hypothesis.

So if you want to stay within the religious sphere you must *struggle*.

1951

God may say to me: "I am judging you out of your own mouth. Your own actions have made you shudder with disgust when you have seen other people do them."

Is this the sense of belief in the Devil: that not everything that comes to us as an inspiration comes from what is good?

Translated by Peter Winch

Karl Rahner

Karl Rahner (1904–84) must rank with Hegel as one of the most difficult thinkers in the German language. His difficulty, however, can be deceptive. His is not a theology or a philosophy of religion that cultivates difficulty for its own sake, an ivory-tower exercise disengaged from the needs of the populace for whom he is writing. On the contrary, his activities as a Jesuit priest and pastor of souls during World War II, when he lost his teaching post, have shaped his entire thought.

Rahner was born in Freiburg im Breisgau on March 4, 1904, and entered the North German Province of the Society of Jesus (Jesuits) on April 2, 1922. After completing the necessary course of studies, he was ordained as a Roman Catholic priest in Munich in 1932 and was then sent for doctoral studies in philosophy at the University of Freiburg, where he was able to attend the seminars of Martin Heidegger. His dissertation was an attempt to fuse the horizons of Thomas Aquinas and Immanuel Kant via a school of epistemology and metaphysics called Transcendental Thomism. His thesis did not meet the approval of his director, and he failed to gain the doctorate in philosophy. His superiors then sent him to Innsbruck for a doctorate in theology (granted in 1936). The dissertation that his adviser had rejected in Freiburg was then published in 1939 under the title *Geist in Welt* (*Spirit in the World*); moreover, his lectures of 1937 in the philosophy of religion also came out in book form under the title *Hörer des Wortes* (*Hearers of the Word*). He joined the faculty at Innsbruck in 1938 and launched an ambitious project for the reformulation of Catholic dogmatics according to his newly developed scheme. But after the annexation of Austria in the Third Reich (the so-called *Anschluss*), the Nazis closed the school, and Rahner had to content himself with private lecturing and pastoral work until the end of the war, when he resumed his professorship after the reopening of the *Hochschule* in Innsbruck; in 1964 he returned to Germany, first as professor at the University of Munich and then later at the University of Münster.

His thought is, as already noted, notoriously difficult, but as the essay to follow makes clear, it is also passionately concerned with the dilemmas so many modern Europeans feel toward Christian revelation:

> Rahner's combination of pastoral work and theological lec-
> turing during the war years gave him a keen appreciation
> of theology's pastoral implications. His personal experience
> of a big-city diocese torn by war and persecution and his
> pastoral contact with large numbers of priests, religious and
> laity during an agonizing and turbulent period in the history
> of Central Europe provoked the theological reflections on the
> diaspora Church, the parochial principle, the charismatic and
> hierarchical elements in the Church, the apostolic spirituality
> of the laity, the formation of priests, and the religious life
> which attracted popular attention to Rahner in the years be-
> fore Vatican II and contributed greatly to his influence on the
> bishops who took part in it.[1]

His primary concern is to heal the breach between the perceived mystery of revelation (in both the good and bad sense) and the ability and willingness of the human subject to accept this mystery — in its full mysteriousness but purged of any accumulated obscurantism that might still pertain to it. In this he is reminiscent of Bultmann, as indeed he is in his proposed solution: like Bultmann he tries to heal the breach with a philosophy of religion that can speak to modern people. And this he does with his so-called transcendental method.

This method bears certain formal similarities to that of Schleiermacher in *Speeches on Religion to Its Cultured Despisers*, inasmuch as it tries to show the inherent connection between man's constitution (as question) and revelation (as answer). There are also certain notable affinities with Hegel, especially in the insis-

---

1. Gerald A. McCool, introduction to *A Rahner Reader* (New York: Seabury, 1975), xix.

tence of both that there is an intrinsic metaphysical connection between the procession of the Word from the Father in the Trinity and the relation of the Word to the world through creation and incarnation.

The selection that follows represents one of Rahner's most concise defenses of this method.

"Theology and Anthropology"

This short paper is intended to show that dogmatic theology today must be theological anthropology and that such an "anthropocentric" view is necessary and fruitful. The question of man and its answering may not be regarded, therefore, as an area of study separate from other theological areas as to its scope and subject-matter, but as the whole of dogmatic theology itself. This statement does not contradict the "theocentricity" of all theology as expressed, for instance, in St. Thomas's doctrine that God is as such the formal object of revelation theology. As soon as man is understood as the being who is absolutely transcendent in respect of God, "anthropocentricity" and "theocentricity" in theology are not opposites but strictly one and the same thing, seen from two sides. Neither of the two aspects can be comprehended at all without the other. Thus, although anthropocentricity in theology is not the opposite of the strictest theocentricity, it *is* opposed to the idea that in theology man is one particular theme among others, e.g., angels, the material world; or that it is possible to say something about God theologically without thereby automatically saying something about man and vice versa; or that these two kinds of statements are connected with one another in respect of their object, but not in the process of knowing itself.

Similarly, this anthropological focus in theology is not opposed to or in competition with a Christological focus. It is not possible to demonstrate this in more detail here; we merely observe that anthropology and Christology mutually determine each other within Christian dogmatics if they are both correctly understood. Christian anthropology is only able to fulfil its whole purpose if it understands man as the *potentia oboedientialis* for the "Hypostatic Union." And Christology can only be undertaken from the point of view of this kind of transcendental anthropology; for in order to say today what the "Hypostatic Union" is without being suspected of merely reproducing no longer feasible "mythologies," the idea of the God-man needs proof of a transcendental orientation in man's being and history under grace. A purely *a posteriori* Christology, unable to integrate Christology correctly into an evolutionary total view of the world, would not find it easy to dismiss the suspicion of propounding mythology.

This anthropology is naturally to be understood as a transcendental anthropology. A *transcendental investigation* examines an issue according to the necessary conditions given by the possibility of knowledge and action on the part of the subject himself. Such an investigation presupposes that the subject of the act of knowing is not simply a "thing" among others which can be made at will the object of a statement including other objects, but which is not present at all — even implicitly — in statements purely about other objects. If I speak of Australia I have not said anything, not even implicitly, about Java. But in such a statement (from the point of view of its content and import) I have said something implicitly about man as its subject (insofar as the statement, in order to be possible at all, necessarily presupposes various things about man). I have expressed and affirmed this by means of subjective implication. Therefore, if one wishes to pursue dogmatics as transcendental anthropology, it means that whenever one is confronted with an object of dogma, one inquires as to the conditions necessary for it to be known by the theological subject, ascertaining that the *a priori* conditions for knowledge of the object are satisfied, and showing that they imply and express something about the object, the mode, method and limits of knowing it.

In general, transcendental investigation does not assume that the material content of the object in question can be adequately deduced from the transcendental conditions whereby it is known by the subject, nor that this content, known *a posteriori*, is unimportant for the subject's existence (his "salvation") and for the truth of his knowledge. It does not regard this content as in itself merely indifferent material whereby the subject experiences his own *a priori* and necessary being. This applies fundamentally and decisively to a theological transcendental investigation and method as well. For instance, not only is it important for a true Christology to understand man as the being who is orientated toward an "absolute Savior" both *a priori* and in actuality (his essence having been elevated and set in this direction supernaturally by grace), but it is equally important for his salvation that he is confronted with Jesus of Nazareth as this Savior — which cannot, of course, be transcendentally "deduced."

On the other hand, to interpret the whole of dogmatic theology as transcendental anthropology means that every dogmatic treatment must also be considered from its transcendental angle, and that one must therefore face the question, what measure of actual material content subsists in the theological subject's *a priori* "structures" implicit in a particular theological statement? In other words it means that the transcendental side of knowledge must not be overlooked but taken seriously. The problem we mentioned of the relationship between transcendental, *a priori* theology and descriptive, historical and *a posteriori* theology is not solved, of course, by what we have just said. The problem only reveals its depth and acuteness when one is aware of the fact that in theology the final *a priori* precondition for the subject's theological knowledge, i.e., grace (ultimately the self-communicating God, acting freely in history), is the real content, or rather, the objective foundation of what is known and experienced *a posteriori* in history. One finds that in theology the *a priori* character of the subject and the *a posteriori* quality of the historical object enjoy an exclusive and unique relationship.

We must now ask *why* this anthropological change of direction in theology is *necessary*. There are fundamental reasons from the nature of the case, i.e., from theology and its object. Besides this there are reasons from the contemporary situation and reasons of basic theology and apologetics.

1. First of all the *reasons* or reason from the nature of the case. As a consequence of the nature of every occurrence of intellectual (and hence also theological) knowledge, the question of the object of such knowledge raises at the same time the question as to the nature of the knowing subject. This inextricable interrelation of the "objective" and "subjective" side of knowledge does not need, of course, to be discussed or to be equally explicit in every sphere of study. A concrete discipline in natural science does not have to investigate its philosophical foundation as well: the latter is con-

cerned with the mode of being and structure of the subject who is concretely engaged in science. But where the study of a particular field becomes really "philosophical" in a specific sense — and theology must do this of its very essence — every question concerning any object whatever also formally implies the question of the knowing subject.

A question is first stated philosophically by being put formally as the question concerning a particular object as such in the *totality* of reality and truth, for it is only in this way that the highest reasons, the philosophical ones, are sought out. If this is done, the subject is also investigated, not only because it is a "material" part of the totality, but because the totality (as that to which man is transcendentally orientated) can only exist in the subject as such according to the latter's own subjective uniqueness. The philosophical question as to a particular object is necessarily the question as to the knowing subject, because *a priori* the subject must carry with it the limits of the possibility of such knowledge. Thus the "transcendental" structures of the object are already determined *a priori*. A really *theological* question can only be put, however, if it is understood as being simultaneously a philosophical one in the sense we have shown. For it is only a theological question as long as it sees the individual object with its origin in and orientation toward God.

But God is not one object among others in the realm of man's *posteriori* knowledge but the fundamental ground and the absolute future of all reality.

As such he can only be understood as the absolute point of man's transcendental orientation. Thus every theology of this kind is necessarily transcendental anthropology; every *onto*logy is onto*logy*.

If one wishes to avoid falling into a heretical and positivistic fideism, what has been said must be applied also to revealed theology. Revealed theology has the human spirit's transcendental and limitless horizon as its inner motive and as the precondition of its existence. It is only because of this transcendental horizon that something like "God" can be understood at all. "Natural," "philosophical" theology is first and last not one sphere of study side by side with revealed theology, as if both could be pursued quite independently of each other, but an internal factor of revealed theology itself; if philosophical theology, however, is transcendental anthropology, so is revealed theology too.

However, the thesis in question can be given a still more direct theological basis. Firstly, revelation is revelation of salvation and therefore theology is essentially salvation theology. What is revealed and then pondered upon in theology is not an arbitrary matter, but something which is intended for man's salvation. By this statement we do not imply the sort of principle (as in the case of a "fundamentalism") according to which certain objects can be excluded at the outset from the sphere of possible revelation, for what salvation really is is determined materially for the first time in the event of revelation. But the statement must be taken seriously. Only those things can belong to man's salvation which, when lacking, injure his "being" and wholeness. Otherwise he could eschew salvation without thereby being in danger of losing it. This does not entail a rationalistic and unhistorical reduction of man to the status of an abstract transcendental being in his merely formal structure as such, as if what is historical and not deducible and what is experienced concretely *a posteriori* had no significance for salvation. It means that everything of significance for salvation is to be illuminated by referring it back to this transcendental being (which is not the same as *deducing* the significance *from* the transcendental being). In this sense, "reduction" does not mean diminution but the process of establishing by reflex investigation. A comparison may clarify what is meant: the concrete beloved person who is the object of my love and in whom it is realized (and without whom it does not exist) cannot be deduced *a priori* from human possibilities, but is rather a historical occurrence, an indissoluble fact which has to be accepted. But in spite of this, such love for this concrete person can only be understood when one comprehends man as the being who must of necessity fulfil himself in love in order to be true to his nature. Even the most unpredictable, concrete love, occurring in history, must therefore be understood transcendentally in this way, in order that it may be what it should be. And this applies above all in the case of salvation. For even if this is a historical event, what it concerns is precisely man's actual nature; it is his nature which is to be consummated in salvation or the loss of it. If revelation and theology are essentially concerned with salvation as such, theology's structure when confronted with any object whatsoever is bound to imply the question as to man's nature, insofar as this nature is susceptible to "saving" influence from the object involved. In other words, a theological object's significance for salvation (which is a necessary factor in any theological object) can only be investigated by inquiring at the same time as to man's *saving receptivity for* this object. However, this receptivity must not be investigated only "in the abstract" nor merely presupposed in its most general aspects. It must be reflected upon with reference to the concrete object concerned, which is only *theologically relevant* as a result of and for the purpose of this receptiveness for salvation. Thereby the object also to some extent lays down the conditions for such receptiveness.

In addition to these more formal considerations there is a decisive and clearly outlined issue. The Council's Decree on Ecumenism emphasizes that not all articles of faith in the "hierarchy" of truths are equally close to the "fundamentals" of the Christian Faith. Thus according to the Council there is a foundation, an inner core in the reality of faith, to which all other realities (and articles of faith) are related. In the nature of the case this "foundation" can only be God himself insofar as he is our salvation through his absolute self-communication, i.e., what we in theology usually call "uncreated grace." Salvation is mediated exclusively in and through this grace. Grace must therefore belong at least to the core of the salvation/revelation reality. If grace and the Trinity are understood, the reality of the triune God as such is given as well. For a full understanding of this grace another important condition must be presupposed: this grace is the grace of *Christ* (and he is not merely external to it as the reason for its being conferred), even in the case of prelapsarian grace. At the same time this means that, within the history of grace (as the self-communication of God acting freely in history), the history of humanity has come *in Christ* to its own historical and eschatological apogee, irreversibly manifested. If Trinity and Incarnation are implicit in the mystery of grace, it becomes intelligible that grace not only *belongs to* the core of the salvation/revelation reality, but *is* this core. (Of course the same could be said of the Trinity, especially *qua* "economic" Trinity, and also of Christ as the apogee of God's self-communication to the world, precisely because these three realities mutually imply each other.)

Now it is only possible to speak of this grace in a meaningful way at all within a transcendental anthropological context. For, without destroying the fact that grace is God himself in self-communication, grace is not a "thing" but — as communicated grace — a conditioning of the spiritual and intellectual subject as such to a direct relationship with God. The most objective reality of salvation is at the same time necessarily the most subjective: the direct relationship of the subject with God through God himself. If what "grace" is must not merely be expressed in a mythological-sounding verbalism which communicates no experience, it can only be understood from the point of view of the subject, with his transcendental nature, experienced as being-in-reference-to the reality of absolute truth and free-ranging, infinite, absolutely valid love. It can only be understood in one's innermost regions as an immediacy before the absolute mystery of God, i.e. as the absolute realization of man's transcendental nature itself, made possible by God in his self-communication.

Without an ontology of the transcendental subject a theology of grace (and hence all theology whatsoever) remains fixed in a pre-theological picture-language and cannot give evidence of a starting-point for transcendental experience. This transcendental experience is indispensable today if theology is to do justice to modern man's question as to whether all the talk of "Divinization," "Sonship," "God's Indwelling" etc. is not merely poetic concepts and indemonstrable mythology. Let us emphasize once more that this transcendental direction in the theology of grace means a similar direction for the whole of theology. For today even ontic Christology itself (in spite of its abiding validity) urgently needs translating into an onto-logical Christology, i.e., one which at the outset understands the "nature" to be assumed not as a thing but as a transcendental spiritual quality. Since nature and being not only "has," but *is* actuality and transcendence, the substantial unity with the Logos must be basically expressible in the terms of actuality and transcendence. It must be translated into these terms in order that what is meant by the "Hypostatic Union" is said really clearly enough and is sufficiently protected from being misunderstood as mythology. All theology stands in need of this transcendental and anthropological change of direction because all theology is dependent upon the mutually determining doctrines of the Trinity, Grace and Incarnation, and these three basic doctrines today fundamentally require a transcendental approach.

2. A considerable objection could be made against what has been said: if it really is so necessary for all theology, surely there must always have been this kind of transcendental anthropological program and method of investigation? — for good theology has not emerged today for the first time. Since, however, there has clearly been no such investigation, the demand for it cannot be legitimate.

First of all we must draw attention to the very basic difference between proclamation and theology, although in practice proclamation always contains an element of theological reflection, and conversely theology can never adequately transmute the proclamation into theological reflection. Modern theological eschatology for instance has been left behind almost totally in a pre-theological stage of proclamation. By and large the ecclesiology of Vatican II has still not progressed beyond a certain systematization of biblical picture-language, apart from particular sections on Constitutional Law. Seen from this point of view it is by no means *a priori* impossible that there is as yet no really scientific, i.e., transcendentally reflected theology in many areas and topics. Why should it be impossible? The fact that there is a lot of thinking, talking, writing and "systematizing" in some way or other in theology (and this is all good and laudable in itself) is no proof that theology has reached that stage of conceptualization and reflection which must differentiate it from proclamation. This qualitative difference only really occurs, however, where and insofar as there is expressly transcendental thought, i.e., where the *a priori* presuppositions for knowledge and realization of the particular realities of faith are explicitly included in one's reflections, determining the choice of terms for theological objects.

At the same time we by no means wish to imply that this transcendental anthropological method has been utterly absent from theology until now. There can be no question of that. We cannot give detailed examples here to show how this transcendental method has been at work everywhere in theology (even if in different intensities), at least since St. Thomas, even if it had not yet become completely aware of itself nor comprehended itself explicitly in formal principles.

But in the end whatever the historical facts may have been, we must say that today's *contemporary situation* demands a transcendental anthropological program and method. Plato, Aristotle and Thomas will remain immortal philosophers from whom we must learn. But this does not alter the fact (even if the kind of philosophy studied in the Church has only taken notice of it in the last forty years or so) that philosophy today and hence theology too *cannot* and must not return to the stage before modern philosophy's transcendental anthropological change of direction since Descartes, Kant, German Idealism (including its opponents), up to modern Phenomenology, Existentialism and Fundamental Ontology. With few exceptions, e.g., Blondel, it can be said that this whole philosophy is most profoundly un-Christian insofar as it pursues a transcendental philosophy of the autonomous subject, who stands aloof from the transcendental experience in which he experiences himself as continually dependent, with his origin in and orientation toward God. But this same philosophy is also most profoundly Christian (more than its traditional critics in modern scholastic professional theology have grasped), for according to a radically Christian understanding man is not ultimately one factor in a cosmos of things, subservient to a system of coordinate ontic concepts drawn from it, but the subject on whose freedom as subject hangs the fate of the whole cosmos: otherwise salvation-history and profane history could have no cosmological significance, and Christological cosmology would be infantile concept-poetry. This inner dividedness is, however, not only a symptom of modern philosophy but of all man's works, and hence a symptom of philosophy in all ages; we must not let it hinder us from seeing what is Christian in this significant epoch of modern culture. We must accept the situation in all its fundamental essence, as a factor henceforward indispensable in a modern Christian philosophy, and so too in modern Christian theology.

Modern man feels that thousands of statements in theology are just forms of mythology and that he is no longer able to believe them in all seriousness. Of course this is ultimately false, but there are real reasons behind the impression. It is due not merely to pride and stupidity on the subjective side, and objectively to the mysterious quality of the truth and reality of faith. Let us look dispassionately at today's real cultural situation: if a modern man who has not been brought up as a Christian hears the words "Jesus is God made man" he will straightaway reject this explanation as mythology which he cannot begin to take seriously nor to discuss, just as we do when we hear that the Dalai Lama regards himself as a reincarnation of Buddha. If this modern man hears of two people dying in similar state and condition, and one is said to go straight to heaven because he happens to be the recipient of a Papal Indulgence, whereas the other spends many years in Purgatory because the Pope, as Keeper of the Keys of Heaven, has not opened up straightaway; he will regard Indulgences, represented in this way, as a clerical invention against which his own idea of God radically protests. It will not be easy to convince him that God desires the salvation of all men, including children dying while not responsible for themselves, even *after* the Fall, and yet is unable to allow children dying unbaptized to approach his face because he cannot dispense with his own rule of the necessity of Baptism.

One could multiply these examples at length. There ought not to be so many. Furthermore, it does not seem to me that theology has dealt with these countless difficulties in a sufficiently intellectual way; above all, not in a way which holds out much promise for the practice of religious education. Let us repeat that in apologetics it is little or no use appealing in a positivistic manner to the "mystery" actually revealed by God. If the *fact* of a verbal revelation were psychologically so absolutely compelling that doubts were utterly impossible, one could impose acceptance of its content in this positivistic manner as a mystery beyond all discussion. But if modern man finds the *content* of revelation unworthy of belief through the fault of theology, he will think himself justified, not illogically, in further doubting the *fact* of revelation. Incidentally these remarks show that we need to strive for a much larger area of mobility for fundamental theology and dogmatics than is usually the case. All these difficulties of modern man can be traced to a common formal structure: theological statements are not formulated in such a way that man can see how what is meant by them is connected with his understanding of himself, as witnessed to in his own experience.

Of course one cannot demand (and it would be heretical Modernism to do so) that the attempt must be made simply to deduce strictly all theological statements *from* man's experience of himself as if they were the latter's objectifying conceptualization and articulation. That is not what is meant, although this problem is more difficult than the traditional opponents of Modernism mostly think for there *is* also an *experience* of grace, and this is the real, fundamental reality of Christianity itself. If we leave this question here, it must be remembered that the connections between man's experience of himself and the content of the statements of dogma must be conceived otherwise than simply as logical connections of deduction or explication. There are correspondences, above all by virtue of the fact that "nature" — understood as personal, intellectual and transcendental — is an inner and necessary constituent not abstractly of grace *per se,* but of the actuality and process by which grace can be conferred. If these connections were uncovered and thought about as the subject-matter required by dogma, rightly understood, dogmatic statements would not only appear more worthy of belief from the point of view of religious education and doctrine; rather, thorough reflection on these correspondences would enable one to penetrate deeper and more effectively to the significance of particular statements and would lead to the elimination of latent misunderstandings, unsuitable schemes of presentation and unjustified conclusions. The discovery of such connections between the content of dogma and man's experience of himself is, in actual fact however, nothing else but the required change to a transcendental anthropological method in theology. Thus today's demand for it is founded on reasons of fundamental theology and apologetics.

Translated by Graham Harrison

Hans Urs von Balthasar

Pascal says that it is a bad sign when somebody's name is mentioned and the first thing one thinks of are the books he has written. This will probably have to remain the fate of Hans Urs von Balthasar (1905–88) for some time to come, as his output outmatches what most people could manage to read in a lifetime. Even to list his works would take up more pages than the selection that is to follow (in fact, the bibliography of his books, articles, and translations is now its own 174-page hardbound book).[1] Not only does his own work comprise over fifty thousand pages, but he was also an editor, translator, and publisher of numerous works of theology, spirituality, and literature (for his translations of such French authors as Paul Claudel and George Bernanos he received the Prix de Traduction from the Fondation Haute Villiers and was also a foreign member of the French Academy).

Characterizing such a prolific output is naturally beyond the scope of these few introductory remarks. Perhaps the most salient feature of Balthasar's writings is their thorough saturation in literature — indeed, he received his doctorate (from the University of Zurich on October 27, 1928) in German literature (*Germanistik*), not theology. Raised in a highly musical family, he found it difficult to decide whether to be a scholar or a musician, but in 1927, just before receiving his doctorate, he made the Spiritual Exercises of St. Ignatius and felt in the midst of this thirty-day retreat a vocation to become a Jesuit. He entered the order on October 31, 1928. After completing two years of novitiate, he studied philosophy in Pullach (near Munich), an exercise he found as dry and

---

1. Cornelia Capol, comp., *Hans Urs von Balthasar: Bibliographie, 1925–1990* (Einsiedeln: Johannes Verlag, 1990).

dull as sawdust, and theology in Lyons, France, where he made crucial contacts with such giants of patristic scholarship as Henri de Lubac, Jean Daniélou, and Gaston Fessard (founders of *Sources Chrétiennes*).

His first assignment after ordination was to be student chaplain at the University of Basel, where he met the Protestant physician Adrienne von Speyr, who converted to Catholicism under his direction. Together they established a "secular institute" (roughly: religious life for laypeople), an establishment that eventually provoked Balthasar to leave the Jesuits (in 1950), as the canonical difficulties of running one religious "order" while being a member of another proved to be unworkable. In 1947 he founded his own publishing house, Johannes Verlag, where most of his own writings have first appeared.

I have chosen the following selection from his book *Heart of the World* because I think it best displays Balthasar's remarkable literary style of writing.

From Heart of the World

Chapter 1
The Flowing Stream

Prisons of finitude! Like every other being, man is born in many prisons. Soul, body, thought, intuition, endeavor: everything about him has a limit, is itself tangible limitation; everything is a This and a That, different from other things and shunned by them. From the grilled windows of the senses each person looks out to the alien things which he will never be. Even if his spirit could fly through the spaces of the world like a bird, he himself will never be this space, and the furrow which he traces in the air vanishes immediately and leaves no lasting impression. How far it is from one being to its closest neighbor! And even if they love each other and wave to one another from island to island, even if they attempt to exchange solitudes and pretend they have unity, how much more painfully does disappointment then fall upon them when they touch the invisible bars — the cold glass pane against which they hurl themselves like captive birds. No one can tear down his own dungeon; no one knows who inhabits the next cell. Conjecture can grope its way from man to woman, from child to adult, even less than it can from human being to animal. Beings are alien to one another, even if they do stand beautifully by one another and complement one another like colors, like water and stone, like sun and fog: even if they do communally perfect the resounding harmony of the universe. Variegation pays the price of a bitter separation. The mere fact of existing as an individual constitutes renunciation. The limpid mirror has been shattered, the infinite image has been shattered over the face of the world, the world has become a heap of fragments. But every single splinter remains precious, and from each fragment there flashes a ray of the mystery of its origin. And infinite good can be detected in the finite good: the promise of greater things, the possibility of breaking through, an enticement so sweet that our pulse falters for keen delight, when the marvel — conferring a boundless bliss — suddenly discloses itself for a few moments, free of its concealment, and presents itself open and naked, stripped of the ashen garment of custom. Here is the seal of its provenance, the kiss of its origin, the pledge of its lost unity. Yet the kernel of this delight always remains incomprehensible and mysterious. If one should snatch at it, he will not grasp it; he will hold the apple of Adam in his hand, not the infinite fruit from the Tree of Life. Smiling sadly, the heavenly image will slip away, effacing itself and dissolving into fumes. What appeared to be boundless again exhibits its stark walls, and both the seeker and the sought slide back into their narrow prison. Once again we stand over against everything, a part of a part, and what we have can only be imparted. No tugging, no weeping can burst open the prison.

But look: hovering, oscillating, inconceivably flowing Time is there no less — the invisible bark going from shore to shore, a rustling of wings from being to being. Come aboard Time: already it is setting out. It carries you along, and you know neither how nor where it is taking you. The rigid ground under you is already beginning to tremble and give way. The hard road becomes supple and alive, and it begins to flow with all the beauty of a river's meandering course. The banks constantly change and vary: now it is woods through which Time rocks you, now far-reaching fields and the cities of men. The stream itself has many forms and modulations: now it flows with a gentle rush, now it plunges wildly into cataracts, then it again flows smoothly and widens into a lake. The movement now becomes imperceptible, and along the banks the water at times flows backward until it is again gripped by the pull from the center.

Space is cold and stiff, but Time is alive. Space divides, but Time brings everything to everything else. It does not course outside of you and you do not swim upon it like a drifting log. Time flows through you: you yourself are in flow. You are the river. Are you grieving? Trust Time: soon you will be laughing. Are you laughing? You cannot hold fast your laughter, for soon you will be weeping. You are blown from mood to mood, from one state to another, from waking to sleeping and from sleeping again to waking. You cannot go on wandering for long. You come to a halt, you are tired, you are hungry, you must sit down, you eat, you stand up again, you begin anew to wander. You suffer: from the distance, unattainable, you glimpse the Deed for which you long. But the stream is constantly moving you and one morning the hour of action has arrived. You are a child, and never (so you think) will you escape the helplessness of childhood, which locks you into four windowless walls. But look: your wall is itself movable and yielding, and your whole being becomes refashioned into a youth. From within yourself there rise hidden springs that leap up to yourself. Possibilities open up before you like flowers, and one day the world has grown all around you. Softly, Time transports you from one curve to another. New vistas and horizons unfold at your side as you pass by. You begin to love the change: you've discovered an extraordinary adventure is afoot. You sense a direction, you feel a new impulse, you can smell the sea. And you see that what changes in you changes also in everything around you. Every point you hurriedly pass by is itself in movement. Every point is being whirled in some direction: its own long history is following its course: but each point knows the ending of its history no more than you know that of yours. You glance up to heaven. Sublime is the rotation of its suns, but these are each heavily laden with their planetary systems as with grapes, and they dash away from one another into already-prepared distances and unfathomable spaces. You smash atoms and they swarm about in more confusion than if you had stamped your foot on an anthill. You seek a mainstay and a permanent law in the temperate mid-region of our earth, but here, too, there is nothing but constant event and changing history, and no one can forecast for you even next week's clouds.

A law does indeed exist, but it is the mysterious law of transformation, to be fathomed by none except the person who is himself transformed. You cannot draw the river onto the dry bank, there to trap its imperative to flow, as if it were a fish. And it is only in the water that you yourself can learn how to swim. The wise among men seek to fathom the foundations of existence, but all they can do is to describe one wave of the current. In their portrayal, the flowing has congealed and can again become true only if they repeatedly release the picture they have painted back into change. The greedy among them have launched many projects: they have thrown rocks into the water in order to dam up the stream: in their systems, they contrived to invent an Isle of Eternity, and then they puffed up their hearts like balloons, all of it so as to catch eternity in the trap of one blissful Now. But they caught only air and they burst, or, turned as if by witchery into an Imaginary Idea, they wholly forgot to live, and the stream calmly washed over their corpses. No: the law is in the river and only by running can you seize it. Perfection lies in fullness of journey. For this reason, never think you have arrived. Forget what lies behind you; reach out for what lies before you. Through the very change in which you lose what you have snatched up you will at last be transformed into what you crave for with such longing.

Trust Time. Time is music, and the space out of which it resounds is the future. Measure by measure, the symphony is created in a dimension that invents itself, and which at each moment makes itself available from an unfathomable store of Time. Space is often lacking: the stone is too small for the statue, the town-square cannot contain the multitude. When has Time ever been lacking? When has it run out like too short a piece of string? Time is as long as grace. Entrust yourself to the grace of Time. You cannot interrupt music in order to catch and hoard it. Let it flow and flee, otherwise you cannot grasp it. You cannot condense it into one beautiful chord and thus possess it once and for all. Patience is the first virtue of the one who wants to perceive. And the second is renunciation. For look: you cannot grasp the melody's flight until its last note has sounded. Only now, when the whole melody has died away, can you survey its mysterious balances, the arcs of tension and the curves of distance. Only what has set in the ear can rise in the heart. And therefore (and yet!), you cannot grasp invisibly in the unity of the spirit what you have not sensibly experienced in the manifoldness of the senses. And so the eternal is above time and is its harvest, and yet it comes to be and is realized only through the change of time.

What strange beings we are! We grow only by being thrust into transiency. We cannot ripen, we cannot become rich in any way other than by an uninterrupted renunciation that occurs hour by hour. We must endure duration and outlast it. Whenever we attempt to stop we violate the very life-principle of nature. Whenever we lose the patience of an existence in time, by that very fact we fall into nothingness. As long as we walk on, a voice whispers to us from the contrary wind we are cleaving; but if we halt in silence the better to hear it, already it is muted. Time is at once a threat and an unheard-of promise. "Let me course on," it calls to us, "otherwise you won't be able to come along! Let go of me, show me your empty hands: otherwise I cannot fill them! Otherwise I will pass you by with my fresh new gifts and abandon you to your outdated baubles. Believe me: you are richer if you are able to end and break off your glee and your hour of triumph, richer if you can be poor and open instead, a beggar at the gate of the future! Don't hold on, don't cling or clasp! You cannot hoard time: let it teach you to squander! Squander yourself what another must otherwise take from you with violence. Then you, the robbed miser, will be richer than a king. Time is the school of exuberance, the school of magnanimity."

It is the grand school of love. And if time is the ground of our existence, then the ground of our existence is love. Time is existence flowing on: love is life that pours itself forth. Time is existence that has been dispossessed, defenseless and unasked; love dispossesses itself and willingly allows itself to be disarmed. Existence cannot help it (this its law and its essence): by its flowing it demonstrates love. And so the way is open for existence to be itself love. We must be patient even if we are perishing from impatience, for no one can increase the span of his life by even the smallest increment, except, that is, by growing... with time. We must renounce things even if, shaking with greed, we clutch our possessions: quietly does deadly Time remove our fingers, and the treasures we've snatched tumble to the ground. Every moment in our life teaches us with gentleness what the last moment must finally enforce with violence: that we ought to discover in the mystery of time's duration the sweet core of our life — the offer made by a tireless love. Strange: we *may* be what we vainly long after. We can realize simply in our existence what we so painfully fail to achieve in our knowing and willing. We would like to give ourselves away, and we have already been given away. We look for one to whom we could abandon ourselves, and already we have long been accepted. And when the heart becomes knotted when it considers the uselessness of all it has lived through, this is but the fear of the bride on her wedding-night when she is robbed of her last veil.

We have been designed as beings who may willingly accomplish what they must unwillingly desire. But what can bring more bliss, what thought can be more intoxicating than this: already to exist is a work of love! And so, it is in vain that I fight being what I have always been.... And even if I should cry out "No!" at the top of my voice, even if my veins should swell with fear as I shout this "No!," even then, in the last corner of the cave, an echo would treacherously say yes: Yes! If, after many a death, we die for one last time, in this act of highest life existence has ceased dying. Only one thing can ever be deadly: to be alive and not to want to die. Every death which is willingly died is a source of life. The cup of love is thus a mixture of life and death. It is a miracle that we do not love: love is the watermark in the parchment of our existence. It is to love's melody that our limbs respond. Whoever loves is obeying the impulse of life in time; whoever refuses to love is struggling (uselessly) against the current. How easy the gesture of giving becomes for us when the golden water of Being constantly runs through us as through the mouth of a wellspring! How easy to become dispossessed when we are bathing in the wealth of a future that flows on inexhaustibly! How easy is fidelity when faithless Time has placed its inviolable ring on our finger! How easy is death when we experience hourly how blessed, indeed, how advantageous it is to pass on! And even aging, anxious aging, which contracts and reduces us, offers as a substitute for exterior mists the inner clarity of poverty. There is nothing tragic about us, for every renunciation is extravagantly rewarded, and the more we approach the pure center of naked poverty, the more intimately do we take possession of ourselves, the more reliably are all things our own.

Thus, we may be what we would like to be. In the mysterious water of Time in which we bathe and which is ourselves, in this liquid of Being, the heart's deeply hated resistance is dissolved and outdone. Only what is fixed is questionable, only what is opaque and stiff and puts up a resistance to every spirit and eye. But the eye is moist and the spirit translucent, and so its rays pierce through and dissolve what is stubborn. While we outwardly armor ourselves with layer upon layer against life's inexorable imperatives, in our inmost being the spring leaps forth and washes away the walls and undermines our most solid fortification. No one can withstand to the end the relentless battering by these billows. Day after day they erode us, gnawing away pebble by pebble at our wasted banks. In the end we collapse. With time even the greatest fool grasps Time. Time hollows out its bed in him and grinds him down with its round stone as the waterfall does a glacier.

Thus it is that you sense Time, and it initiates you into its highest mystery. You come to feel Time's rhythm, now rushing on, now withdrawing. Under the form of the future it approaches you, overwhelms you, bestows on you an immeasurable bounty; but it also robs you and demands that you give everything. It wants you to be at once rich and poor, ever richer and ever poorer. It wants you to be more loving. And if you were once to follow wholeheartedly the law and imperative of your very being, if you were once fully yourself, you would live solely on this gift that flows out to you (this gift which you yourself are), and you would do this by giving it away in turn, in holiness without having defiled it through possessiveness. Your life would be like breath itself, like the lungs' calm and unconscious double movement. And you yourself would be the air, drawn in and exhaled with the changing measure of the tides. You would be the blood in the pulse of a Heart that takes you in and expels you and keeps you captive in the circulation and spell of its veins.

You sense Time and yet have not sensed this Heart? You feel the stream of grace which rushes into you, warm and red, and yet have not felt how you are loved? You seek for a proof, and yet you yourself are that proof. You seek to entrap him, the Unknown One, in the mesh of your knowledge, and yet you yourself are entrapped in the inescapable net of his might. You would like to grasp, but you yourself are already grasped. You would like to overpower and are yourself being overpowered. You pretend to be seeking, but you have long (and for all time) been found. Through a thousand garments you feel your way to a living body, and yet you insist you cannot feel the hand that nakedly touches your bare soul? You jerk about in the haste of your unquiet heart and call it religion, when in truth these are the convulsions of a fish struggling on shipboard. You would like to find God even though it be with a thousand sorrows: what humiliation that your efforts were but an empty fuss, since he has long held you in his hand. Put your finger to the living pulse of Being. Feel the throbbing that in one single act of creation at once claims you and leaves you free. Feel the throbbing that, in the tremendous outpouring of existence, at the same time determines the precise measure of distance: how you ought to love him as your most intimate friend and how you ought to fall down before him as the all-high Lord; how in one and the same act he clothes you out of love and strips you out of love; how, along with existence, he presses all treasures into your hand, and the most precious jewel of all: to love him in return, to be able to give him a gift in return; and how he nevertheless (not afterward, in a second movement, in a further step) again takes away everything he has given so that you love not the gift but the giver and so that you know, even in giving, that you are but a wave in his stream. In the same split instant of existence you are near and far; in the same moment a friend and a master is set before you. In the same moment you are child and slave. You will never go beyond this first state of things. In eternity you will live as that which you have been. For, even if your virtue, your wisdom, your love towered immeasurably, even if you were to grow beyond men and angels straight through to the highest heaven: even then you would never leave your point of departure. Yet nothing is more blessed than this first moment, and would that on the longest arc of development you would but constantly be curving back to this marvel of your origin! For love's full reality is inconceivably glorious.

And life, to be sure, strives away from its origin. It seeks itself and believes that it finds itself where it is safe from the dangers of its beginnings. The seed seems to be all too unprotected; it seems to need a strong bark, and the moment of generation appears all too close to nothingness. But an iron law compels all linear motion back into the circle. Life awakens to its own reality and rises up in a great, slender arch; it then seeks to assert itself on this narrow ridge. Blood flows mightily through the narrow door of an individual's life, making his heart and brain swell. Possessed by a sense of self-importance and of mission, his hands proudly dispense, as if they had created what has in fact come to him from afar, from the unknown roots of his forebears. But the summit of the pass has been reached, and while for others the sun may still be climbing, his path begins to descend and plunges into the afternoon of cooler woods, and again he hears it murmuring — a small brook at first: the memory of younger days, now almost buried, begins to swell up in him; a longing for primal times softly comes to life; a presentiment swells up; love is in the ascendancy; and unawares, precipitously, a waterfall suddenly plunges into the abysmal night of the Beginning. All of that marvelous separate existence dissolves, like the course of different rivers, in the One Ocean of death and life. In the One Ocean the waves rise and sink; body floats past body; figures and generations, century after century, are all so much foam falling prostrate on the broad beach of eternity in a most tremendous obeisance.

The meaning of our life: to show our recognition that we are not God. Thus, we die unto God, for God is eternal life. How could we attain to it other than through death? In our life, death is the pledge that we are touching on something that outlives this life. Death is our life's profound bow, the ceremony of *proskynesis* before the Creator's throne. And, since the creatures' innermost being consists of the praise and service and awe which they owe their Creator, a drop of death is commingled in every moment of existence. Because time and love are so closely intertwined, however, creatures also love their dying, and their being does not refuse to perish. But even if the small, individual life should be fearful and our darkened self-will should struggle against death, existence itself — the deep sea-swell that raises and lowers it — knows its Master and gladly bows down before him. For it knows intuitively that autumn comes only to prepare for the spring, and that in this world there willingly wilts whatever bears the promise of blossoming in God.

Thus does the creature die unto God and rise up unto God. We rush into the light and are drawn on in ecstasy; but the fire which no one may approach holds us in its spell. We plunge into the flames, are burnt through and through, but the flame does not kill: it transforms us into light and burns on in us as love. This is love that knows the depths. It lives in us, establishes itself within us as a center; we live from it; it fills and nourishes us; it draws us into its spell, clothing itself with us as with a mantle and using our soul as its organ. This is no longer ourselves: in a most immediate, hardly distinguishable proximity, this is the Lord in us. A loving fear grows within us, fear which again and more urgently forces us to our knees, into the dust of nothingness. Mightily, more roaring than Time itself, the Heart of love hammers on. It pulses and unites Two into One, or again divides One into Two. Thus do we live from God: he draws us mightily into his glowing core and robs us with his lordliness of every center that is not his own. But we are not God, and, in order the more mightily to show us the power of his center, he hurls us out imperiously — not alone, not powerless, but endowed with our own center and in the power of his mission. God claims us jealously; he wants us solely for himself and for his honor. But, laden with his love and living from his honor, he sends us back into the world. For it is not the rhythm of his creation that it should go out from God as by regress and return to its source as by regress. Rather are both these things as one, inseparable, and the going forth is no less unconditional than the return, nor the mission less God-willed than the longing for God. And perhaps the going forth from God is still more divine than the return home to God, since the greatest thing is not for us to know God and reflect this knowledge back to him as if we were gleaming mirrors, but for us to proclaim God as burning torches proclaim the light. "I am the light of the world," says God, "and without me you can do nothing. And, beside me, there is no light and no god. But you are the light of the world, a borrowed but not a false light; burning with my flame you are to enkindle the world with my fire. Go out into the furthest darkness! Take my love like lambs into the midst of wolves! Take my gospel to those who cower in the dark and in the shadow of death! Go out; venture beyond the well-guarded fold! I once brought you home when you were lost lambs and were bleeding among the thorns. Then did I bring you home on my good shepherd's shoulders. But now the flock is scattered and the gate of the pen gapes wide: this is the hour of mission! Out! Separate yourselves from me, for I am with you until the end of the world. For I myself went out from the Father and, by going out from him, I became obedient unto death, and by obeying I became the perfect image of his love for me. The going out itself is love; the going out itself is the return. Just as the Father has sent me, so do I send you. Going out from me as a ray from the sun, as a stream from its source, you remain in me, for I myself am the ray that flashes forth, the stream that is poured out from the Father. To give is more blessed than to receive. Just as I radiate the Father, so also are you to radiate me. So turn your face to me that I can turn it out into the world. You are to be so separated from your own ways that I can place you on the way that I am."

This is a new mystery, inconceivable to mere creatures: that even distance from God and the coolness of reverence are an image and a likeness of God and of divine life. What is most incomprehensible is, in fact, the truest reality: precisely by not being God do you resemble God. And precisely by being outside of God are you in God. For to be over against God is itself a divine thing. As a person who is incomparable you reflect the uniqueness of your God. For in God's unity, too, there are found distance and reflection and eternal mission: Father and Son over against one another and yet one in the Spirit and in the nature that seals the Three of them together. Not only the Primal Image is God, but also the Likeness and the Reflected Image. Not only the unity is unconditional; it is also divine to be Two when there is a Third that binds them together. For this reason was the world created in this Second One, and in this Third One does it abide in God.

But the meaning of creation remains unexplainable so long as the veil covers the eternal Image. This life would be nothing but destiny, this time only sorrow, all love but decay, if the pulse of Being did not throb in the eternal, triune Life. Only then does the spring of life begin to leap up also in us: it speaks in us of the Word, becomes itself Word and Language, and communicates to us — as a greeting from God — the task of proclaiming the Father in the world. Only then is the curse of solitude also resolved: for, to-be-over-against is itself divine, and all beings — man and woman and animal and stone — are not, by their particular existence, excluded from the common life, rather are they oriented to one another in their very form. They are not locked up in a dark dungeon from which their oppressed yearning seeks to escape out into the unbounded: rather, as God's messengers accomplishing a resplendent work of completion, they are rounded out into the one Body whose Head rests in the bosom of the Father.

Beat on, then, Heart of existence, pulse of Time! Instrument of eternal love! You make us rich and, then again, you make us poor. You draw us to yourself only then yourself to withdraw from us. But, through the surges of the tide, we remain the festal ornament you wear. Majestically you roar on over us; you reduce us to silence with your stars; you fill us to overflowing, to the very brim, and you empty us down to the dregs; to the point of collapse. And whether you roar or keep silence, whether you fill up or empty out, you remain the Lord and we your household servants.

Translated by Erasmo S. Leiva

ACKNOWLEDGMENTS

Every reasonable effort has been made to locate the owners of rights to previously published works and the translations printed here. We gratefully acknowledge permission to reprint the following material:

Immanuel Kant, *The Conflict of the Faculties,* translated by Mary J. Gregor. New York: Abaris Book, Inc., 1979. By permission of the publisher.

From *Religion in History,* translated by James Luther Adams, copyright © 1991 T & T Clark, Ltd. Used by permission of Augsburg Fortress.

From G. E. Lessing, *Theological Writings,* by permission of A & C Black.

From *Jewish Perspectives on Christianity,* edited by Fritz A. Rothschild. Copyright © 1990 by Fritz A. Rothschild; from Karl Rahner, *Theological Investigations,* volume IX, copyright © 1972 by Darton, Longman & Todd. Reprinted by permission of The Crossroad Publishing Company, New York.

From Arthur Schopenhauer, *The World as Will and Representation,* translated by E. F. J. Payne. By permission of Dover Publications, Inc.

"Myth and Science" from "Myth and Religion" by Karl Jaspers from *Myth and Christianity* by Karl Jaspers and Rudolf Bultmann. Copyright © 1958 by The Noonday Press, Inc. Copyright renewed © 1986 by Farrar, Straus & Giroux, Inc. Reprinted by permission of Farrar, Straus & Giroux, Inc.

Excerpt from *Philosophical Faith and Revelation* by Karl Jaspers. Copyright © 1967 in the English translation by Karl Jaspers; excerpts from *On the Eternal in Man* by Max Scheler, translated by Bernard Noble. Copyright © 1960 by SCM Press. Reprinted by permission of HarperCollins Publishers Inc.

From Hans Urs von Balthasar, *Heart of the World.* By permission of Ignatius Press, San Francisco, California, © 1979.

From T. Bottomore, *Karl Marx: Early Writings* (1963) by permission of McGraw-Hill, Inc.

THE GERMAN LIBRARY
in 100 Volumes

Wolfram von Eschenbach
Parzival
Edited by André Lefevere

Gottfried von Strassburg
Tristran and Isolde
Edited and Revised by
 Francis G. Gentry
Foreword by C. Stephen Jaeger

German Medieval Tales
Edited by Francis G. Gentry
Foreword by Thomas Berger

German Mystical Writings
Edited by Karen J. Campbell
Foreword by Carol Zaleski

Seventeenth Century German Prose
Edited by Lynne Tatlock
Foreword by Günter Grass

German Humanism and Reformation
Edited by Reinhard P. Becker
Foreword by Roland Bainton

German Theater before 1750
Edited by Gerald Gillespie
Foreword by Martin Esslin

Eighteenth Century German Prose
Edited by Ellis Shookman
Foreword by Dennis F. Mahoney

Eighteenth Century German Criticism
Edited by Timothy J. Chamberlain

Sturm und Drang
Edited by Alan C. Leidner

Immanuel Kant
Philosophical Writings
Edited by Ernst Behler
Foreword by René Wellek

Friedrich Schiller
*Plays: Intrigue and Love
 and Don Carlos*
Edited by Walter Hinderer
Foreword by Gordon Craig

Friedrich Schiller
Wallenstein and Mary Stuart
Edited by Walter Hinderer

Friedrich Schiller
Essays
Edited by Walter Hinderer
 and Daniel O. Dahlstrom

Johann Wolfgang von Goethe
*The Sufferings of Young Werther
and Elective Affinities*
Edited by Victor Lange
Forewords by Thomas Mann

Johann Wolfgang von Goethe
*Plays: Egmont, Iphigenia in Tauris,
Torquato Tasso*
Edited by Frank G. Ryder

German Romantic Criticism
Edited by A. Leslie Willson
Foreword by Ernst Behler

Friedrich Hölderlin
Hyperion and Selected Poems
Edited by Eric L. Santner

Philosophy of German Idealism
Edited by Ernst Behler

G. W. F. Hegel
*Encyclopedia of the Philosophical
Sciences in Outline and Critical
Writings*
Edited by Ernst Behler

Heinrich von Kleist
Plays
Edited by Walter Hinderer
Foreword by E. L. Doctorow

E. T. A. Hoffman
Tales
Edited by Victor Lange

Georg Büchner
Complete Works and Letters
Edited by Walter Hinderer and
 Henry J. Schmidt

German Fairy Tales
Edited by Helmut Brackert and
Volkmar Sander
Foreword by Bruno Bettelheim

German Literary Fairy Tales
Edited by Frank G. Ryder and
Robert M. Browning
Introduction by Gordon Birrell
Foreword by John Gardner

F. Grillparzer, J. H. Nestroy,
F. Hebbel
Nineteenth Century German Plays
Edited by Egon Schwarz in
collaboration with
Hannelore M. Spence

Heinrich Heine
Poetry and Prose
Edited by Jost Hermand and
Robert C. Holub
Foreword by Alfred Kazin

Heinrich Heine
The Romantic School and other Essays
Edited by Jost Hermand and
Robert C. Holub

Heinrich von Kleist and Jean Paul
German Romantic Novellas
Edited by Frank G. Ryder and
Robert M. Browning
Foreword by John Simon

German Romantic Stories
Edited by Frank Ryder
Introduction by Gordon Birrell

German Poetry from 1750 to 1900
Edited by Robert M. Browning
Foreword by Michael Hamburger

Karl Marx, Friedrich Engels, August
Bebel, and Others
German Essays on Socialism in the
Nineteenth Century
Edited by Frank Mecklenburg and
Manfred Stassen

Gottfried Keller
Stories
Edited by Frank G. Ryder
Foreword by Max Frisch

Wilhelm Raabe
Novels
Edited by Volkmar Sander
Foreword by Joel Agee

Theodor Fontane
Short Novels and Other Writings
Edited by Peter Demetz
Foreword by Peter Gay

Theodor Fontane
Delusions, Confusions and The
Poggenpuhl Family
Edited by Peter Demetz
Foreword by J. P. Stern
Introduction by William L. Zwiebel

Wilhelm Busch and Others
German Satirical Writings
Edited by Dieter P. Lotze and
Volkmar Sander
Foreword by John Simon

Writings of German Composers
Edited by Jost Hermand and
James Steakley

German Lieder
Edited by Philip Lieson Miller
Foreword by Hermann Hesse

German Essays on History
Edited by Roll Sältzer
Foreword by James J. Schechan

Arthur Schnitzler
Plays and Stories
Edited by Egon Schwarz
Foreword by Stanley Elkin

Rainer Maria Rilke
Prose and Poetry
Edited by Egon Schwarz
Foreword by Howard Nemerov

Robert Musil
Selected Writings
Edited by Burton Pike
Foreword by Joel Agee

Essays on German Theater
Edited by Margaret Herzfeld-Sander
Foreword by Martin Esslin